Stupendous, Miserable City

Stupendous, Miserable City

Pasolini's Rome

John David Rhodes

UNIVERSITY OF MINNESOTA PRESS
Minneapolis · London

Chapter 3 was previously published as "Scandalous Desecration: *Accattone* against the Neorealist City," *Framework* 45, no. 1 (Spring 2004): 7–33. Reprinted with permission of Wayne State University Press.

Excerpt from "The Tears of the Excavator," from Pier Paolo Pasolini, *Poems,* translated by Norman MacAfee (New York: Farrar, Straus and Giroux, 1982). Translation copyright 1982 by Norman MacAfee. Reprinted by permission of Farrar, Straus and Giroux, LLC.

Published by the University of Minnesota Press
111 Third Avenue South, Suite 290
Minneapolis, MN 55401-2520
http://www.upress.umn.edu

Library of Congress Cataloging-in-Publication Data

Rhodes, John David, 1969–
   Stupendous, miserable city : Pasolini's Rome / John David Rhodes.
     p.   cm.
   Includes bibliographical references and index.
   ISBN 978-0-8166-4929-7 (hc : alk. paper) — ISBN 978-0-8166-4930-3 (pb : alk. paper)
   1. Pasolini, Pier Paolo, 1922–1975—Criticism and interpretation.   2. Rome (Italy)—In motion pictures.   I. Title.
   PN1998.3.P367R54   2007
   791.4302'33092—dc22
                                            2006100453

Printed in the United States of America on acid-free paper

The University of Minnesota is an equal-opportunity educator and employer.

12 11 10 09 08 07   10 9 8 7 6 5 4 3 2 1

Contents

Introduction

This Cinema, *This* City

Rome is at the heart of Pasolini's cinema. That is, very simply, this book's central premise. Pasolini's first two films, *Accattone* (1961) and *Mamma Roma* (1962), are as much "about" Rome as they are about anything else, and the power of their specific historical, political, and aesthetic interventions remains inaccessible without some knowledge of the Roman urban and architectural context out of which they emerged and to which they respond. Similarly, the full significance of later films like *La ricotta* (1963), *Hawks and Sparrows* (*Uccellacci e uccellini,* 1966), *La terra vista della luna* (The earth as seen from the moon, 1966), and *La sequenza del fiore di carta* (The paper flower sequence, 1969), Pasolini's only other films to privilege Roman location shooting, cannot be grasped without a knowledge of their relationship to Roman urban history.[1] Furthermore, the shift in Pasolini's filmmaking from a practice grounded in contemporary everyday life to a practice predicated on allegory needs to be understood as a departure from Rome, a departure that is only fully comprehensible within the Roman-ness of the earlier films. To tell as fully as I can the story of the profound connection between Pasolini's filmmaking and Rome is my project in this book.

The films that are studied in detail in this book were set and shot for the most part in the marginal landscape of Rome's periphery, the most dynamic and rapidly changing domain of the city in the years after World War II. The story of the periphery's rapid and reckless growth, legible in countless anonymous apartment buildings and housing projects, is the story of Rome's redefinition in the postwar period. This redefinition was a rapid acceleration of a process of urban expansion that began after Rome was made the capital of united Italy in 1870, continued up through the years of fascism, and then resumed with abandon in the 1950s and 1960s. Pasolini's Roman films are among the most significant and compelling aesthetic responses to and documents of the Roman periphery as it existed in the 1960s. The films grew out of Pasolini's engagement with the periphery that consisted of his living in and writing about this same environment during the decade of the 1950s.

Pasolini's enormous literary production of the 1950s is marked by the intensity of its engagement with the city of Rome. Having left his home in the region of Friuli in northern Italy, Pasolini arrived in Rome in 1950, seeking a new life like so many other postwar immigrants to the capital city. Later in the year of his arrival, he had produced an intimate poetic diary, recording both his entrapment inside the house of his own consciousness and his dislocation inside Rome's alien but alluring landscape. Soon thereafter he was making what little money he could by teaching and writing freelance journalistic pieces in a fury of anxious activity. A brief look at one of the earliest of these essays reveals not just Pasolini's interest in the city that was his new home but also how this interest bears, from a very early moment, the mark of the cinema. Here is a passage from a sort of hybrid documentary essay/short story produced in 1951, "Studies on the Life of Testaccio":

> You will always see a murky, dazzled sky over Testaccio. Springtime warmth still on the chilly side; the green surface of the trees spotted with violet or with the indigo of fruit saplings, with the charm of a Japanese landscape. Panoramic opening from above, as in some French film classic, René Clair—: Porta Portese, the Juvenile Reformatory—of a solid, discolored Roman baroque—high, deserted Tiber embankments. But this in passing: the camera will immediately focus on the Testaccio side. Ponte Testaccio. Bare shore, of a poisonous green, above the water of the Tiber, still swollen from the winter flooding. Long yellowish block of five- or six-story houses, early twentieth century, with a northern, seaside look. Asphalt of the streets near the river.[2]

Significantly, this vision of Rome does not resort to the familiar picturesque traditions of looking at the city. There is no dome of St. Peter's here; there are no Spanish Steps. Instead we have an aerial shot of something less appealing: a juvenile prison, a flea market. But even these places, "shot" only "in passing," are passed over in favor of a prospect still less welcoming—that of Testaccio, whose bulky and forlorn apartment blocks, set down in a rigid grid in the late nineteenth and early twentieth centuries, make up Rome's first official working-class district. In a sense, Pasolini's entire aesthetic could be deduced from this passage. In it we have evidence of his eschewal of the usual itinerary of Roman sights; of his interest in working-class milieus, in mass housing and its architecture; of his passion for the unlovely. Moreover, the abrupt transitions among views, details, and objects of description in the passage, here self-consciously framed as cinematic, are consonant with the rough surfaces and jarring ellipses of his films, demonstrating the ineluctable entwinement of Pasolini's literary and cinematic production. Just as the neighborhood of Testaccio is only a prelude to the seediness and immensity of Rome's later-blooming peripheral neighborhoods, so does "Studies in the Life of Testaccio" only hint at the enormous concentration of energies that Pasolini would bring to bear on the subject of Rome and its periphery.

This book situates the films Pasolini made in and about Rome in two informing contexts: first, that of modern Roman urban and architectural history, and second, that of his literary production of the 1950s. *Accattone* was shot largely in Roman peripheral neighborhoods known as the *borgate,* a pejorative term denoting the large fascist-era mass housing projects built outside the city center. The term is also often used interchangeably to refer to the swarming clusters of huts and hovels built by new immigrants to Rome along the outskirts of the city. *Mamma Roma* was shot in a public-housing project built in the 1950s, one of many constructed to address the needs of Rome's underhoused citizens, many of them residents of the borgate like the ones seen in *Accattone. Hawks and Sparrows* features scenes shot on the furthest outskirts of Rome where the newly completed Autostrada del Sole (Italy's equivalent of an interstate highway) still had the air of a construction site. Because of the obvious imbrication of Pasolini's filmmaking with these several instances of urban and architectural history, I have grounded my analyses of these and other films in the historical contexts of several episodes from Rome's urban development in the twentieth century, chief among these the following: the history of the construction and growth of the borgate under fascism; the large-scale public-housing projects of the 1950s that ambitiously sought to address Rome's housing shortage and were also the breeding grounds of the "neorealist architecture" movement; and the construction of the Autostrada and its redefinition of urban and territorial space as well as its impact on Roman urban planning of the 1960s.

The second informing context is that of Pasolini's literary production in the 1950s. As we have already seen in the passage above, there are strong links between Pasolini's literary and cinematic work. For instance, I establish Pasolini's poems and letters in which he first begins to articulate his attitude toward Rome (and especially the Rome of the borgate) as context in conjunction with the history of the borgate. I interpret at some length Pasolini's long poem "The Tears of the Excavator," from his celebrated volume of poetry *Le ceneri di Gramsci* (The Ashes of Gramsci, 1957), in connection with the history of public-housing construction in postwar Italy. This poem's central image is that of a construction site at which a housing complex, perhaps like the one pictured in *Mamma Roma,* is being built. This context of historical-biographical literary analysis and urban history is the matrix out of which the analyses of the films emerge.

The book's first chapter, then, offers an introduction to twentieth-century Roman urban history, tracing the major developments of immigration to Rome by poorer rural Italians, most of whom settled along the city's periphery, and the expulsion of lower- or working-class Romans out of the city center and into peripheral slums and housing projects during the years of fascism (1922–42). This chapter also considers the representation of the Roman periphery in neorealist cinema in order to establish neorealism as one of the key contexts to which Pasolini's filmmaking responds.

Chapter 2 moves into a history of Pasolini's arrival in Rome in 1950 and an analysis of his first attempts to come to terms with the city and its awesome, squalid periphery in his poetry and prose, paying special attention to his diaristic poetry, his letters, and his novel *The Ragazzi* (*Ragazzi di vita,* 1955). It also considers Pasolini's work as a screenwriter in the 1950s. All of this work is clearly the experimental laboratory from which the filmmaking emerges.

In chapter 3 I analyze *Accattone,* which was shot, with very few (but significant) exceptions, entirely in Rome's borgate. This chapter argues that the film cannot be understood (at least fully) outside the specific geographical, architectural, and historical context of the Roman borgate. I attempt to show, as well, that the film, despite its participation in the tradition of Italian cinematic neorealism, is in fact a critique of neorealism, at least as Pasolini understood it. Furthermore, I argue that its critique of neorealism is coterminous with its representation and documentation of the dull nightmare of life in the borgate.

An analysis of "The Tears of the Excavator," a poem that throws into question the "progress" embodied by the new construction that was redefining the look of the Roman periphery, starts the next chapter. The construction that the poem describes seems to be that of a large-scale housing project or mass apartment building. The chapter, therefore, moves from literary analysis to a history of the housing projects that were built in the 1950s under the INA Casa scheme to alleviate the dire need for habitable housing in the Roman periphery. This history is interwoven with contemporary commentators' critical responses to the aims, methods, and architectural practices embodied by these projects. Several INA Casa projects, including the one that provided the location for *Mamma Roma,* were exemplars of what has been called (by its practitioners and its critics) architectural neorealism. The resonance of this term is investigated in this chapter.

Chapter 5 focuses on *Mamma Roma* and explores the possible meanings of Pasolini's decision to locate the film in the Tuscolano II housing project, an INA Casa development that has often been considered under the aforementioned rubric of architectural neorealism. The interaction of Pasolini's camera with the architecture of this environment receives special attention. Here I concentrate especially on the film's consistent confounding of the establishment of a subjective character point of view vis-à-vis the architecture of the INA Casa development and its surrounding neighborhood of high-rise apartment buildings. I argue that the film's shooting style expresses a profound skepticism toward the project of architectural neorealism and that this skepticism toward Rome's built environment attaches itself to and is consonant with the film's corrosive take on cinematic neorealism, whose legacy is everywhere alluded to in the film, from its title to its casting decisions.

The last chapter concludes with a consideration of the few films that followed *Accattone* and *Mamma Roma* which made use of Roman locations. *Hawks and Sparrows,* for instance, begins in the outskirts of Rome, in terrain very similar to that of *Accattone* and *Mamma Roma.* Quickly, however, the film moves into the landscape (if it can be called that) of the Autostrada, which, at the time the film was shot, had only recently been constructed in order to serve the needs of the country's increasingly mobile and automobilized population. The film's setting in a kind of nowhere is symptomatic not only of changes in Italian culture but also of shifts in Pasolini's preoccupations. While this film flirts openly with allegory, so do other of Pasolini's films from the mid- to late 1960s move away from a mode related to realism to embrace a mode of full-blown allegory. I interpret the nature of Rome's appearance in several of these films—*La ricotta, La terra vista dalla luna,* and *La sequenza del fiore di carta*—in order to trace Pasolini's movement toward allegory. Under-standing how and why the direction of this movement is begun in Rome is key to understanding the movement's ultimate destination. As the Ital-ian city became ever more derealized by the "progress" suggested by the Autostrada, Pasolini turned from documentarily specific representations of Rome to a mode of allegorical representations that are located else-where, often in Africa. Postwar Roman development, therefore, which was very much a phenomenon of limits and their surpassing, embodies a limit or boundary in Pasolini's own aesthetic practice.

Scholarly work on the city and cinema has, for the past several years, prospered as a vibrant field of scholarly research, and while Pasolini scholars have consistently pointed out the centrality of the city of Rome to his filmmaking, there does not exist a thorough consideration of the complex particularity of his films' relationship to and representation of the city of Rome as a complex material reality. Recent studies of film's intersection with the city have largely focused on several overlapping areas of research, among them: dazzling evocations of cities in the "city films" of European modernists such as Dziga Vertov, Jean Vigo, and Wal-ter Ruttman, whose films' rapid, paratactic editing patterns have often been understood to convey the shocks and ecstasies of urban living; Weimar "street films" whose cities are usually artificial set constructions and whose narratives are often preoccupied with the moral challenges of urban modernity; postmodernist evocations of virtual cities, such as Ridley Scott's *Blade Runner* (1982); sociological studies of the cinema as a source of knowledge about city living; historical studies of the cinema as an urban industry and studies of the urban situation of much film production and reception.[3]

The attention to the city in recent film scholarship has been excit-ing, invigorating, and long overdue, especially given the closely imbri-cated histories of the film medium and the cities that serve as film loca-tions and are home to film production. This book stands slightly to one side from most of the work on the cinema and the city by virtue of its sustained attention to one filmmaker's relationship to one particular city. Often discussions of cities and cinema assume a rather abstract, diffuse character; often the "city" might even be only an imagined city—a fabrication of set design and cinematography. Inspiring this book is the belief that each instance of interaction between a city and a cinematic practice is entirely specific and unique unto itself.[4] Furthermore, I am interested in Pasolini's treatment of an actual concrete urban milieu—peripheral Rome—not a phantasmatic piece of set design built on a backlot in Cinecittà or Hollywood. I treat the images of Rome in Pasolini's films as a kind of material archive of the city, as a record of how the city was used and inhabited—what it looked like and felt like at a particular point in time. Of course, the films are also records of Pasolini's own thinking about Rome, for his films are not transparent documents but elaborate inventions and interventions. However, I reject the belief, nearly dogma in many studies of Pasolini, that Pasolini's Roman locations were solely aesthetic inventions, in Sam Rohdie's words "poetic metaphors for what was missing in the modern world, not real locations, not actual places."[5] Such an understanding of Pasolini's Rome errs in two ways. First, it overstates the degree to which the profilmic is overwhelmed by aesthetics (i.e., Pasolini's original and idiosyncratic techniques of shooting, framing, editing, and so on): despite Pasolini's high-contrast black-and-white cinematography, his elliptical editing, the spatial deformations of his film form, we still sense strongly a real, historical Rome that is being offered to us on film. Second, such an approach to Pasolini's Rome must ignore or at least displace the evidence of Pasolini's intense attachment to and knowledge of Rome, and his awareness of contemporary architecture and architectural debates. Pasolini's films offer us both Rome and a version of Rome: the city itself and a way of thinking about it—both aesthetically and politically.

Pasolini, I believe, understood Rome in a way similar to Henri Lefebvre's conceptualization of the city: a "centre . . . of social and political life where not only wealth is accumulated, but knowledge, techniques, and oeuvres (works of art, monuments). This city is itself 'oeuvre.' "[6] Lefebvre aligns his term *oeuvre* with the concept of use value. As oeuvre, the city is a site traversed by a multitude of practices—economic, governmental, artistic, familial—that amount to more than what can be represented in an image. Much of Lefebvre's writing on cities, however, is motivated out of his distress over the fact that cities have been almost wholly converted into arenas of consumption, theaters in which the serial tragedy of sheer exchange value is played out day after day. This state of affairs occurs as historic centers of many cities (particularly European) become exclusively the homes of the rich, open to other classes only as sites used for the consumption of commodities, whether these be cultural, comestible, or otherwise. The city center itself, once divested of any meaningful relationship to its actual inhabitants, comes to exist as nothing more than a product, ready and waiting to be consumed. Studies of the city "in film" that are not responsible to the historical and material specificities of actual cities may run the risk of treating the city as nothing more than an evocative visual commodity. In doing so, of course, such studies only recapitulate what Lefebvre laments: that the city is often, in fact, no more than a site of commodity consumption and itself a consumable commodity.

T. J. Clark, in his stunning analysis of late nineteenth-century French painting, shows that one of the ways Impressionist painting came to be considered modern was that it reflected the "spectacular" nature of the city.[7] Clark's use of the word *spectacular,* of course, implicitly nods to Guy Debord, whose notion of the spectacle he (Debord) epigrammatically expressed thus: "The spectacle corresponds to the historical moment at which the commodity completes its colonization of social life. It is not just that the relationship to commodities is plain to see—commodities are now all that there is to see."[8] Although Rome was a latecomer to industrial urban modernity, its development in the late nineteenth and early twentieth centuries bears some affinities to the sort of changes that Clark describes.[9] Sections of central Rome, for instance, were redesigned and developed first by the government of unified Italy that made Rome its capital in 1870, and next by Mussolini's fascist regime, which sought to expunge working-class citizens from Rome's center. These citizens were forcibly removed from the center and their homes destroyed to "sanitize" the city and make room for new urban spaces and monuments. Of course, Rome's countless ancient fountains, palaces, piazzas, and other monuments were originally constructed as signifiers of power and were also intended to generate visual pleasure in the eyes and minds of their beholders, which is to say that Rome, even ancient Rome, has always participated in the spectacular, if not, in Debord's and Clark's terms, the "spectacle." The spectacle in Debord's terms is "mere representation," and its effect of "unreality" is predicated on the estrangement of people from the world "directly lived."[10] The image that Rome—ancient, medieval, Renaissance, baroque, even fascist—

offered to or impressed upon its citizens and visitors was concretely subtended by the power that resided in the city itself. Across the second half
of the twentieth century and up to the present day, the city (like most)
has been reduced to a field of play for the signifiers of capital whose
origins and destinations may have hardly any "brick and mortar" address
or any concrete relation to the city itself. The city's material reality—its
conglomeration of urban and architectural voids, thoroughfares, and
monuments—has been derealized into a consumerist pleasure ground.
This derealization is especially true today of Rome's city center, which
has basically become a district of high-priced apartments, luxury bou-
tiques, and other institutions that cater almost exclusively to tourists and
middle-class residents who can afford to live there.[11]

Central Rome's derealization along these lines was already pronounced by the dawn of the 1960s when Pasolini began to shoot his first
film, *Accattone*. Fellini's decision to shoot much of *La dolce vita* (1960), a
film set in and around Rome, on a sound stage at Cinecittà, is interesting
in this respect. Rather than shoot his film on location on the Via Veneto,
he chose to build an elaborate simulation of this street on a studio lot.
The film's fake Via Veneto was built to the exact dimensions of the Via
Veneto itself. This fantastic production decision suggests that the city
center might be, for all intents and purposes, indistinguishable from its
representations; its structures drained of meaning to the extent that they
need only be observed in the service of representation.[12]

Pasolini's *Accattone* scarcely visualizes the city's ancient center. Most
of its action takes place at Rome's periphery, where those expelled from
or repulsed by the city live in squalid fascist borgate or else have constructed abject homes of mud and scavenged brick and lumber. Pasolini
offers us this world and impresses on us a visual and spatial knowledge of
it. The center of Rome might have been derealized by 1961, but *Accattone*
insists on the borgate as a landscape all too real. Pasolini regarded the
borgate and their inhabitants as outside or prior to history; something
as yet unredeemed by the profane miracles of the spectacle to which
Rome's center had been given over. The movement from *Accattone* to
Mamma Roma, the film he made one year later, shows Pasolini recording
a shift from prehistory to history and from an immersion in material
reality to the seductions of the derealized spectacle. This movement is
embodied in the new government-subsidized apartment building that
is central to *Mamma Roma*'s thematic and visual construction. Careful
explication of both the nature and history of the urban sites that appear

in Pasolini's films and of his politico-aesthetic approach to these sites is, therefore, the key to understanding these films' meanings. A study of these films that does not take into account simultaneously the details of Roman urban history and the specific formation of Pasolini's aesthetics misses what is most important about these films both as aesthetic artifacts and as political arguments.

One cannot approach the subject of the city and cinema without somehow reckoning with the figure of Walter Benjamin, whose work on the modern city (most significantly Paris) has been central to much recent scholarship in this area. Readers may find Benjamin conspicuously absent from this book. This absence is due to the difficulty one encounters in reconciling meaningfully Benjamin's Paris with Pasolini's Rome.[13] Simply put, Rome is not Paris, nor is it Berlin or any of the other stereotypically "modern" cities whose rush of stimuli so excited Benjamin's theoretical reflection. Urban modernity came later to Rome than it did to, say, Paris, and when it did, it either came in piecemeal, lopsided installments—the expansions needed to make Rome a modern capital, the fascist renovations, for example—or else it arrived at the city's periphery, fast, furious (as in the postwar period), and far away from the patterns of typical, bustling flânerie so central to Benjamin's theorization of modernity. There were very few structures in Rome like Benjamin's cherished Parisian arcades and department stores.[14] Rome's center to this day maintains a sense of itself as a product of ancient, medieval, Renaissance, and baroque planning. The city is, however, traversed and carved through by several modern interventions. The Corso Vittorio Emmanuele, the Via Nazionale, the Piazza Venezia, and the Vittoriano towering above it: all are products of postunification urban planning. But as historian Denis Mack Smith writes, despite the reinvention of Rome (until 1870 a backwater ruled by the Vatican) as "Roma capitale," "Rome lacked the resources to become industrial and remained provincial in culture." The city did not offer quite the same shocks, attractions, thrills, and abrasions that are central to Benjamin's theory of urban modernity. Despite being the nation's capital, according to Mack Smith, "Rome remained a city of the past—ancient, medieval, or baroque. It was not a town of theaters and banks, but of churches, palaces, and monuments."[15] Furthermore, later planning interventions, especially those authored by Mussolini like the Via dell'Impero (now called the Via dei Fori Imperiali, a massive wasteland of a street overlooking the Forum, bordered by no shops or residential buildings and created to accommodate automobile traffic and to pronounce the link between Mussolini's seat at the Palazzo Venezia and the Coliseum—symbol of ancient Rome—which lie at either end of the street), did not create flâneur-friendly boulevards where fashion and commerce could display themselves to transitory, peripatetic passersby.

Anthony Vidler, in a study that rigorously investigates the usefulness of Benjamin's writing on the Parisian arcades to contemporary thinking about architecture and overlapping aesthetic discourses, articulates some of the idiosyncrasies of Benjamin's work that demonstrate how difficult it is to harness his thinking to the Roman context. Vidler pays special attention to Benjamin's *The Arcades Project,* the famously inchoate and yet encyclopedic tissue of impressions, quotations, and images of and about nineteenth-century Paris. Benjamin conceives of the Parisian arcades, built of iron and glass, forerunners to the shopping mall, as the allegorical harbingers of advanced modernity and advanced capitalism. According to Vidler, the arcades are "purely textual spaces. . . . [T]hey possess an architectonics of their own, all the more special for its ambiguous status between textual and social domains; they are, so to speak, buildings that themselves serve as analytical instruments."[16] Vidler also conceptualizes Benjamin's *The Arcades Project* itself as a proto-cinematic endeavor. From *The Arcades Project* Vidler cites the following passage:

> Could one not shoot a passionate film of the city plan of Paris? Of the development of its different forms [Gestalten] in temporal succession? Of the condensation of a century-long movement of streets, boulevards, passages, squares, in the space of half an hour? And what else does the flâneur do? (115)

Vidler follows this quotation by wondering:

> In this context, might not the endless quotations and aphoristic observations of the Passagen-Werk [The Arcades Project], carefully written out on hundreds of single index cards, each one letter-, number-, and color-coded to cross-reference them to all the rest, be constructed as so many shots, ready to be montaged into the epic movie "Paris, Capital of the Nineteenth Century"...? (115)

Vidler supposes that this imaginary film would give concrete realization to "the flâneur's peripatetic vision": fleeting, fragmentary, "Vertov-like" (116).

Rome, I'm afraid, does not nourish such visions of itself. As Marco Bertozzi has noted, Rome received scant attention from early filmmakers like the Lumiére Brothers, who specialized in the production of touristic "view" films, perhaps because "Rome's marvels did not guarantee the dynamism" so delightful to early film spectators.[17] One could, of course, choose to picture Rome as "Vertov-like"; the work of a good film editor could turn the lazy Mediterranean capital into something more nervous and frenetic, but doing so would be purely an imposition of vision, not something inspired by or grounded in the city itself.

Pasolini chose to picture a Rome that was, in fact, very much a modern phenomenon and a product of the city's modernization. The borgate were indices of Rome's growth in the nineteenth and twentieth centuries as much as the Vittoriano (the giant gleaming altar to the Italian nation state that presides over the Piazza Venezia) or the Via dell'Impero. However, as will be explained in the next chapter, often tram and bus lines did not even extend all the way out to the borgate. The landscape of peripheral Rome, as Pasolini lived, understood, witnessed, and represented it, was a place of long slow walks to and from the tram's or the bus's last stop, of large buildings and bedouin-like villages stranded at the edge of things: more impoverished, quasi-agrarian languor than neurasthenic shock.

Thus on the basis of the foregoing, we can see that Rome—at least Pasolini's Rome—and Benjamin sit uneasily together. The length of this explanation indicates how central Benjamin has become to studies of the city and the cinema. Unfortunately, the Benjaminian approach to urban space (especially in relation to cinema) has become a cliché of film studies. My reluctance to pick up Benjamin in the present work is actually informed by a desire to see his work used more carefully and thoughtfully, and in contexts where his allegorical hermeneutics of Parisian modernity are best suited to the rigors of that context and the rigors of his exhilarating thought. Furthermore, this book stages an attempt to interpret a particular instance of modernity through what I would call an indigenous set of hermeneutic tools. Rather than "apply" a theory to Rome and to Pasolini's treatment of it, I have attempted to understand these films through a set of archival and historical materials that better illuminate what was and remains specific about Roman modernity and Pasolini's approach to it.

Within Pasolini studies proper, there is a noticeable trend of addressing the significance of Rome in Pasolini's work, both literary and cinematic. Keala Jewell has seriously investigated Pasolini's poems from *The*

Ashes of Gramsci, commenting on their depiction of "the Roman architectural and urbanistic configuration as a splendid palimpsest."[18] In scholarship specifically concerned with Pasolini's filmmaking, Lino Micciché's *Pasolini nella città del cinema* (Pasolini in the city of cinema) evocatively considers Pasolini as citizen of several "cities"—not the least of which are Rome and Cinecittà. He also rigorously analyzes Pasolini's method of shooting the peripheral landscape.[19] Angelo Restivo's *The Cinema of Economic Miracles: Visuality and Modernization in the Italian Art Film* displays a vivid awareness of the specificity of Pasolini's relationship to urban space in Rome, particularly to the tensions between center and periphery in *Accattone.*[20] These last two books offer much to the study of Pasolini and/ in Rome. Neither book, however, is as interested in marrying formal analysis to a thoroughly researched context of urban and architectural history as I am here. The present book, thus, fills a gap in Pasolini studies and Italian film studies. I hope this book will be seen as an addition to the valuable work I mention above and to the ongoing investigation (both historical and theoretical) of the modern city's relationship to modernist aesthetic practices

My own interpretive methodology is in some ways quite simple, although it draws on a wide number of varied and complex discourses. First I should clarify that my approach is, to some degree, an intentionalist one. That is to say, I credit Pasolini's poetry and films with a high degree of authorial coherence and I furthermore believe that Pasolini's representation of Rome in word and image constitutes an investigation into and interrogation of urban space and architecture that is highly conscious of itself as such. I hold that the continuity of Pasolini's investigation of Rome across media and genres proves that regarding this investigation as anything less than intentional would be a mistake. Italian and Roman contemporary life were dominated by questions of urban growth and expansion, public housing, and the conservation of city centers. We need only look at the pages of the special May 1961 issue of the important architectural journal *Casabella* to understand the cultural and political significance of architecture and urbanism in the period and how these matters were understood to be complexly intertwined with film history.[21] The issue published the responses of leading Italian and international architects and critics to several questions about the state of Italian architecture. The text of these responses sits side by side with architectural elevations, photographs of projects, Italian cities, and, significantly, stills from postwar Italian films. The life of Italian cities was bound up with their cinematic representations; both were objects of an ongoing cultural conversation. Pasolini was not only aware of this cultural conversation, he was a vibrant contributor to it.

My desire is to set up Pasolini's work in relation to other historical and theoretical discourses and aesthetic practices (most contemporary to his work, some not) in the hope that hearing their "voices" in concert will help us to hear and see, perhaps for the first time ever, the specific contribution that Pasolini's films make to film history, to the history of Rome and its representations, and, more generally, to the history of representations of urban space.

I am compelled to mention a work that comes from far outside the field of film studies that has deeply informed my desires and my methods in writing this book: Marvin Trachtenberg's *Dominion of the Eye: Urbanism, Art, and Power in Early Modern Florence.*[22] In this masterful study Trachtenberg reconceptualizes trecento Florentine urban planning, which had always been perceived as the somewhat hapless antecedent of "ordered" Renaissance planning. By performing exhaustive analyses of piazzas and monuments, by immersing himself in theoretical and archival literature, and by comparing urban sites to their representation in trecento painting, Trachtenberg is able to reveal what had been hiding in plain sight: that trecento planning was in fact a rigorous and analytical practice that sought to design the city so as to create perspectival views for its inhabitants. The coherence of trecento planning had been obscured by scholars' conceptual inability to perceive it. In this book I hope to restore to Pasolini's films their complex meanings as aesthetic and urban historical documents, similar to the way in which Trachtenberg restored to the trecento piazza its ingenuity.

At this point I want to mention another work again, one that has been influential on this book: T. J. Clark's *The Painting of Modern Life.* In a typically elegant passage Clark expresses the desire that his work "be partly a matter of looking at Impressionist pictures again and being struck by their strangeness."[23] Not unlike the trecento piazza before Trachtenberg and the work of Manet before Clark, much of the significance (urban historical, architectural historical, and film historical) of Pasolini's films has long been hiding in plain sight. These films' strangeness and richness as art and argument, as bearers of the marks of a specific urban history, have been obscured by critical commonplaces and by a scarcity of knowledge of their rich historic context. I hope that this book can do something in the way of illuminating Pasolini and Rome the way Trachtenberg and Clark have illuminated Florence and Paris, the piazza and *Le déjeuner sur l'herbe*. I believe that what we know of Pasolini's filmmaking practice and what we know of Rome can be deepened, refreshed, and enlivened by bringing both Pasolini and Rome into rigorous historical intimacy.

Chapter 1

A Short History of the Roman Periphery

Rome's conversion into newly united Italy's capital in 1870 was the event that dragged into modernity a city that for years had been a backwater administered by the papacy.[1] Prior to 1870 Rome's population consisted mainly of a clerico-bureaucratic class, an ancient land-owning aristocracy, a small white-collar professional middle class, a sizeable merchant and artisan class, and a large subproletariat. Missing, of course, was a proper working class, whose nonexistence was owed to Rome's almost total lack of industrial economy.[2] Becoming the nation's capital required Rome to accommodate a substantial influx of state bureaucrats and to commence a number of large-scale construction projects that would house the new national government and its employees. This construction in turn demanded the importation of laborers from the rural areas surrounding the new capital. All of this new economic activity acted as a magnet for more immigration, apart from the immediate importation of the laborers needed for new construction projects. The national government made efforts to discourage the industrialization of the city, however, acting on the belief that the introduction of a proletariat into the city might naturally occasion the introduction of radical proletarian political movements.[3] The building industry, therefore, became a dominant force in Rome, and it employed a largely unskilled labor force, very different from the skilled laborers working in the industries in the north of Italy.[4]

The construction of government buildings and middle-class housing for government employees did not take place outside the old city center, but rather right in its core. A plan was introduced to build a monumental zone of government buildings to the east of the center near Termini Station, but only the war and finance ministries opted to locate there.[5] Many other ministries and offices found homes in palaces and monasteries, acquired by the state from Rome's noble families or the church and situated in diverse sections of the city's center. Because the government would be located firmly in Rome's center, it was generally felt that a bit of sprucing up was in order: old streets needed to be widened, new streets planned, "unhygienic" ghettoes destroyed. The Corso Vittorio Emmanuele II, beginning near Piazza Venezia and running west to the Tiber, was created by enlarging narrow pre-existing streets of Renaissance and Medieval origin to form an uneven axis with the newly built Via Nazionale, which ran east toward Piazza della Reppublica, near Termini.[6] The "creation" of Corso Vittorio (as the street is commonly called) meant the displacement of many members of the artisanal and merchant classes who had since time immemorial called this area home. Similar displacements resulted from demolitions around the Piazza del Popolo, the construction of Via Cavour, the renovation of the old Jewish ghetto, and other like projects. The displaced, if they could afford it, found housing in large apartment blocks that were being built just outside the Aurelian walls. Those less fortunate improvised dwellings out of scrap lumber, brick, and mud, buildings that came to be called *baracche*, or what we call shacks or shanties in English. These baracche made up the first peripheral neighborhoods, which are often called *borgate*.

The term *borgata* does not have an exact equivalent in English. Dictionary translations usually offer something to the effect of "working-class suburb." The term, pejoratively derived from the word *borgo*, which simply means "district" or "neighborhood," was coined as an official term by the fascists. As Italo Insolera has written, "Borgata is a subspecies of borgo: a piece of the city in the middle of the country, that is not really one or the other."[7] *Borgate* is a loosely used term and can refer usually to either unofficial borgate[8] or official borgate. When one thinks of unofficial borgate, images of abject, crudely made, single-story houses come to mind. These are baracche, which, lumped together, come to form unofficial borgate. Official borgate, on the other hand, are those large housing projects built under fascism. Both unofficial and official always carry with them the implicit sense of being peripheral to the center. One may occasionally hear or read the terms *borgate* and *periphery* (in Italian, *periferia*) used almost interchangeably.

In the years between Rome's installation as the capital and the turn of the century, the city nearly doubled in size, growing from 226,000 (the number counted by the last papal census in 1870) to over 400,000 by 1900. During this time of rapid growth, however, the city administration failed to follow through on any relatively strict regulatory plan to guide urban development. It also repeatedly chose not to buy up undeveloped land for later use as was the practice in other European capitals, in London and Paris, for instance, and instead allowed private landholders (many from the still politically influential nobility) free rein to profit from a more or less unregulated real estate market.[9] A system of housing imbalance had occurred by the 1880s, thanks to the reign of the city's free-market attitude. Private speculation was responsible for the construction of most new housing. This housing was largely of the middle- and upper-middle-class variety—obviously because such housing would guarantee the greatest return on the speculators' investment. Entire new neighborhoods, composed of large apartment buildings, were designed and built which in scale and style sought to emulate Piedmontese building types. This mimetic urbanism paid homage to the Turinese origins of the House of Savoy and unified Italy's new royal family. The neighborhood of Piazza Vittorio Emmanuele II is a good example of the importation to Rome, on a grand scale, of this essentially foreign form of design and construction. As Insolera points out, these developments were clearly Roma Capitale's effort to imitate the nineteenth-century architectural programs of other European capitals.[10] Given that so much of modern Rome bears evidence of the Piemontese influence, one must work hard today to imagine how very strange an imposition on the Roman landscape these buildings would have seemed in the late nineteenth century. As more and more buildings went up (the decade of the 1880s is remembered for its "building fever," or *febbre edilizia*), more and more workers were attracted to Rome to build these structures, but there was little construction dedicated to housing these same workers. For workers who had migrated to Rome, each new middle-class apartment building, therefore, concretely figured both their incorporation into and exclusion from Rome's spatial and material economy. Ironies of this sort season modern Roman urban history.

One major exception to this lack of attention to workers' housing was the Testaccio district, whose creation was first proposed in 1872, but not commenced until 1883.[11] The area was developed through a joint public-private initiative as a neighborhood to house workers employed by a few light industries—slaughterhouses, dairies—both situated just out-side the ancient city walls to the south around "mount" Testaccio.[12] The adjacent Aventine hill and the ancient Roman archeological zone conve-niently acted as agents to buffer the middle-class neighborhoods in the center from both these industries and the people who were employed by them. Testaccio remained incomplete for over two decades due to lack of private initiative in finishing it. Of thirty-six projected apartment blocks, only nine were completed up until 1907 when, in addition to completing the planned construction, certain basic amenities such as gas and paved streets were also installed. Schools for the neighborhood's children did not arrive until about the same time.[13] But despite its many abuses—chiefly its tardiness and its institutionalization of geographic class apartheid—the neighborhood comes off well in comparison to the misery of the unofficial borgate and the later official borgate of the fas-cist years.[14]

To return to the subject of the unofficial borgate, these were what, in the earlier years of the twentieth century, one saw upon entering Rome, whether by train or by car, especially if traveling from or to the south, the area of their densest concentration. Borgate were also visible from inside the Aurelian walls that marked the ancient boundaries of the city. The visibility of such squalor from inside Rome's walls was intolerable to Mussolini's fascist regime, which, after Il Duce's ascent to power in 1922, sought meticulously to create a fascist visual culture that would proclaim order, beauty, and power, through (among many other things) parades, public spectacles, monuments, architecture, and public spaces. Fascism's predilection for visual and symbolic splendor demanded that the bor-gate inside the walls be torn down and replaced at a further distance from the city center with what were called *borgate rapidissime*—literally (very) quickly built suburbs. Furthermore, Mussolini was obsessed with the significance of Rome's ancient patrimony, most vividly expressed, he felt, by the ruins of the forums around the Capitoline hill. The majority of these ruins, however, had been covered by centuries of urban growth in the form of dense, mostly lower-class housing. In the 1920s Mussolini initiated an extensive process of *sventramento*—disemboweling—which entailed the demolition of housing (as well as churches and other public structures and spaces), much of it medieval in origin, so that the ruins of the Forum and other prized monuments could be "freed" from their burial in the urban fabric. The people who had lived in the areas marked for sventramento were sent packing to the borgate rapidissime.

Mussolini expressed his vision of a new Rome, befitting the age of fascism, in his New Year's Eve address of 1925:

> In five years Rome will appear beautiful to everyone in the world; vast, ordered and powerful as it was under Augustus. You will liberate the trunk of the great oak from everything that encumbers it. You will open up the areas around the theater of Marcellus, the Pantheon, and the Campidoglio; everything that was created during the centuries of decadence must disappear. In five years one must be able to see the Pantheon from the Piazza Colonna. You will also free the majestic temples of Christian Rome from their parasitical constructions. The millennial monuments of our history must stand isolated and majestic.[15]

Mussolini, however, was not merely isolating monuments so that they could gain visibility; he was displacing and, thus, isolating lower-class people so as to render them invisible from inside the city center and controllable in their new homes outside it. "Liberating" Rome's historic center meant the destruction of more than 5,500 livable dwellings, which forced tens of thousands of inhabitants into borgate built for them in Rome's periphery.[16] Almost all of the demolitions destroyed housing inhabited by the lower classes. Mussolini's regime profited from this radical disruption of the urban fabric in two principal ways. First, Mussolini was dedicated to the project of emphasizing the history of ancient imperial Rome; thus, we can, in part, take his desire to "free" the ancient forums at face value. Freeing them involved the sventramento that left open spaces that were converted into large piazzas and avenues suitable for the mass demonstrations and parades that were the stuff of fascist Italy. In a sense, the Mussolinian sventramenti and other forms of urban "improvement" were no different from the planning and construction pursued in the postunification period in which Rome was remodeled as capital of the nation. However, Mussolini's project was more vast, more hyperbolic, both ideologically and architecturally.

The example of the sventramenti of neighborhoods that lay between Piazza Venezia and the Coliseum will demonstrate the nature of fascist urban planning. What is now called the Via dei Fori Imperiali, but was referred to during fascism as the Via dell' Impero, a street mentioned briefly in the introduction, runs from Piazza Venezia, the site Mussolini chose to stage his massive rallies, on past (really, on top of) the ancient fora, continuing beyond the Coliseum and on to the southwest. The road runs toward the sea, which gestured toward Mussolini's imperial desire to re-establish the ancient Roman "mare nostrum."[17] Interventions like the creation of this new avenue by destroying an existing neighborhood were the means by which Mussolini was able to place himself, as Diane Ghirardo has said, "in a direct line of descent from the Roman emperors, especially Augustus Caesar, architect of the greatest moment of the Roman Empire."[18] However, this same street, which seems at first to privilege the ancient Roman past by hugging the Forum and the Coliseum on its way to the Tyrrhenian, in fact suppresses as much as it valorizes. After so much housing was demolished to allow for the archaeological excavations of the glorious ancient past, most of what had been brought to light quickly disappeared again. Eighty-five percent, or 76,000 square meters, of the fora that had been uncovered was buried again and paved over by the Via dell' Impero.[19] So much for privileging the ancient past. Reburying the ruins, however, served Mussolini's ambitions more powerfully than their excavation; by paving over them, "Mussolini symbolically both acknowledged and at once claimed precedence over the works of Roman emperors."[20] Certainly the grand and cruel gesture of displacing thousands of humble Romans put his actions on par with the worst excesses of ancient Rome's emperors.

The sventramenti entailed the demolition of lower-class neighborhoods, coinciding with Mussolini's desire to make Rome's center predominantly bourgeois in class composition. Doing so would keep the city within the walls free of the rabblerousing, strife, and other unpleasantness that the regime associated with the working class, particularly with the period of worker unrest that immediately preceded and precipitated fascism. The state militia escorted inhabitants of sites set for destruction to their new homes in the borgate rapidissime. Most often these new neighborhoods were also located near newly constructed military posts and police barracks as a further means of exerting social control.[21] If these factors were not insulting enough, the fascist borgate were cheaply made of the worst materials, often with no running water and with only communally shared toilets. Some were even built beyond gas and electric lines.[22] The first fascist borgata was the neighborhood of Acilia, built fifteen kilometers outside the city to the northeast on a malaria-infested plot of land. This was the borgata that housed those displaced by the sventramento of the fora.[23] It is difficult to imagine the psychological damage and material privation wrought on the first inhabitants of a place like Acilia. To have lived, not just in the city's center, but literally at its navel, and then to see your home destroyed while you are forcibly expelled from the city and forced take up residence in an alien landscape of monumental tawdriness—the historical imagination reels.

Fortunately we do have some famous and widely accessible documents of these experiences. The particular experience of the aftermath of the sventramento and resettlement in the borgate, which may seem somewhat recondite to most readers, has in fact been witnessed by generations of foreign-film buffs and first-year film students. I mean here Vittorio De Sica's *Bicycle Thieves* (*Ladri di biciclette*, 1948). Very often, even in Italian contexts, this film is cherished more for its exposition of humankind's generic cruelties and kindnesses or for its demonstration of the power of familial love than it is for its documentation of historical experience. Apart from an obvious acknowledgment of the film's representation of post–World War II economic misery, the imbeddedness of its images in a specific *urban history* has seldom been discussed. The great exception here is Pierre Sorlin's compelling, rather breathless account of the film in his *European Cinemas, European Societies, 1939–1990*. Sorlin considers *Bicycle Thieves* and several other Italian neorealist films "as documents" of Roman urban experience in the postwar period. As Sorlin astutely interprets, "Distance is a fundamental feature of the film."[24]

In the film's opening scenes we see the main character, Antonio Ricci, in what seem rather strange environs. In every direction that the camera points there stretch out before its gaze monotonous rows of multistory buildings: blank, rigid, merciless, glaring down at the dusty plots that separate each from the other. These are the borgate rapidissime. In fact these are the borgate of Val Melaina, built to the city's northeast between 1935 and 1940, one of the last of the projects to be built by the fascists. These were constructed in the period during which demolitions took place around the Mausoleum of Augustus, areas lying between Piazza Navona and the Pantheon (space cleared to become the Corso del Rinascimento), and the Borgo Pio, near the Vatican and Castel Sant'Angelo.[25] Italo Insolera's generic description of the borgate built in this period might well be a verbal transcription of the establishing shots that open *Bicycle Thieves:*

> The panorama offered by these borgate is always the same:
> houses all plastered in yellow—the cheapest color—with green
> shutters, all lined up in a fashion that clearly denounces the

The opening credit sequence of *Ladri di biciclette (Bicycle Thieves):* the blocks of the borgata Val Melaina are visible behind the film title, barren countryside surrounding all.

spiritual poverty and lack of culture of the technical offices that designed them; in the open spaces the only embellishment are the clotheslines and a few spindly shrubs, scorched by the sun in summer and frozen by the wind in winter, in spaces that offer their inhabitants no shelter, no protection.[26]

If we were to accept, for the moment, the film's characters as actual historical people, we would suppose that by 1948, when *Bicycle Thieves* was shot, Ricci and his wife would have been living in Val Melaina for only about a decade, having been relocated from one of the aforementioned zones of sventramento. Ricci's young son Bruno would have been born there; he would have been a stranger to the city center.[27] To eyes untutored in the history of Roman urban history, the film's setting, a material embodiment of a very recent (at the time the film was shot) and highly specific trauma, might look instead like a "natural" location for its near-mythic tale of woe.

The film's narrative hinge—the loss of a bicycle—expresses, as Sorlin's comment on the film's preoccupation with distance suggests, what was perhaps the greatest insult the borgate's inhabitants were forced to endure: their spatial displacement from Rome's cultural and economic center. In reading the film's title—*Bicycle Thieves*—then, the mental stress should fall on the word "bicycle." This is a film not about petty criminality, but about an unjust distortion of urban space perpetrated by fascist urban interventions.[28] In the film's opening scene, unemployed men are clamoring for job assignments being handed out by a bespectacled bureaucratic functionary. When he calls Ricci's name, one of the men runs to find Ricci who is discovered some distance away, sitting sulkily on the ground. Such immobility and impoverished languor might have been the normal state of affairs for a man forced to pawn his only means of connection to the city—his bicycle—in order to raise money to feed his family, as we soon learn is the case with Ricci. The job offered to Ricci requires that he have a bike; he takes the job anyway, lying about the fact that it is sitting in hock.

Although the picture of economic despair that the film presents us with in its very first images must obviously be read in relation to the depression of the immediate postwar years, things might not have been much different in Val Melaina and areas like it a few years earlier under fascism. Many of the people forced out of the city and into the borgate were not industrial workers who could have changed addresses while continuing to report to work in the same factory, but rather members of the servant class or else small tradesmen and artisans who depended for their survival on the delicate ecology of the old neighborhoods and their proximity to the districts of the middle and upper classes for whom they worked and with whom they traded.[29] The official fascist borgate were even further out than the earlier settlements built by the first workers who migrated to postunification Rome. As mentioned before, these early borgate, closer to the city's center and often even located inside the Aurelian walls, were also demolished to make way for the construction of middle-class housing and to make the city *dentro le mura* (within the walls) more visually tidy. Put simply, residents of the borgate were more than simply displaced; they were nearly quarantined. In many cases it would take years for the municipal transportation system to reach some of the new neighborhoods, and even when they did, commutes on the buses and trams might cost a worker two hours a day or more in transit, on top of their actual monetary cost.

Of the variety of abuses committed by the borgate, none was worse than what their material configuration did to their inhabitants' mental ability to conceive of some form of social, civic life. More damaging than far-flung inconvenience and the mere lack of indoor toilets was, in Insolera's words,

> the sense that the relationship between the people and the world was different for them than it was for others, as if their lives had been filtered through a screen that had kept something from them and gave everything the feeling of having been improvised and left incomplete, of abandonment and humiliation.[30]

Feelings such as these must have been sharp indeed for that first generation of borgate dwellers evicted from the city's familiar and meaningful contours.

The historical context I have laid out here saturates every frame of *Bicycle Thieves*. The film is much more than a tale of personal humiliation and the flicker of universal redemption that we get at its conclusion when Bruno slips his hand inside that of his humiliated father. Not that this humanist, universalist reading should be rejected, for such an interpretation is warranted by the film's quite real pathos (and its frequent lapses into sentimentality). But an understanding of the film as a historical essay on and document of the deformations of fascist urbanism should be held alongside more standard symbolic interpretations. I want to return a bit later in this chapter to consider the centrality of Roman urban history to Italian neorealism and particularly the work of De Sica.

Wave after wave of migrants from rural Italy continued to break on the borgate throughout the years of fascism, despite the regime's initiatives to keep people in the country. The bleakness of underclass existence in Rome was still an improvement over the conditions of literal starvation in the countryside.[31] The fascist regime, despite its bloated statist rhetoric, was significantly in thrall to private interests, and so despite nominal efforts at directing the city's growth, Rome continued to grow in "oil stain" fashion.

In stressing the bitterest aspects of fascist city planning and housing construction in Rome, I have not intended to offer the reader too narrow an understanding of what fascist architectural and urban constructions and culture were like. A proper understanding of fascist contributions to architectural and urban culture would encompass not only the regime's unhappiest episodes, but would also account for some of its important successes. It was under the fascist regime, for instance, that urbanism was first recognized as a theoretical discourse. INU, or the National Institute for Urbanism, was established in 1930 along with its banner publication, *Urbanistica,* which became an organ of progressive architectural and urbanist thought in the postwar period and continues to be published today.[32]

One of the regime's most grandiose and controversial projects to be essayed in Rome was E'42, later and ever after referred to as EUR, short for Esposizione Universale di Roma, a World's Fair–type of exhibition, meant to showcase the marvels of fascism on its twentieth anniversary, projected to open in 1942, but unfinished until after the war. The design of EUR was an often awkward cross between classical monumentality and modern rationalist construction. As a piece of urban planning, EUR was intended to create a new urbanized center outside the city that would solve some of its overcrowding and housing shortages. As has often been noted, however, the project's location to the southwest of the city center ended up contributing to the overdevelopment of the city in that direction, doing nothing to stem the oil-stain pattern of construction.[33] The neighborhood is now a staunchly middle-class address and home to a number of financial institutions and government ministries. Its most famous appearance in film is in Michelangelo Antonioni's *The Eclipse* (*L'eclisse,* 1962); Pasolini made his home there from the mid-1960s until his death in 1975.[34] EUR continues to be a controversial project, but it is nonetheless an interesting one that continues to draw the attention of contemporary architectural historians.

Rome is, of course, home to many other fascist-era architectural monuments of remarkable rigor and interest, among them, Adalaberto Libera's post office on the Via Marmorata (1933–35) and the Città Universitaria (1932–35), the seat of the University of Rome (La Sapienza), the design of which was presided over by Marcello Piacentini and which included design contributions by Italy's leading architects, including Gio Ponti and Giuseppe Pagano. The fascist contributions to Roman architecture are various; some are even stunning. However, it is the unjust history of the borgate that will be most important in understanding the landscapes and buildings we see in Pasolini's films.

Rome's population grew under fascism and continued to do so in the postwar period. In 1936 the city's population numbered 1,155,722. By 1951 this number had reached 1,651,754. By 1960 Rome reached the two million mark.[35] This means essentially that Rome doubled in size in the space of less than thirty years, adding one million inhabitants to its population. Rome's growth was an effect of what is called the Italian "economic miracle," or, popularly, "il boom." The postwar period was, of course, a period of enormous economic and urban growth across Western Europe and America, what the historian Paul Ginsborg calls "the golden age of international trade."

Expressing wonder at Italy's unprecedented growth in this period, Ginsborg asks the question that has often been the object of historical speculation and research: "How was it that Italy, far from playing a minor role in this great era of expansion, became one its protagonists?"[36] A comprehensive answer to this question cannot be essayed here, but a short answer—the one offered by Ginsborg himself—would mention at least some of the following factors: the influx of American investment under the Marshall Plan; the ending of fascist-era protectionism and the opening and deregulation of Italian markets; the discovery and subsequent production of cheap fuel on the Italian peninsula; the aggressive entrepreneurship of Italy's automobile and consumer goods industry; and the cheap price of Italian labor.[37] Even though Rome has remained forever undeveloped as an industrial center, its growth was similar to that of the northern industrial cities due to its becoming a banking and finance center and to the growth of the postwar governmental bureaucracy. While these sectors are traditionally middle class, Rome still attracted waves of subproletarian migrants who sought work in the construction and service industries. The rapid influx of inhabitants would change the look of the city and the feel of its material reality. One of the ways it did this was through its making necessary (as immigration has throughout the history of modern Rome) the construction of housing to shelter the city's newest citizens—of middle-, working- and subworking-class origins. But the growth of the construction industry and the demands placed upon it functioned in a sort of Moebius strip manner: the housing industry was coddled by the state and given total autonomy in order to promote its growth so as to create jobs for new migrants; this growth in jobs attracted more migrants who, in turn, increased the need for more housing. Housing developments—public and private, middle and working class—spread like architectural cancer in massive blocks and rows, creating dense, inchoate outgrowths of the city center that continued to be concentrated in the southern, southwestern, and, to a lesser degree, the northeastern reaches of the city.

Most of this development was the result of real-estate speculation in the private sector. During the boom years of the 1950s and 1960s, the government, in its desire for economic growth at any cost, chose to look the other way as developers disobeyed building codes and zoning laws. Structures were built on sites unsuitable for large-scale development, and high-density high-rises were thrown up in areas zoned for low-density inhabitation. Where well-planned low-rise apartment buildings might have spread out in neighborly order, skyscrapers aggressively rubbed their hypertrophied shoulders against one another.[38] Like the immigration statistics from these years, the number of dwellings built in a short space of time is stultifying: 73,400 in 1950, 273,500 in 1957, 450,000 in 1964.[39] The construction industry was one of the most profitable sectors of the economy in this period, an integral participant in the boom.[40] The Italian government did institute several housing schemes in the postwar period, the most important of these—both architecturally and in terms of the needs it met—was the INA Casa housing scheme. This program, which will be discussed in detail in chapters 4 and 5, added a number of large complexes of lower- and lower-middle-class housing in Rome's peripheral neighborhoods and in some cases acted as a magnet for private developers.

Neorealist films, especially those films shot in Rome and set in the postwar period (rather than those depicting the Nazi occupation and partisan resistance, like *Rome, Open City* [*Roma città aperta*, Roberto Rossellini, 1945]), are heavily invested in the history of the borgate, the crises of housing shortages, the growth of the periphery, and the concomitant redefinition of Rome's geography in the postwar period. De Sica's *Umberto D.* (1952) and *The Roof* (*Il tetto*, 1956), both shot in Rome, are manifestly and primarily *about* housing conditions in the capital.[41] The same is true of De Sica's *Miracle in Milan* (*Miracolo a Milano*, 1951), though it relocates these concerns to the northern Italian metropolis. Likewise, housing conditions in the Roman periphery figure prominently in the omnibus film *Amore in città* (Love in the city, 1953), a project overseen by Cesare Zavattini, De Sica's regular collaborator on screenplays and a theoretician of neorealism. The film featured short films directed by Zavattini himself, Carlo Lizzani, Michelangelo Antonioni, Dino Risi, Federico Fellini, Francesco Maselli, and Alberto Lattuada.

This interesting and understudied piece of neorealist filmmaking reflects the diversity of filmmaking practices among directors who understood themselves or were understood as neorealists.[42] The most interesting episodes in the film blur the line between documentary reenactment, documentary interviews, and reportage. Antonioni's contribution,

"Tentato suicidio" (Attempted suicide), exemplifies compellingly and hauntingly this mix of techniques. An interest in the borgate and the landscape of the periphery obtains generally across the seven episodes. In the first episode, directed by Carlo Lizzani, "L'amore che si paga" (Love that is paid for), several prostitutes are interviewed and photographed "at work" as they linger along the embankments of the Tiber, on buses and trams, at bars and on streetcorners. The film finally follows the last of these subjects home, to a small shanty built onto the side of one of the aqueducts that are found along the Rome-Naples train line, not far from the Via Tuscolana.[43] Such a dwelling would have been on the absolute lowest scale of habitation in the borgate. The film does not treat the location (and it is a real location) melodramatically. Though a sense of plaintiveness reigns, the presentation of this woman's house is matter-of-fact; it speaks for itself. In the second episode, "Tentato Suicidio," both the sound and image tracks direct our attention to the architecture of the periphery, specifically that of the borgate rapidissime. This episode is broken into several smaller episodes, each a narrative of a woman's botched attempt at suicide, attempts essayed in each instance as a result of romantic disappointment. Each, as well, is clearly situated in the periphery: punctuating the film are shots of large housing projects sitting forlornly next to empty fields. The last of these tells the story of Maria, who is involved in an unhappy love triangle. The film clearly grounds this story in the neighborhood of Val Melaina, the aforementioned fascist borgata that served as the location for *Bicycle Thieves*. Again, this rather desolate landscape of very large buildings in the middle of what appears to be nowhere is clearly meant to underscore the unhappiness of these lives. But rather than simply employ the landscape as metaphor, the film seems to suggest the material as well as psychic challenge to happiness that living in such a place would present.

The last of the episodes, "Gli italiani si voltano" (Italians turn around), directed by Alberto Lattuada, seems, in its first minutes, to be playing in a different key. Essentially the film begins as what might have been a rather stupid pun: the italiani who are turning around are actually italian*i*— that is to say, Italian men—whose "turning around" consists of ogling the abundance of buxom women to be seen on the streets of Rome's center. The film gives us a cheery (but really rather creepy) montage of such shots, with the women's bouncing breasts and bottoms made cartoonish by a cheery, mickey-mousing musical score. The pun, of course, is that we might have thought "italiani" to refer to *all* Italians, men *and* women (as the plural ending *i* can stand for male and female), and the "turning around" to refer to Italy's nascent postwar economic recovery, which would very soon develop into the economic miracle. Just as—or rather, long after—this extended joke begins to pall, the film shifts registers: a young woman gets on a bus bound, we discover, for the periphery. In the crush of human bodies all standing uncomfortably together, she realizes she is being molested by a middle-aged man—an average, middle-class, rather pathetic-looking man in a suit. As the bus empties after several stops, she is able to move away and sit apart from him, although he continues to stare at her. As we see the uneven landscape of the periphery roll by outside the window (glimpses of old farmhouses encroached on by large apartment blocks), she tries to deflect his unwanted attention by pulling her short skirt over her knees. Finally, she gets off at her stop, only still to be followed by the man. The environs of this bus stop are little more than a crossroads and a construction site—a desolate and provisional place. The feeling at this moment would be quite sinister were it not leavened by the return of the bouncy score that had accompanied the earlier montage of stares and décolletage. The man follows briskly on the woman's heels, but she finally runs into the doorway of her building, a large, brand-new apartment building that sits alone at the edge of this anonymous nowhere. The film ends with a long shot of the man outside the building, nothing else around, really, save for power lines, and, far in the distance, more large, new apartment buildings. The film is clearly an expression of an anxiety about what exactly this "turnaround" will mean for Italy. Playful prurience in Rome's center turns into squalid perversion—perhaps even real physical danger—at the city's (new, expanding) periphery. We wonder whether such a new Italy will come to any good. My intention in lingering over this rather slight film is to show that even in a film as silly as this, the subject of postwar urban development emerges as central to the film's concerns. Peripheral Rome is clearly much more than a setting or a backdrop to these stories; indeed, it *is* the story.

Amore in città and the other films I've mentioned (and to which I shall turn in later chapters) all also demonstrate that the changes taking place in Rome's geography were intertwined with the vicissitudes of film culture of the postwar period, particularly neorealist filmmaking. Thus film history and urban history together constitute a rich context that precedes, informs, and is visible in Pasolini's novels and poetry, and in *Accattone* and *Mamma Roma*. Pasolini was witness to this history—to both the sordid conditions of the borgate and to the rapid transformation of the uneven peripheral landscape into what Eleanor Clark, the writer and sometime Roman, calls "a howling wilderness of new apartment complexes . . . of instant slums, pushing out farther every day like some malign vegetation disguised in steel and stucco."[44]

Chapter 2

"Rome, Ringed by Its Hell of Suburbs"

Shortly after the close of World War II, Pasolini was living in Friuli, the northern Italian region of his maternal ancestry, where he had waited out the war's devastation with his family, managing to avoid active duty on a student's dispensation. He had taken up residence in the village of Casarsa, his mother Susanna's hometown, when at last— after the war's interruption—he received his *laurea,* his degree, from the University of Bologna, where he completed a thesis on the nineteenth-century Italian poet Giovanni Pascoli. In Casarsa Pasolini threw himself into the idylls of rural village life. He rode his bicycle everywhere, seeking out the company of the peasant boys whose earthy liveliness he admired and desired. He joined the local communist cell and worked actively inside it. He taught the local schoolchildren, using innovative and creative pedagogical techniques—inventing fables to teach Latin lessons, asking students to bring him folksongs for literary analysis—that won him the love of his students and the gratitude of their parents. He began as well to take an especially keen interest in the "mother tongue" of the region, Friulian, a local dialect possessed of its own, ever more local subdialects. Pasolini seized on Friulian as a vehicle for his own creative purposes, but the Friulian that Pasolini began to compose in was an invention all his own. As a spoken language, Friulian varied across short distances; in the region "it was possible in ten minutes by bicycle to pass from one linguistic area to another more archaic by fifty years, or a century, or even two centuries."[1] Pasolini strained his experiences of Friulian's various dialects through his own linguistic sieve to create a personal poetic patois. Pasolini's intention, in his own words, was to perform a "semantic expansion operated on sound pushed to the limit of transferring meaning into another linguistic domain, from which it returns gloriously indecipherable."[2]

The lyrical voice predominates in the Friulian poems, and an overwhelming sense of premature nostalgia pervades. We often see Pasolini lamenting the forfeiture of something that he has yet to lose and perhaps never possessed in the first place. Images and scenery blur in the fading light of dusk. Today the poems seem rather distant—faintly clinical for poetry so personal and cathected on so many levels (familial, linguistic, geographical). The insistence on composing in a dialect not really his own[3] emits of academic preciosity, perhaps even of unwitting anthropological condescension. As John Ahern has written, "Pasolini chose dialect not to get a better grip on reality, but as absolutely pure language. . . . He worried Friulano into a delicious music."[4] But we should endeavor not to miss the fragrance of political and cultural resistance that the poems exuded in the period of their production and earliest publication. Official fascist culture had sought to unify a geographically and linguistically fragmented Italy through a variety of means, not the least of which was through the government's insistence that everyone speak in proper standard Italian (really, Florentine) and that dialect speech be refrained from if not suppressed. Given this state of affairs, Pasolini's effort to write in Friulian was a (timid, perhaps) slap in the face of fascist officialdom and a celebration of a language that was surely dying. Thus the Friulian poems should be seen as an admixture of pure poetry, political resistance, and ethnography. When his first small volume of poems, *Poesie a Casarsa,* was published in 1942, the poet Gianfranco Contini could not publish his appreciative review of it in an Italian newspaper on account of fascist censorship. Instead Contini's review appeared in a Swiss paper.[5] Pasolini's political gesture, however minor, had not gone unnoticed, at least by the fascist censors.

My intentions here for considering Pasolini's Friulian poems lies not so much in the poems themselves, but in their difference from the poetry and other literary work that Pasolini was to produce in Rome. A brief look at a few of his Friulian poems will prepare us to appreciate the astounding impact that Rome exerted on his poetic and linguistic imagination.[6]

The first poem of *Poesie a Casarsa,* "Il nini muàrt" (The dead little boy), begins on an oxymoronic note of death and rebirth, evoking a twilit world of lowly pastoralism. The imagery and the parsimonious economy of diction are, however, as affected as affecting:

> Luminous evening, in the ditch
> the water rises, a pregnant woman
> walks through the field.

> I remember you, Narcissus, you had the color
> of evening, when the bells
> toll death.[7]

Clearly we are in the realm of the decadent. The apostrophe to Narcissus uttered in Friulian combines a cosmopolitan voluptuousness with a lexicon of rural imagery.[8] The clipped succession of images might bear some kinship to the poetry of Pascoli or Montale. The self-conscious mythological reference feels positively *fin de siècle*. This poetry is perhaps closest to the work of the Symbolists, particularly to Paul Valéry, who Pasolini self-consciously adopted as a poetic role model.[9] Edmund Wilson's remark about a poem of Valéry's, "Profusion du Soir," in which the landscape "the poet is watching is assimilated to his state of mind until it seems only a set of images for a complex of emotions and thoughts,"[10] could also serve as an apt description of the note struck in "Il nini muàrt." Another example, this one from a volume published in 1949 and entitled *Dov'è la mia patria* (Where my country is), "El cuòr su l'aqua" (The heart of the water), gives more evidence of the poetry's contradictory cosmopolitan pastoralism:

> It is Sunday! I am alone
> in a small boat on the Lemene.
> the Burino seems velvet.

> Everyone is celebrating and I alone,
> half-naked in the heart of the Lemene,
> warm my rags in the velvet sun.

> I don't have a cent. I own only
> my golden hair on the Lemene
> full of little velvet fish.

> Full of sins is my solitary heart.[11]

Three words are repeated in each stanza: alone, Lemene, and velvet. These are respectively: a word describing the condition of the subject, a place name, and the name of the fabric most seductive to the touch of the fetishist. The speaker is alone, gloriously, self-pityingly so, while the landscape against which both mind and body rub themselves is all cut of the same voluptuous cloth. This is the autoerotic ego remaking nature in its own image. Different from the identification with nature as might be performed in Romantic poetry, here nature is subsumed by the ultra-refined and narcissistic ego of the speaker—an action more closely identified, again, with the decadent poetry of the fin de siècle. Both of these poems involve themselves in the compilation of a series of images, all of which together point at some meaning which remains unexpressed or inexpressible.[12] And it is the landscape that seems at once to be harnessed into the service of poetic expression and also that thing whose meaning poetry cannot penetrate. These observations should be borne in mind when I return later to analyze Pasolini's Roman poems. Pasolini continued to compose verse more or less in this vein until the fragile tissue of his Friulian pastoral began to unravel precipitously.

In the years immediately following the war, Pasolini kept busy writing, editing, teaching, and organizing for the local PCI (Italian Communist Party) cell. He was a stock figure in the villages around Casarsa: the intense, idealistic young schoolteacher, always on his bicycle. Pasolini's bicycle allowed him the mobility to pursue his microlinguistic study of Friulian, and also to cruise for sexual encounters with the local young men. His relationship with one younger boy, Tonuti Spagnol, was the basis of an autobiographical fiction he composed in these years, which was not published until 1982 under the title *Amado mio* (My beloved). The nature and extent of Pasolini's sexual activities is not really clear, although the prolific nature of his later, better-documented sexual life would seem to point the imagination in a suitable direction. By the summer of 1949, however, there were rumors afloat of his sensual inclinations. These attached themselves to the consternation that his fervid communism inspired in the more conservative citizens of Casarsa and environs.[13] Any of Pasolini's detractors had ample reason to decry him after the events of September 30, 1949, became public.[14]

In the hamlet of Ramuscello, near Casarsa, Saint Sabina's Day was celebrated with a dance held on a wooden platform set amid farmland. Pasolini was there; he was a regular at most events where the local boys could be expected to turn up. What happened that day is a matter of public record, but the clipped confessions and testimonies still present us with only a vague picture of what actually transpired. Pasolini evidently approached a young man he had met before. Somehow this boy and three others ended up accompanying Pasolini to a nearby copse of trees in an adjacent field where he and the boys masturbated themselves and each other. Two boys were sixteen, one fifteen, and the last fourteen years of age. Seemingly the whole affair went down without any trouble—as usual, perhaps. But three weeks later, on October 22, charges were filed against Pasolini at the local carabinieri (state police) station: "corruption of minors" and "obscene acts in a public place."[15] Only one week later, before the charges were ever even heard in court, Pasolini was stripped of his membership in the PCI. *L'unità,* the official national PCI daily newspaper, published this summary of the party's attitude toward the matter:

> We take as our starting point the bringing of a serious disciplinary action against the poet Pier Paolo Pasolini in order once again to denounce the deleterious influence of certain ideological currents coming from Gide, Sartre and other decadent poets and literati, who seek to present themselves as progressives but in reality bring together the most harmful aspects of bourgeois degeneration.[16]

Pasolini quickly thereafter lost his teaching post as well. Casarsa, which had been a paradise, changed overnight into a claustrophobic dystopia. The charges never stuck, but the damage was done; Pasolini could not go on living in Friuli. Three months after his fall from grace, on January 28, 1950, Pasolini and his mother took the train south, toward Rome. Pasolini's father, Carlo Alberto, of whom the war had made a mess and a monster, was left sleeping in his bed; he would wake to find his wife and son had disappeared. Pasolini's uncle Gino Colussi lived in Rome with his lover, a successful German dentist. These two men helped to settle Pasolini and his mother in Rome. They found Susanna a situation as a nanny in the household of an architect and Pasolini a room in a flat in Piazza Costaguti, an irregular little elbow of a piazza in the heart of the Jewish ghetto. Thus, under an inauspicious cloud of scandal, Pasolini began his life as a Roman.

Pasolini's first home in the city was actually right in its historic center. The Jewish ghetto in Rome is tucked away in relative obscurity, but bounded at its irregular frontiers by the Campidoglio, the Largo Argentina, and the Tiber. The ghetto is a neighborhood—medieval in its narrow-streeted intimacy—very much like many of the older neighborhoods destroyed by Mussolini's *sventramenti.* Areas adjacent to and overlapping with the borders of the ghetto, in fact, were heavily redesigned under fascism, making the ghetto an interesting nodal point from which to survey the fascist interventions in the fabric of the city. Poetically it was a fitting home for the exiled Pasolini. Despite the close confines of his single room, his lodgings were particularly well located for the pursuit of pleasure. Nearby were both the Monte Caprino and the Circo Massimo, both cruising grounds for anonymous gay pickups and outdoor sex. Nearby also was the Tiber, with its pissoirs and bathing scene in the summer months, all of which offered a plenitude of options for easy sex. And there were the trams that led directly from the Largo Argentina, just around the corner, to the peripheral neighborhoods beyond Trastevere. In the periphery, soon to become home to the exiled young poet and his parents, Pasolini began to discover the culture of the Roman subproletariat. For Pasolini this culture—and he came to insist on its uniqueness as a culture apart from bourgeois Italian life—still possessed a premodern vitality that he believed he had found in Friuli and lost in leaving it. In many ways, Pasolini transferred his love of the Friulian peasantry and its strange regional tongue directly to the subproletariat of peripheral Rome and its linguistic specificity. Indeed, as critics have pointed out, there is a great deal of conceptual continuity between Pasolini's Friuli and his borgate.[17] The borgate of Rome's periphery would change Pasolini's life. He would come to devote the better part of an entire decade of productivity to representing life in the borgate, studying its dialects, courting its boys.

The most significant poetry that Pasolini wrote in this early Roman period spent in the ghetto is his *Rome 1950, A Diary (Roma 1950, diario)*. The poems that make up this collection—only fifteen in all—manifest Pasolini's extreme melancholy and sense of geographic and spiritual dislocation during his first days in Rome. The volume was not published until a decade after the poems were written, well after Pasolini had earned considerable fame and notoriety as both poet and novelist. Anthony Oldcorn, the first translator of the diary into English, claims that the poems "document a moral crisis, precipitated by his recent experience of social ostracism." Oldcorn understands this moral crisis to be essentially about Pasolini's effort to reconcile his difference—in part expressed by his homosexuality—with the traditions—religious, literary, cultural, familial—he had inherited. Oldcorn ascribes the poems' "bleached voice" to Pasolini's intention to resist the tradition of Italian modernist hermeticists whose diction and imagery tend toward the gemlike. Instead, Oldcorn places the poems closer to the literature of neorealism—then flourishing, alongside neorealist cinema—and its unaffected, popular language.[18] If Oldcorn is right, then the lowered tone of the poems might be an early sign that Pasolini has departed literarily from the earthy empyrean of his Friulian idyll. Certainly the first poem of the series begins on an abrupt, declamatory note, much closer to spoken language than any of the Friulian delicacies Pasolini had been in the habit of whipping up:

> An adult?—Never; like existence
> that does not ripen, is forever green
> from glorious day to glorious day.
> My only course is to be true
> to the awesome monotony of the unrevealed.
> That is why, happy, I never knew abandon,
> why, in the anxiety of my guilt,
> I never truly entertained remorse.
> Faithful ever faithful to the unexpressed
> at the root of what I am.[19]

The refusal to mature, to grow, would seem to draw its strength from the trauma of the events that "brought" Pasolini to Rome.[20] Although no specifically urban images appear here (quite the opposite, in fact, is true: the only imagery is horticultural), there are two tropes worth noting that will figure largely in Pasolini's subsequent attempts to grapple poetically with the city of Rome. The first of these is contained in the lines: "My only course is to be true / to the awesome monotony of the unrevealed." Oldcorn's measured rendering of these lines must, perforce, lose some of their specificity, which might be more literally rendered in English as "I cannot but be faithful / to the stupendous monotony of the mystery." *Stupendo* in Italian carries the same connotations as the English "stupendous": stunning, provoking wonderment, amazement. However, stupendo/stupendous connotes a notion of enormous scale, something so large as to be out of proportion. As we shall understand later, the word figures importantly in one of Pasolini's most significant poems, "The Tears of the Excavator," lines from which this book's title is taken. "Stupendous monotony" gets us closer than "awesome monotony" to an idea important to Pasolini: that the monotony he describes is one that resists representation and does so because of its incomprehensible size.

The last lines add to this same sense of representational crisis. Evident here is Pasolini's notion that something inexpressible defines the core of his experience. Thus there is a link between "the stupendous monotony of the mystery" and the "unexpressed at the root of what I am." I linger here not to quibble unnecessarily with Oldcorn's translation, nor to make claims for this poem's (aesthetic, philosophical) singularity. I emphasize here simply the fact that in one of his very first pieces of creative work to be produced in Rome, Pasolini announces the themes of "stupendous monotony" and of ineffability, two themes that he will join more forcefully in his later attempts (literary and cinematic) to represent Rome's expanding peripheral neighborhoods.

As explained above, Pasolini wrote the poems of his "Roman diary" while living in the cramped but nonetheless picturesquely medieval confines of the Jewish ghetto. The core of the ghetto, to a considerable extent, survived the pickaxe that destroyed other ancient working-class neighborhoods all around it.[21] We might recall that the first official peripheral housing developments housed people who were displaced by Mussolinian sventramenti. Interestingly, in his first years in Rome, Pasolini's residential itinerary—living first in the center and then moving on to peripherally abject Rebibbia—traces the same one mapped by Rome's indigenous proletariat. But the ghetto was his first home, and despite the extremity of his poverty, he was initially spared the periphery's squalor, rich and strange as it was—or at least as he would find it. Thus in these first poems the urban images, when they appear, depict the city as a rather benign and somewhat generically European place. Witness these lines from the fourth poem in the diary's series:

> brisk and sluggish a motor moves away
> over the wet cobbles—the street vendor
> with his pushcart cries and cries—
> beneath the fluttering laundry, the chorus
> is disjointed, blind.[22]

These lines could have been written in a hundred other cities. And the same could be said for much of *Rome 1950: A Diary* in terms of the vagueness of the urban imagery that Pasolini employs. What bears observation in these poems is the way that a certain structure of thought and feeling begins to attach itself to the contours of a city that the poet's mind has not quite penetrated or managed to grasp. Holed up in the ghetto, keeping company with pain and self-pity, Pasolini has not begun really to experience Rome as he would come to know it, or at least we have yet to see the fruit of such experience in these early Roman poems.[23] There are, however, intriguing images that are not specifically or necessarily urban, but that proleptically suggest the way the city would be described and visualized in the later poems and in the films. A significant instance of such imagery occurs in the third of the Roman diary poems, which I give here in full:

> When people's happiness resounds
> more clearly in the narrow streets,
> against walls drenched in sunlight,
> and pushcarts go by, among children,
> kittens, young people arm in arm . . .
> how emptily my destiny echoes in my mind,
> a halo edging things with gloom.
> And if a sound should lift itself
> more sharply against death—a song, a child's
> cry—if on the street the sun,
> dimmed by a dazed cloud, should become
> more gentle. . . . No! You must not think about it![24]

The poem is evidence of a mind that will not be consoled and that refuses the small consolations offered to it. The city bestows this poem's soliloquy with its casual yet busy mise-en-scène: sun-drenched walls, streets, passersby. The image that unevenly divides the poem is the "halo edging things with gloom." Again I wish only to poke gently at Oldcorn's translation which I believe slightly occludes this image's and the poem's most interesting resonances.[25]

The image of the halo follows the brief litany of urban sounds. Next the speaker turns from the exteriority of the city and its sounds to the aural landscape of the inner life. A very literal translation might read: "How destiny echoes more deeply in my mind, that squalid halo of things." Pasolini's mind is exalted and debased—"squalid," and yet its figure is that of a seraphic crown. The particular shape and texture of the image of the squalid halo beckon us to assimilate it to the urban landscape that will become Pasolini's central subject matter, for what else better describes the hapless and haphazard borgate and developments that encircle Rome than the phrase a "squalid halo of things"? Strictly speaking, the image describes only Pasolini's depressed state of mind, but it is this same mind that will find the analogue of its terrors and pleasures in the landscape of the Roman periphery. The "squalid halo of things" also anticipates Pasolini's later evocation of the periphery as a hybrid of the sacred and the profane, the stupendous and the miserable. No wonder, then, that the words used to describe the poet's mind could also so aptly describe the exterior landscape that so enthralled it.

In the penultimate poem of the fifteen that constitute *Rome, 1950: A Diary,* Pasolini employs another suggestive image that functions not only to describe his mental depression and spiritual isolation but also the texture of the Roman periphery. The following lines close the poem:

> and over the outlying districts, from
> Testaccio to Monteverde, dank
> and listless, festers a hum of motors
> and passing voices—the desolate crust
> formed by our world on the silent universe.[26]

Pasolini actually names the neighborhoods outright—the only time specific Roman place names are used in the diary—and he employs the term *periferie*—the periphery, or peripheries, more exactly. This is, as far as I know, the first real mention of the Roman periphery in Pasolini's literary production. The poem evinces a city that becomes less coherent as one approaches its outlying reaches: the rumor of engines, passing voices—all a swish pan of sound and movement. And yet things seem to coagulate into a city of a different order. There is a kind of solid materiality to the phrase Pasolini uses to describe the phenomenal world before him, which, of course, is the world of Rome. This phrase is "desolate crust," or, more suggestively in the original, "*sperduta incrostazione.*" The use of crust or encrustation is almost topographical, belonging to landscape, but also hints at the body and its functions; the root word *crosta* means "scab" in Italian. *Sperduta* might also be translated as "lost," "out of the way," "ill at ease." As Pasolini's eyes direct themselves from the city center that was his short-lived home in that first Roman year to the periphery—Testaccio, Monteverde, and beyond—which would become his spiritual and physical home, his imagery speaks beyond its immediate context and begins to announce a kind of ars poetica of the city—of Rome, that is. "Sperduta incrostazione": a mis- or displaced scab, an index of an injury, a dried clump of bodily fluids, a desultory scatter of homely huts plopped down on packed Roman dirt—all of this floating uneasily on the "silent universe." Pasolini's identification with the city is already apparent in this image that would seem equally apt in describing the borgate or a cum stain (that emblematic glyph signifying a successful trip to the borgate). The scab-like image also suggests a dawning awareness of the political injustice and collective pain that was embodied by the borgate. At this point in the poems, though, these things are still very much only suggestions. In time—a short time—Pasolini's experience of Rome and its periphery would sharpen his sensitivity, hone his language, and provoke his outrage in response to the concrete experience of the development of the city's margins.

Pasolini's letters from this same period express the dawning of Rome's profound impact on his imagination and his creative activity. The letters to his close friend and confidante Silvana Mauri reveal Pasolini at the height of his epistolary powers.[27] Silvana and her brother Fabio were Pasolini's companions from his adolescence and early adulthood in Casarsa. At one time Pasolini and Silvana had idly toyed with the idea of becoming lovers—an idea that, for obvious reasons, bore little fruit. Pasolini's letters to Silvana in the aftermath of his removal to Rome are among the most expansive and most intimate of all of those to be found in his collected letters. His second letter to her after settling in Rome expresses only the newness of the city, its lack of definition in his mind:

> It seems to me that everything has remained in Friuli, like the landscape. Rome stretches out around me as if it too had been drawn in an empty space but yet it has a strong power to console; and I immerse myself in its noises without in that way hearing my own out-of-tune notes.[28]

These sentiments are hardly remarkable. The new arrival often feels himself lost amid the broad novelty of a large city. By the same token, it might strike us as significant that in one of his earliest descriptions of Rome he should be aware of its distension, its "stretching out." In a letter written to Silvana two years later, Rome has, as we would expect, become a much more specific and sensually concrete place for Pasolini. By this time Pasolini had been living for some time in the far-removed suburb of Rebibbia and so is able in the letter to catalog offhandedly the sense impressions of peripheral squalor:

> I have just opened the window on to the balconies of that room . . . that sad builder's site of a room suspended over the mud. . . .
>
> Opening these balconies and colliding breast to breast with spring, which is already adult, almost faded, the true tremendous Roman spring, which you know, and the scent is like an enormous mudguard baked in the sun, a piece of metal, of rags wetted and then dried in the heat, of old iron, of burning heaps of rubbish, I immediately thought of you with a choking flood of sweetness. Some tatter of adolescence remains attached to the skeleton: and all that is needed is the smell of the madeleine. . . . In my case an atrocious madeleine of the outskirts of town, of the houses of the evicted, of warm rags. Altogether I feel the excitement (but without the abundant softnesses of childish fat, of sex ardent with freshness

and unconfined violence) which I felt on Sunday morning in
Bologna, when I had to go to the Imperiale for the retrospec-
tive screenings of the cine club (Machaty, Feyder).[29]

Rags, iron, burning rubbish: not the usual Proustian mnemonic cues.
Pasolini's memory in this passage actually does not work in typical Proustian fashion. There could have been no "atrocious madeleine" in his
childhood to correspond to the borgate's filth. Instead the excitement
itself—sensual, sexual—repeats an earlier sense of excitement and that
excitement (in the Italian Pasolini uses the word *orgasmo*) attaches itself
to the textures and odors of peripheral Rome. Significantly, Pasolini's
exultation in the sensations of his Rebibbian Sunday gives way immediately to thoughts of the cinema. The city and its periphery, desire and
the cinema are all here rather sensually—even carnally—intertwined.
Despite the poverty of his living conditions, Pasolini, as we witness in this
passage, found joy and value in the periphery's squalor. Often this joy
might merely have been sexual; in this same letter to Silvana, Pasolini
mentions the possibility of spending the day watching some boys playing
soccer and then getting drunk with them. But Pasolini also began to find
philosophical and aesthetic stimulation in a terrain that might just as
easily have been understood as an affront to both knowledge and art.

In a letter written to Silvana only a few months later, Pasolini begins
to squeeze from his sense experience of peripheral Rome the first drops
of metaphysical nectar that will flavor much of his production, both literary and cinematic, based in or on the borgate:

For two or three years I have been living in a world with a
"different" feel: an extraneous body and therefore defined
in this world, to which I am adapting myself, and very slowly
coming to terms with. . . . I find myself here in a life which is
all muscles, turned outside in like a glove, which is always un-
folded like one of these songs which I once detested, absolutely
stripped bare of sentimentalism, in human organisms so sensual
as to be almost mechanical; in which one does not know any
of the Christian attitudes, pardon, meekness, etc., and selfish-
ness takes permissible—virile—forms. In the northern world
where I have lived there was always—at least so it seemed to
me—in the rapport between one individual and another, the
shadow of a kind of piety which took the forms of timidity, of respect, of deep anxiety, of strong affection, etc.; in order to break
off a love-relationship only a gesture, a word, was needed. Since
the interest in the intimate, in the goodness or wickedness that
is within us had the upper hand, it was not an equilibrium

between one person and another that was sought but a recip-
rocal impulse. Here among these people who are much more
the victims of the irrational, of passion, the relationship on the
other hand is always well-defined; it is based on more concrete
facts: from the muscular force to social position. . . . Rome,
ringed by its hell of suburbs, is stupendous in these days.[30]

This passage is perhaps the clearest of Pasolini's early articulations of
what we might call his "poetics of the periphery." Here we see that Pasolini has already begun to conceive of the borgate as an absolute world
of archaic values that he opposes to the world of the industrial north
(and by implication, any place ruled by the values of the bourgeoisie,
of capitalism). Rome's peripheral neighborhoods succumbed easily to
Pasolini's allegorical desire.[31] And the colonial imaginary is clearly at
work in his construal of the life of the borgate as inherently more primitive, more "concrete" than life elsewhere. But at the same time, Pasolini
did, indeed, live in these areas, inhabit their spaces, move among and
fraternize with their inhabitants. His writings and his films document
them in a way that cannot simply be dismissed as a mere projection of
colonialist fantasy.

Let us return to the specifics of the passage and the notion of a
"poetics of the periphery." In the borgate Pasolini lives inside out; he is
all nerves and feelings, all sensation. Whereas in the north, exchanges
between people were conducted on the basis of reason, of politesse, of
signs, in the borgate life is fed by "passion" and the "irrational." "Concrete facts" supersede the claims of any civilized discourse.[32] The last lines
that I have quoted seem to spring forth as the summarizing statement
of all that Pasolini has just said: "Rome, ringed by its hell of suburbs,
is stupendous these days" ("Roma, cinta dal suo inferno di borgate,
è in questi giorni stupenda"). Living with one's insides exposed, being
directed by the passions, by the irrational, centering one's life on the
concrete—all of this is implicit in that one sentence, whose incantatory
power begs repetition: "Rome, ringed by its hell of suburbs, is stupendous these days."

The sentence rehearses territory by now familiar: "the squalid halo
of things." Infernal circles. We know from Dante that one reaches the
frozen heart of hell by circling downwards. And like a circle, hell and
its torments have no beginning and no end. Of course, the same can
be said of paradise, and Sam Rohdie is perhaps correct in saying that
the borgate were "Paradises Lost" for Pasolini.[33] However, what makes

peripheral Rome stupendous is actually its specificity, its concreteness, its profusion of material reality. "Stupendous" expresses both the pleasure that the periphery gives to Pasolini, its inhabitant and observer, while also suggesting an element of painful excess.

As the 1950s wore on, Pasolini's desire for success, both critical and financial, was increasingly gratified. This period of furious creativity (though every period of Pasolini's life might be described in such terms) is also the moment at which he enters the cinema as a screenwriter and dialogue consultant on a number of films. The sequence of events is very hard to pick one's way through: when was he working on his novels, and when his poetry? When was he applying himself to commissions that arrived from the world of Cinecittà? For my purposes here, which are not strictly genetic, I would prefer to see all these domains of activity as overlapping and mutually reinforcing, and in fact, Pasolini was probably working at all of these things at once. In Enzo Siciliano's formulation: "These were years of hectic and parallel activity that resists chronological treatment. One gets the impression of simultaneous whirlpools, of work resolutely executed on several keyboards."[34] It is necessary to see the earliest literary production in Rome (including the letters) as a vital prelude to this stage of production. But once he embarks on his literary/cinematic blitzkrieg, trying to figure out which piece of writing neatly paves the way for which successor is more difficult. What follows is, therefore, an account of these intertwined areas of creativity. However, for purposes of conceptual clarity, I will focus in this chapter mostly on his novel *The Ragazzi* (*Ragazzi di vita* [literally, The boys of life], 1955), some of his nonfiction pieces, and his early screenwriting activity. These elements of his work bear most directly on *Accattone,* Pasolini's first film and the subject of the next chapter, whereas *A Violent Life* (*Una vita violenta,* 1959) and *The Ashes of Gramsci* will be taken up later as they bear more significantly on *Mamma Roma.* Separating discussion of these closely related literary works might appear at first problematic. But, as will become apparent later, Pasolini calibrates *Accattone* with the world of *The Ragazzi,* and *Mamma Roma* with *Violent Life.* The relation of each book to its cinematic counterpart is signaled by geographical correspondences between the settings of *The Ragazzi* and *Accattone* and between *Violent Life* and *Mamma Roma.* I will make much of these interrelationships, whose complexity can be better understood by approaching them in two nexuses.

The Ragazzi is perhaps, more than anything else, an experiment in and on language. Just as Pasolini's Friulian poetry attempted to render in written literature a language that had so far eluded precise transcription, so does this novel attempt to push romanesco, or Roman dialect, specifically that variant of it spoken in the borgate, out of pure orality and onto the page. Like Friulian, romanesco had (and has) no single, stable lexicon; thus Pasolini's written version of it is to some extent as much an invention as was his Friulian. But the book is still subtended by a fierce realist, even ethnographic impulse: to render this world of the borgate, if not exactly as it was, at least as truthfully and specifically as could be possible within an aesthetic project. The novel is a hybrid combination of document and invention. It has a concatenating structure that seeks to efface itself as structure. *The Ragazzi,* set during the last gasp of the Nazi occupation of Rome and the early days of the postwar period, chronicles the petty thievery, hustling, and other unglamorous crimes of Riccetto, Marcello, and a chorus of other characters, all children of the borgate, who come in and out of focus in the various episodes of the novel. Certainly there are repetitions of similar events that mark the novel as a product of extreme artifice (e.g., Riccetto's saving a swallow from drowning in the Tiber in the novel's first chapter and his decision not to save Genesio from drowning in the Aniene in the final chapter). But much of the novel seems to move forward as a nearly meaningless accumulation of events that, in its seeming directionless-ness or lack of obvious moral or narrative telos, both fulfills and undermines the nature of narrative fiction as such: narrative *is,* after all, nothing more than one thing after another, and yet narrative fiction generally shapes events so that they seem to amount to something. In this sense, the novel's realism—its endless reporting and relaying of the sensual and linguistic immediacy of the borgate—is consonant with that version of the modernist sensibility that relishes the accumulation of narrative fragments as such and disdains any obligation to produce a whole or a sense of totalizing meaning. In Pasolini's fiction, as in his cinema, there is little sense in maintaining realism and modernism as binary terms. In fact, one of the fruitful byproducts of his work is the blurring and the problematizing of these reified critical categories.

Ultimately, Pasolini is more interested in capturing the linguistic rhythm of life in the periphery than he is in reporting on it visually. Although the setting in both is always the periphery, its visual qualities are rendered irregularly—mostly in occasional flashes of description. And yet setting is absolutely vital to *The Ragazzi,* which sticks close to the periphery's landscape of humble barracche and fascist borgate. When geographic detail is offered, it is done so with an incredible degree of specificity; we are reminded repeatedly of precisely where characters are and how they get from one place to another. Geographic detail is not, in and of itself, unusual in the tradition of the novel. What strikes us in *The Ragazzi* is that Pasolini so insists on the precise coordinates of areas of Rome that were, to most readers in Italy of the 1950s, relatively or completely unknown and unheard of. In reading Alberto Moravia's 1949 *The Woman of Rome,* for instance, the novel's geography often remains for us rather vague, as if Moravia wants only to communicate the respectably shabby and impoverished conditions of the life of the narrator and protagonist, a young woman who falls into prostitution, rather than root us too concretely in a specific place. Witness Adriana, the narrator, describing the situation of her home in the novel's early pages:

> We lived in a small flat on the second floor of a long, low building, erected for the railwaymen fifty years earlier. The house was situated on a suburban avenue pleasantly shaded by plane trees.[35]

That such a house is near the train station and suburban tells us, apparently, all we need to know about the unenviable but still generically very familiar conditions of this life. When Moravia has Adriana report more specifically, she remains on a Roman map that is supremely accessible, legible:

> So we took a streetcar and got off at the top of Via Nazionale. When I was a little girl, mother used to take me for walks along this street. She used to begin from Piazza Esedra, on the right-hand pavement and proceed slowly, looking attentively into every shop window until we reached Piazza Venezia. Then she would cross over and return to Piazza Esedra.[36]

Compare Moravia's heroine's geography with that of Riccetto, *The Ragazzi*'s main character, in that novel's very first paragraphs:

> It's a short way from Monteverde Vecchio to the Granatieri. You go by the Prato, and cut in among the buildings under construction around the Viale dei Quattro Venti: garbage piles, unfinished houses already in ruins, great muddy excavations, slopes heaped with junk. The Via Abate Ugone was just down the way.[37]

This would be unknown terrain for most readers in the mid-1950s. The passage names and depicts what were, during the period in which the novel is set, the furthest reaches of urban development in southwest Rome. At the time the novel was published, these areas (very near to where Pasolini was living at the time in the Via Fonteiana, a street running parallel to the Viale dei Quattro Venti, which lies two blocks to the east) were still close to the furthest edges of southwest urban expansion. The neighborhood comprised the outskirts of petty bourgeois decency and the beginnings of the borgate. It was a landscape that was only coming into (and out of: "house already in ruins") existence, new not only to readers but to Rome itself.[38] In case readers might have found themselves needing to get to the Via Abate Ugone from Monteverde Vecchio, they now knew how. Of course, Pasolini almost mockingly assumes we won't want or need to know this, thus the specificity of the instructions act to scold the provincialism that believes Rome to be only about the Pantheon, the Vatican, the Piazza Farnese. There is something Adamic at work here, as well, as if Pasolini wants to be the first to utter these names in the land of fiction, and thereby to document them factually, to bring them into the realm of our consciousness.

Similar emphases on particular topographical knowledge occur throughout the novel:

> Riccetto and Marcello . . . went down along the Via Ozanam, and slouched along half dead under the burning July sun toward the Ponte Bianco, where they could hitch a ride on the number 13 or the number 28.[39]

A pity he doesn't give us the time of the trams as well! The most exaggerated example of such topographical specificity in the novel is the following passage:

> [A]fter they had elbowed their way to the grade crossing, they found a line of police there, blocking the street. Agnolo and Riccetto tried to argue their way past, on the ground that they lived in Donna Olimpia, but the cops had orders to let no one through, so the boys had to turn back. They tried to go down from the Viale dei Quattro Venti on the side where there was a sheer drop, taking the path that the workmen had made, down past the grade crossing. But there were policemen stationed there too. The only thing left to do was to go the long way around to Donna Olimpia by Monteverde Nuovo. Agnolo and Riccetto returned to the Ponte Bianco, where still more people had gathered by this time, and went up the hill by the

> Gianicolo, taking turns riding on the handlebars, and doing
> long stretches on foot when the hill was too steep. It was at
> least a mile and a quarter to the piazza at Monteverde Nuovo,
> and then another quarter-mile downhill, across fields, by the
> barracks-like buildings housing the refugees, and the con-
> struction lots, to get down to Donna Olimpia from the oppo-
> site side.[40]

Pasolini is not only documenting this part of Rome for us, he is documenting his knowledge of it. The anal, obsessive, concrete specificity is
rivaled perhaps only by Leopold Bloom's Dublin. Yet here with Pasolini,
the point is not just the documentary specificity itself, but the documentary specificity of a place that was not on most people's radar. "Pay
attention to these places," Pasolini is saying. "Here, too, life exists." Or
as David Ward has explained:

> The almost obsessive logging of street names, names of Rome's
> suburban quarters, bus numbers and routes, cinemas, etc., that
> allows us to follow the meanderings of the *borgatari* on a street
> map, reminds us that Pasolini wants to establish a very real
> connection between his text and the city. Clearly, the Rome
> Pasolini gives us in *Ragazzi* and *[A Violent] Life* is not a city born
> of fantasy but one of historical fact.[41]

This preoccupation with places and spaces, with the geography
of an ever-expanding Rome, is a defining feature of Pasolini's literary
production across the 1950s. In a story written in 1953–54 called "Dal
vero" (From life), Pasolini narrates the events inside a long bus ride
from Rebibbia toward the center of Rome, ending at the outskirts in
San Lorenzo (the working-class neighborhood near the University of
Rome where much of *Rome, Open City* was shot). Place names and bus
stops are announced as the narrator describes, proto-cinematically, the
changes in the landscape that occur as the bus moves from periphery
to center.[42] In May 1958, a series of three essays by Pasolini appeared in
Vie Nuove (New pathways), a weekly associated with the PCI. Although
Pasolini had not been a member of the PCI since his expulsion in 1949,
he was allowed to publish in the magazine's pages. This series of articles
was entitled "Viaggio per Roma e dintorni" (Voyage through Rome and
its surroundings), and in these impressionistic but polemical pieces,
Pasolini addresses the miserable living conditions and the rapid development in Rome's periphery. The first of the series, entitled "The City's
True Face," begins abruptly by asking:

> What is Rome? Where is the true Rome? Where does it begin
> and where does it end?[43]

The question of Rome's indeterminate, expansive borders is consonant with Pasolini's depiction of the city in the Roman poems and letters. That these questions should constitute the first lines of his investigation suggests how central the conception of Rome as spatially incontinent was to Pasolini's understanding of the city and its expansive periphery. The Rome that he is interested in is not the city's center, rather the "immense" city that is "unknown to tourists, ignored by the right-minded, and nonexistent on maps" (166). He then goes on to evoke this immense, unknown city in a rough torrent of nouns and adjectives—a squalid visual spectacle available even to tourists and the right-minded who, on the condition that they deign to peer out the window of the train as it pulls into the city, will see:

> . . . clusters of hovels . . . expanses of shacks like Bedouin camps,
> collapsed ruins of mansions and sumptuous cinemas, ex-
> farmhouses compressed between high-rise buildings, dikes
> with high walls, narrow muddy alleyways, and sudden empty
> spaces, empty lots and small fields with a few heads of live-
> stock. Beyond all of this, in the burned or muddy countryside,
> marked by little hills, ditches, old pits, plateaus, sewers, ruins,
> trash piles and dumps. (166–67)

This discontinuous landscape of redundant baseness is the setting of *Accattone*. It is a landscape that, in Pasolini's own words, was "a Rome that wasn't Rome"—an alien territory that circled what is perhaps Europe's best-known city.

The article that was published after "The City's True Face" is entitled "The Concentration Camps." In this article Pasolini gives a brief sketch of the conditions of the fascist borgate rapidissime, describing the poorness of their construction and the unjustness of the regime that built them. He is struck by the way that the housing built by the Christian Democrat regime seems, to his thinking, hardly different from that of the fascists.[44] Here is Pasolini describing what he saw during a visit to the old fascist borgate with new construction going up around them:

> We recently returned to the *borgata* of Gordiani. It is being
> torn down. Where there were lines of atrociously sad, dirty,
> inhuman shacks there is now an expanse of reddish crushed
> stone. And beyond it shimmers, weirdly, the front end of the
> Centocelle neighborhood. . . .

> Most of the inhabitants of these houses have been
> moved . . . to the newly built Villa Gordiani and the Villa Lan-
> cellotti on the Via Prenestina, not far from the old *borgata.*
> I went to see them. In reality nothing has changed. In-
> stead of the small one-story shacks with a little courtyard in
> front, there are brand new buildings. . . . What are the stylistic,
> sociological, or human criteria of these new buildings? They
> are the same as before. This is still a concentration camp. . . .
> The people were transferred *en masse* from an old concentra-
> tion camp to a new one. (174–75)

These two neighborhoods—the borgate Gordiani and Centocelle—are
not just any two neighborhoods. The first is the neighborhood in which
many key scenes of *Accattone* were shot. The second is an INA Casa housing project, Villa Gordian, built in the early to mid-1950s, very much
like the INA Casa project in which *Mamma Roma* is set, the INA Casa
project of Tuscolano II. In fact, the same architect, Saverio Muratori, was
responsible for much of the design of both. Clearly these articles and
the research Pasolini did to write them figure as a necessary link to his
film work and a necessary context within which to understand that work.
The more Pasolini wrote about the periphery, and the more specific and
preoccupied with its material concreteness that that writing became, the
more he seems to be pushed toward cinema as the necessary and vital
mode within which to apply himself to the aesthetic and political issues
that so mattered to him. This notion that it was the Roman periphery's
sense of physical expansiveness and economic, political injustice that
pushed Pasolini toward the cinema is made even more explicit in this
passage from "The City's True Face":

> When one observes this phenomenon of the city that grows
> from year to year, month to month, day to day, the only way to
> comprehend it is through the eyes. The visual spectacle is so
> distressing, grandiose, and senseless, that is seems possible to
> resolve it only through intuition, by a series of uninterrupted
> observations, almost like cinematic "takes"; an infinite num-
> ber of very particular close-ups and infinite number of bound-
> less panoramic shots. (167–68)

In the last of the *Vie Nuove* pieces on the periphery entitled "The
Shantytowns of Rome," Pasolini begins by complaining that the images
of the borgate in 1950s Italian film never depicted the actual squalid
conditions of life in peripheral Rome:

You've seen them in *The Roof*, by De Sica and in Fellini's *Nights of Cabiria*, as well as in the various minor products of Neorealism. There is no one in Italy who does not have at least a vague picture in his mind of the shantytowns around Rome.

But it's always the same: Italian culture in this last decade has been anything but realist, except in the specialized fields of the essay and investigative reporting, inspired by Marxist thought. This realism has only indirectly filtered into the artistic genres: movies, novels, and poetry.

. . . The fact remains that the shantytowns one sees in most more or less courageous Italian films are not the same as the *real* shantytowns.

In fact, I don't think that any writer or director would have the courage to fully represent this reality. He would find it too ugly, too inconceivable, and thus would be afraid of dealing with this "particular," or marginal specific phenomenon. Certain low points of humanity seem impossible to treat in art; apparently certain psychological deviations resulting from abject social surroundings cannot be represented. (177–78)

Pasolini complains here of what might also be called a kind of dilettanteism and sentimentalism in the representation of the poverty of the postwar period by neorealist directors, as he understands their work. Pasolini, as will become clearer in the following chapters, engaged himself in an Oedipal struggle with his neorealist forbears (whose films he sometimes worked on). His characterization of neorealism cannot, therefore, be trusted entirely. For instance, he seems not to recall the use of "real" hovels in *Amore in città*, discussed above, which surely is an impressive exception to the tendency he is describing. And in the case of De Sica's *The Roof*, surely Pasolini might have admitted that the film is committed to representing a serious social problem—the shortage of housing for lower-class citizens of Rome. The film depicts a young couple, Natale and Luisa, who struggle to find their own house in Rome. They settle on a desperate option: build an illegal house on public land during the night. If they manage to finish it, complete with its roof, by morning, the police will not be able to evict them due to an obscure detail in the Italian legal code. The film's narrative deadline—that the house must be completed by dawn—while it should be felt as an awful, tyrannical burden, is actually experienced in the film as the cause of narrative suspense, a goad for narrative action that is at turns comic, pathetic, and finally sentimental. The house completed, a new day breaks over the

Roman periphery, and our couple is—though still impoverished and disenfranchised—content. The film's happy ending has a kind of fullness that, in spite of the degrading circumstances of which it is a part, pushes the broader causes and implications of this situation outside the frame and outside the field of our critical reflection. Similarly, Fellini's *Nights of Cabiria* wants to picture the borgata where Cabiria lives as a kind of metaphysical, rather than social and economic, landscape. The odd peripheral landscape, like Cabiria herself, comes across as a poetic exception to normal life, which is elsewhere.

Pasolini worked on the dialogue of *Nights of Cabiria*. He also collaborated on a number of other screenplays at the time—most notably those in which there were some scenes set in the periphery. Mauro Bolognini's *La notte brava* (The great night, 1959), on which Pasolini collaborated, has a few important scenes in the borgate in which we see the usual "hovels" with newer apartment buildings hovering just nearby. Such scenes in the film function in relief to the scenes that take place in the historic center or on the Via Veneto. While they acknowledge the desperate reality of the borgate, they do not represent them as an urgent reality; they exist more as metaphorical counterpoint to life that, again, is elsewhere. They are exercises in the picturesque of the impoverished.

Working on such films introduced Pasolini to the world of filmmaking, to the formal and technical exigencies of the craft, to its material and financial conditions of production. But clearly such filmmaking could not satisfy his relentless desire to represent the borgate and peripheral existence in all their specific material detail as he had in *The Ragazzi*. Just as his literary work seems to have exhausted itself in trying to grapple with Rome ("the only way to comprehend it is through the eyes"), so too his work as screenwriter and collaborator on mainstream films of the 1950s seems to have propelled him out of such an (ultimately) unsatisfying collaborative domain and into a territory hitherto uncharted in cinema. At the end of "The Shantytowns of Rome" Pasolini describes the vision of a little boy standing outside one of these hovels, who, upon seeing Pasolini and his friends pass by his miserable dwelling, "put his little grubby hand to his mouth, and happily and affectionately, on his own initiative, blew us a kiss" (181). This gesture leads Pasolini to close his article with the following:

> The pure vitality that is at the core of these souls is the combination of evil in its purest form and good in its purest form, violence and goodness, depravity and innocence, despite every-

thing. And for this reason something can, and must, be done
for them. (182)

This is more than the conclusion—perhaps rhetorically overloaded—of
an article written for a communist paper. Beginning as the article does,
as a reflection on what has been lacking in Italian cinema until now,
clearly the "what" that must be done is the production of Pasolini's own
films about these same conditions. His turn to filmmaking is a political
action that springs directly out of an urgent encounter with the material
experiences of those people living in Rome's peripheral suburbs.

Furthermore, and as I shall argue in the next chapter, the landscape of the periphery is not merely recorded by Pasolini's camera. His
bold stare is starkly different from the skittish glance of his imaginary
tourist looking out from his train seat, or from that of a Fellini or a De
Sica. Rather, this landscape left its imprint on Pasolini's aesthetic—his
mode of seeing and representing; the periphery's uneven and dilating
contours can be felt in the formal manufacture of his films themselves.
Furthermore, the encounter of filmmaker and landscape is not merely
the encounter between a viewing subject and an object of vision. Embedded in this encounter is also a confrontation between a film director
and his cinematic forbears—between Pasolini and the legacy of Italian
neorealism.

Chapter 3

"Scandalous Desecration":
Accattone against the Neorealist City

Pasolini's first film opens with a close-up of a man's vulgar laughing face, its mouth missing teeth, a bouquet of flowers bunched next to it, crowding the frame. The shot is simple, crude, abrupt; its function is difficult to interpret. Rather than express anything discursive or psychological, this opening close-up, in Geoffrey Nowell-Smith's words, expresses only "the enigma that is the human face";[1] in other words, the face just "is"—and furthermore, it first appears to us dislocated from both its body and its immediate surroundings. As the film cuts to this face's interlocutors, we see the character in his physical milieu. The first image of the film gives us absolutely no clue as to its location; the laughing face is abstracted from its surroundings by means of the close-up. Obviously, this is Italy; people are speaking Italian—or some version of it—and, what's more, a group of men is seated outside a bar, a ubiquitous tableau of Italian social life. (Actually, if we were skilled in the dialects of the Italian peninsula we might pick up that the characters are speaking some form of romanesco.) There are buildings in the background lining a seedy street that extends back and away. It is an urban location of sorts, that much seems true: taller, newer buildings—apartment high-rises—glower over one-story shanties. It seems safe to say that we are not in the middle of some *centro storico*. It is difficult to work out exactly where we are. This is because we are in the borgate, that zone where city meets field and high-rise meets hovel.

Spatial illegibility in the opening shot of *Accattone.*

But to pause again at the first shot of the laughing face: it interests us not so much for what the face expresses—humor, a sociological type, an enigma. Rather, the shot is remarkable for what it is not. It is not an establishing shot, the stock-in-trade of fiction films, especially films that are set in cities and that, like *Accattone,* are principally about characters traveling to and from different locations in the city. There is no knowing where we are in that first shot; space and location are, as yet, unquantifiable and unintelligible. And once we get a bit more information, we are still fumbling toward some recognition of place. Perhaps I risk overstating my case, but let us compare this film's opening shots with those of another film that is "about" Rome: *Rome, Open City.* In that film, our first image is of German soldiers crossing the well-trod and easily recognized pavement of the Piazza di Spagna. The effect of such a shot: "This is Rome."[2] The initial shot of Pasolini's first film proposes the same thing, only we recognize this in retrospect. "This is Rome"; yes, but this is a Rome yet unknown to most, one of toothless grins, lowly streets, proliferating shacks, and unmarked open spaces whose names we cannot guess. The location is more disorienting, for example, than the shots of the fascist borgate that open *Bicycle Thieves* because in that instance, the apartment buildings of the Val Melaina project at least firmly anchor the shots inside the recognizable iconography of mass (urban) housing.

In *Accattone*'s initial scene, after the man who is the subject of that first close-up has continued on his way, the men seated outside the café discuss (with an earnestness and intensity perhaps unwarranted by their subject) the danger posed by swimming too soon after eating. Among these men is the title character, Accattone (played by Franco Citti), who wagers he can eat a full meal and swim back and forth across the Tiber (really just a ploy on his part to get a free dinner). A simple cut ends this scene. Pasolini finally gives us the security of knowing we are in Rome in the next shot. This shot is a close-up of Accattone stuffing forkfuls of potatoes into his mouth; behind this activity we clearly see one of Gian Lorenzo Bernini's angels that line the Ponte Sant'Angelo, and behind this, the grim, crenellated battlements of the Castel Sant'Angelo. A cut to one of Accattone's companions, also stuffing himself, shows the Ponte Vittorio Emmanuele II's bronze allegorical statues hovering not too distantly. From their spatial position below and between the two bridges we infer that Accattone and his mates are on some sort of barge anchored in the Tiber.[3] Citizens, students, and tourists of Rome can recognize these landmarks quite easily. They may not announce "Rome" as markedly as, say, a shot of the Pantheon or St. Peter's, but these are very visible points on the Roman map. The upshot of all this, then, is that within the space of a single cut Pasolini has moved us from the geographic obscurity of the borgate to the legible, intelligible center of historic Rome. Such a move, perhaps, is not remarkable in and of itself; one of cinema's greatest prerogatives is to change locations boldly across the interval that separates two frames of celluloid. But Pasolini's cut from urban obscurity to urban intelligibility strikes us because he handles it with so little fanfare. In the transition to the film's second scene at the Tiber, there is no establishing shot; we are "established" only by the background — the Castel Sant'Angelo and the two bridges. Thus, despite the valorized nature of this second location, Pasolini does not shoot it in a manner that differs appreciably from how he shoots the lowly landscape of the borgate. His decision to shoot and edit in this way is not necessarily radical, but it is significant.[4] It suggests disdain for the typical fantasies inspired by Rome's cultural and architectural patrimony. The structures and sites that Pasolini will probe most carefully do not appear on any typical tourist itinerary. In fact, this scene is one of the very few times that Pasolini ever offers any sustained view of heroic, typically recognizable Rome. From this scene on, almost entirely, Rome, for Pasolini, is elsewhere.

Parataxis reigns through much of Pasolini's cinema. We have already witnessed one example in the cut from the first scene in the borgate to

Accattone eating his potatoes beneath the Ponte Sant' Angelo.

the second at the Tiber. From a shot of Accattone laughing, vaunting his courage to stuff himself and swim across the river, food dangling from his masticating maw, the film cuts to a medium-long shot of Accattone on the balustrade of the Ponte Sant'Angelo. On screen left, one of Bernini's famous angels is visible from its waist up; the angel wields a cross like a truncheon. Its marble head is angled away from Accattone's body, which is fully visible at the very center of the frame and clothed in a short bathing costume. This shot has received a fair amount of attention by commentators on the film. Since this scene is one of the few in Pasolini's cinema to utilize one of Rome's historic monuments, it deserves comment. Although Pasolini's camera gives this location only cursory treatment, some sense must be made of Pasolini's decision to locate this scene here and so intentionally to utilize the Ponte Sant'Angelo as a signifying element in the scene.

The Ponte Sant'Angelo was designed by Bernini as part of a seventeenth-century urban planning project that clarified the approach to St. Peter's and the Vatican, linking the pope's residence with the city's other pilgrimage churches. The bridge was intended as the first grand stage in a procession that would lead from the historic city center, across the Tiber, opening onto the Borgo Pio, which led to the outstretched arms of Bernini's colonnaded Piazza San Pietro. The Castel Sant'Angelo, which sits guard over the bridge, is actually a structure that survives from ancient Rome and has been in continual use ever since. Designed by

Accattone and one of Bernini's angels atop the Ponte Sant' Angelo.

the emperor Hadrian to serve as his mausoleum and begun after his death in A.D. 128, the building originally boasted a skin of fine marble and was crowned with exquisite statuary and pine trees planted over its upper levels. Later it was stripped of its marble (put to use adorning the basilicas of Christian Rome) and used as a fortress and papal residence. When *Accattone* was shot, the Castel Sant'Angelo was in use as a museum, which remains its function today.

One could run the risk of overinterpreting a film's location, but it is unlikely that this location was chosen casually. The bridge has a special resonance as a testament to a grandiose form of urban planning. Centuries after the bridge was built, the fascist regime, in one of its phases of the aforementioned *sventramenti*, razed the buildings along the Borgo Pio and began radically widening the street and building unimpressive but massive travertine buildings along it, renaming it the Via della Conciliazione, as a testament to the accord reached between the regime and the Vatican in 1928. The project was interrupted by the war and completed in the early postwar period. This project displaced thousands of working-class Romans (many whose families had been situated in the neighborhood for centuries) who were re-housed in the borgate in Rome's periphery. This is the history that lies just outside the borders of the image of Accattone on the bridge. Furthermore, this historically dense site is exactly the kind of urban space from which Accattone and his companions are excluded.

Critics and scholars have often paused over the significance of the seeming symbolism of the bridge scene, but only rarely have they discussed the bridge as a specific, concrete urban site with its own history. In Pasolini scholarship we usually encounter a mention only of "Accattone's dive from the bridge with the statues of angels,"[5] or something like the mistaken observation that "when Accattone plunges into the Tiber, the spectator is offered images of his body cross-cut with that of the sculpture of an angel on the bridge."[6] A reader might assume that the Ponte Sant'Angelo could be any bridge with an angel attached to it, instead of the very specific urban site that it is. More recently Angelo Restivo has considered the specificity of the location.[7] Maurizio Viano also lingers over the scene on the bridge:

> [T]he frame with Accattone and the angel reinforces the notion that he does not really belong to his own world. It is a shot that nobody can miss and that many remember, as attested to by critics' frequent mention of it. Is Accattone the "real" angel? Or is this a premonition of his salvation? Or, again, is it an indication that he will stoop low and that the angel will fly high? Whatever the meanings generated by such a contrast, one thing is beyond doubt: the angel is there as a conventional sign of loftiness against which we are to measure Accattone.[8]

I quote this passage at some length and, in so doing, pause over this moment in the film, not necessarily because the sequence is the most interesting in terms of the film's urban discourse, but because it helps to clarify what is particular to my approach to Pasolini's Roman filmmaking. While there is no doubt that Pasolini's choice to frame Franco Citti with the Bernini angel behind him summons (if, perhaps, only to upset) the opposition of sacred and profane, such a metaphorical reading tends to occlude what may be going on at the metonymic level—that is to say, what the site as a physical location may be telling us. I do not reject the legitimacy of Viano's interpretation. However, I prefer instead to bracket questions of metaphor, so that the issues pertinent to the film's material reference to Roman urban history can come to the fore.

A few more things should be noted about this remarkable sequence on and around the Ponte Sant'Angelo that lasts only seconds. Its abrupt temporal hiccup (the cut from Accattone eating to his standing on the balustrade); its rapid shift, from one shot to the next, between close-ups and long shots; its brusque sensuality: these elements all conspire to transmit a sense of dislocation and unease. While we know we are in Rome, we do not know how we get from one space to the next, even within a narrow spatial circumference. The lack of spatial coherence between shots suggests that, at some level, our sense of space in the film—and perhaps in Rome—suffers some deformation. These are actual places; nothing is shot on a set. But the experience of space lacks the coherence associated with good, legible urban design of which the Ponte Sant'Angelo is such a striking example. In this sense, the space photographed by the camera in the scene is put at odds with itself. The film's documentation of a specific and densely historical and iconographic site serves to underscore the way in which the editing and framing derealize it as a legible space.

Shortly after surviving his plunge into the Tiber, Accattone learns that his whore Maddalena, who has just suffered an accident, has her leg in a cast and awaits him at home. Accattone returns to his hovel in the peripheral neighborhood of Pigneto, an area to the east of the city center, off the Via Casilina. Pasolini often published his screenplays at about the same times his films were released. A working screenplay was always, of course, written prior to the film's production and release, but Pasolini made no effort to reconcile the proposed scenes with what was actually filmed.[9] His plans for this scene, in which Accattone returns home, describe a more dramatic urban landscape than the one he ended up using:

> A pile of little Moroccan hovels, each with four cinder block walls and a tin roof: sunk among molting gardens, where the sun bears down furiously.
>
> Accattone arrives among the hovels in the millequattro, on a street thick with dust (all around, vertiginous high rises— new, black and white).
>
> He gets out of the car, passes through two or three little kids—gorgeous as little angels, dressed in rags, who play in the dust—he enters one of the hovels.[10]

In the scene as it exists on film there are no children. There is dust. There are miserable dwellings and pathetic gardens. But there are no high-rises, only a three-story building that flanks the hovel Accattone calls home. The high-rises are a significant omission. Certainly they are prominently visible in many key shots and entire scenes later in the films. Some can even be glimpsed in the first shots of the film. Their mention in the screenplay, though, suggests the degree to which Pasolini's imagination of the film was ordered by an awareness of the dramatic juxtapositions—between high-rise and hovel, for instance—in the peripheral landscape. The lack of visible new construction in this particular scene is not as important as the evidence in the screenplay of an overriding concern to represent and criticize it, which becomes more apparent later in the film and in *Mamma Roma.*

Later that night Maddalena is out walking the streets, somewhere outside the city walls.[11] A gang of Neapolitans, introduced earlier and in Rome to settle a score with Maddalena, comes to pick her up, and she grudgingly, skeptically, goes along with them. Inside the car the first Neapolitan tells Maddalena that she will have no say in choosing their destination. He starts the car, and they depart. The image track cuts to a panoramic pan from left to right, slow and even, that shows a nighttime landscape: pitch black in the foreground; in the middle distance a strand of white apartment high-rises, in various states of completion, with cranes standing at attention next to them and a sparse parade of streetlights and passing traffic before them; in the far distance the dark gray night sky. Following a shot taken inside a moving vehicle, this pan tempts the spectator to read it as an index of that same car's movement, as if the car were moving from left to right and we were able to see it onscreen. In fact, the image is shot at too great a distance to distinguish any one car from the others that pass in the middle plane of the image. From this pan, there is a cut to the car coming over a hill and onto a wild field of grass and nearby rocks. In the far distance are streetlights, hanging luminous and disembodied at the top of the image. The distant streetlights suggest that this might be more or less the location from which the pan was shot. In this wild place, harshly lit by the car's headlights so that the characters swim in light while the background remains benighted, Maddalena is used and then beaten by the Neapolitans. Her beating is an awkward, hieratic ballet, scored only by the sounds of fists on flesh and cries of "Oddio! Mamma! Aiutame!" In the middle of this, the film cuts to another pan of the landscape. The pan cues a shift in the soundtrack, now overtaken by Bach's "St. Matthew Passion," which played briefly before when Maddalena first climbed into the Neapolitans' car.[12] The pan follows exactly the same movement as the one before; this shot differs only by being a little bit darker (perhaps it was shot later?) and being a little shorter in duration, although for all intents and purposes, they might as well be the same shot. The repetition clearly dissociates the shot from any grounding in point of view or character psychology; rather, it expresses a sense of formality and, quite literally, distance.

The scene in the film differs markedly from how it is described in the screenplay. This difference displays the way in which Pasolini's use of the urban landscape seems to have become more interesting and complex in the interval between writing the script and making the film. Indications for the first pan are not given in the screenplay. The only directions for a similar shot are linked to character point of view and appear before the Neapolitans begin to savage Maddalena:

> A few minutes have passed, five, ten. The Neapolitans are sitting around on the dry grass, around the car. They keep quiet, menacingly. Only the second Neapolitan hums, lying stretched out, leaning on his elbow, his legs crossed. He hums, looking around . . . toward the immense circle of twinkling, anguished lights of the city.[13]

How different and how much more complex is what happens in the actual film. That look toward the "anguished lights of the city" has become instead two mysterious and majestic shots, which, to be understood, cannot be linked to a character's eyesight, but to the vision of the film itself. The first one might be understood as an establishing shot, but usually establishing shots are not nearly so opaque: they establish and do so clearly. The second pan is more disorienting because it interrupts the beating scene for no immediately apparent reason.

Pasolini discusses his use of the pan in *Accattone* in an essay entitled "Confessioni tecniche" (Technical confessions). The essay finds Pasolini pondering the meaning and effects of his camera style. He makes much of the crudeness and simplicity of *Accattone*'s cinematography:

> With *Accattone*, inexpert in the cinema as I was, I reduced as much as possible . . . [the] objective simplicity [of the cinematography]. And to me the result seemed—and in part, it was— sacredness: a technical sacredness that then had a deep effect on the landscapes and characters. There is nothing more technically sacred than a slow panning shot.[14]

This sacredness obviously suggests that Pasolini intended shots like the ones that punctuate the scene of Maddalena's beating to possess their own legitimacy and urgency, quite apart from performing any function in advancing the film's narrative, something they clearly do not do. Nor do they provide, through point of view/reverse field cutting, subjective, psychological identification with the character. Rather than *identify with* Maddalena, we are made to *witness* her victimization and the landscape in which it takes place. The shots, in fact, weld Maddalena's victimization to the peripheral landscape. Going further, however, we might wonder whether they also suggest that the landscape itself—the periphery—is the story here. Although our view of it is wide and far away, the peripheral landscape imaged here asserts its primacy through its mere brooding presence, oddly made even more menacing by the stiff, slightly robotic sweep of the camera's movement. Regardless of what particular meaning we might attach to these shots of the periphery, the interpretive challenge that they pose ("what do they mean?") is itself evidence of the fact that the meaning of the film is drenched in the subject of the periphery.

Shortly after this scene, with Maddalena in jail for falsely identifying a few of Accattone's companions as her attackers, Accattone is, so to speak, out of work. He tries to pay a visit to his estranged wife and son to beg for money. The scene begins with a shot of a long, straight, and wretched boulevard, lined with streetlamps and telephone poles. On either side of the road are squat, decrepit hovels, which, despite their squalor, were obviously constructed as a housing project: they sit in regular, one-storied rows running perpendicular to the street. The only trees in sight appear stunted and filthy. The shot lasts only one or two seconds before it begins to pan slowly to the left, revealing in its movement more of this impoverished landscape of dirt and lowly housing. The camera pans a full 180 degrees to cast its gaze exactly opposite to its original direction. The view reveals, still, more of the same, but with just two differences: in the far background, high-rise, newer large apartment buildings and, moving toward us in the foreground, Accattone, all in black. We are in the Borgata Gordiani, the neighborhood mentioned at the close of the last chapter.[15]

This borgata was built in the early 1930s to house those dispossessed by the sventramenti in Piazza Venezia. This was one of the most pitiful and insulting of the borgate rapidissime. The buildings had no running water or electricity, and were built of the cheapest materials. Their poverty of means is obvious in the images we have of them in *Accattone:* only thirty years old when the film was shot, the constructions look to be three times that age, falling apart, many in ruins. As well, the neighborhood was built several kilometers to the southeast of Stazione Termini, in complete isolation from the city.[16] At the time Pasolini was shooting *Accattone,* the neighborhood was still undergoing the demolition process that he describes in his 1958 essay, "The Concentration Camps." This film, in fact, contains perhaps some of the very last images of the neighborhood before it disappeared altogether. Urban historian Italo

Insolera observes acerbically that "it is an enormous weight on Rome's conscience that they even lasted thirty years."[17]

Visiting the area even today, there remains a sense of isolation and desolateness. Where the buildings we see in *Accattone* used to be, there is now (in 2005) a temporary settlement for recent immigrants; this camp is surrounded by a chainlink fence. Nearby, going toward the Via Casilina, the main arterial link to the city center from this part of the periphery, is the latter-day borgata of the Quartiere del Casilino, an imposing housing project–cum–new town, completed in 1973 and designed by Ludovico Quaroni, an important figure in postwar architectural history who will appear in the next chapter. In short, while everything has changed in the Borgata Gordiani since 1961, so is it the case that nothing, really, is all that different.

After the shot of Accattone, the film cuts to a dolly shot that moves alongside him in medium close-up as he walks past Balilla, one of the characters we have been introduced to already in Accattone's haunts.[18] As Accattone passes him, Balilla awkwardly makes the sign of the cross, the action performed by a Catholic when a dead body crosses one's path, mentioning to Accattone that the cemetery is in the other direction.[19] Accattone says tersely, "Tell it hello for me." Balilla joins up with Accattone to walk with him awhile. The camera maintains its observation of their steady progress through a series of medium shots, reverse-field medium close-ups, and long shots, all dollying, in motion. Behind their heads in the far background are visible again the large, new apartment buildings, whose sheer newness stands in such contrast to the squalor of the surrounding borgata. This is really the first time the film has offered a clear and expansive vision of this landscape; the sight is hardly welcome. There is something at once desolate and dense in the rows of dwellings wedged against each other in wretched intimacy, interrupted by the occasional vacant lot. The sight stretches on and on into the distance, like something that should end, but can't or doesn't know how to.

In the course of a long, backward-dollying two shot of Balilla and Accattone, the former peels off from our hero to address a child who is seated in front of an abandoned house. Accattone keeps moving, looks back at his errant companion, curses, spits, keeps moving. His actions and the camera's continual movement might distract us from noticing a salient visual detail. Scrawled in large black letters on the wall of the house where Balilla has stopped are the words "Vogliamo una casa civile":

Accattone in the Borgata Gordiani. Note the graffito on the wall of the house: "Vogliamo una casa civile" ("We want a decent house").

"We want a decent house." And behind the house, Accattone and Balilla are the still-visible but distant palazzoni. In the simplicity and solemnity of this scene, Pasolini has managed—merely through careful framing and movement—to fashion a powerful discursive statement from the borgata's raw material.[20]

Accattone continues on a bit, then stops his progress and looks ahead. The camera cuts to a long shot of a funeral procession—acolytes and priest with black hearse and mourners behind—moving across the road (from right to left onscreen) on which Accattone is standing. The procession looks to be a good fifty meters in front of Accattone's point in space. Next we cut back to a medium close-up of Accattone's face, still seemingly looking in the same direction, but rotating his head slightly to the left as if to follow the movement of the procession, which, to judge from the position of his head, would seem to be suddenly at his left and somewhat behind him. Next, a cut to a medium shot of the acolytes and priest, followed by a cut back to a long shot in which are visible the procession in the middle distance, Accattone in the foreground, looking over his shoulder, and in the far distance the outline of the large apartment buildings. I have broken down this sequence (which lasts no longer than twenty seconds) in such detail because temporally and spatially it is "impossible." When Accattone first notices the procession, as explained before, it is a good fifty yards from his position in space and moving across the screen and across his field of vision. Only two shots and a few seconds later the procession has already passed him, moving in a direction opposite to the one he has traveled. Like the fleeting appearance of the scrawled plea for shelter on the abandoned house, the spatio-temporal trick played on us by the sequence is fairly subtle and may escape an inattentive viewer. But once we register an awareness of it, this instability in spatio-temporality unsettles us and asks to be understood.

One reason why the spatio-temporal impossibility of the sequence might go unnoticed is that the editing seems to follow the conventions of optical point-of-view editing, in which we are offered a shot of a character's face, and then what we assume to be a shot of what that character is looking at. Between the shots of Accattone's face and those of the procession, there is an acceleration of time, a hiccup in the spatio-temporal unity of the fiction. But more than this, the lack of correspondence between the shots actually begins to undermine the work of traditional point-of-view editing to which the sequence alludes but does not conform.[21] Similar to what happens in the scene of Maddalena's beating in which a point-of-view pan that was called for in the screenplay becomes, in the film, a depsychologized, repetitive gesture, in this sequence the conventions of camera and editing that are usually used to construct point of view are thrown off balance and into question. I believe that the implications of the film's undermining of point-of-view editing are intertwined with the landscape of the periphery.

The representation of point of view is one of the prerogatives, if not requisites, of narrative cinema. The use of optical point-of-view shots in which spectators assume that they see what (and as) the character sees is a fine way of encouraging audience identification, of involving spectators in the texture of the fiction. Following a line of argument set up by Edward Branigan, Stephen Heath has suggested that point-of-view shots taken from an "impossible" place—positions that could not be inhabited by characters, or could not reflect properly the spaces they occupy—increase our awareness of "film as process."[22] I have described the sequence of shots that represent Accattone's encounter with the funeral procession as "impossible" to read as point of view. Thus, at this moment in the film, the transparent legibility of the narrative clouds over; the film asserts its own existence as a document of itself, and this assertion impedes our access to character subjectivity.

This breakdown in the spatio-temporality of subjectivity is, therefore, grounded in a conceptualization of the space of the periphery—a space we would hesitate to call either urban or suburban. In this borgata, where Accattone's "funereal" encounter (for it also foretells his own death at the end of the film) occurs, the contours of space do not cohere in a reassuring manner. All is too close and too far away. Empty space surrounds the neighborhood, while the individual dwellings that constitute them crowd in on one another. Meanwhile, the city itself (those large buildings in the background of the image) keeps its distance. The borgate figure a miserable limbo. How fitting, therefore, that Pasolini chooses lines from Dante's *Purgatorio* as the film's epigraph.[23] In the borgate, one is not in the "here" of the city center, but neither is one exactly banished to the "there." What is "there," or "out there," is still somehow "here," meaning that the borgate still belong to the orbit of the city as much as they are excluded from its core. Both the borgate themselves and Pasolini's method of filming them embody this confusing sense of dislocation. In short, the borgate (both as they existed historically and as we experience them in *Accattone*) do not possess what the urban design theorist Kevin Lynch would call "good city form."

Lynch's object of study is the postwar American city whose distinctive character was destroyed by the automobile. He laments the freeways that so brutally cut swathes through older city centers and the endless suburban development that grew along the veins and traffic arteries leading into and out of the city. His work manifests an implicit phenomenological approach to urban space, an approach signaled by the title of his first major book, *The Image of the City*. The city's image, or rather, its ability to generate an image of itself for its inhabitants, is one of Lynch's chief concerns. Lynch explains the significance of the city's image thus:

> Obviously a clear image enables one to move about easily and quickly: to find a friend's house or a policeman or a button store. But an ordered environment can do more than this; it may serve as a broad frame of reference, an organizer of activity or belief or knowledge. . . . Like any good framework, such a structure gives the individual a possibility of choice and a starting point for the acquisition of further information. A clear image of the surroundings is thus a useful basis for individual growth.
>
> A vivid and integrated physical setting, capable of producing a sharp image, plays a social role as well. It can furnish the

> raw material for the symbols and collective memories of group
> communication. A striking landscape is the skeleton upon which
> many primitive races erect their socially important myths. . . .
>
> A good environmental image gives its possessor an impor-
> tant sense of emotional security. He can establish an harmoni-
> ous relationship between himself and the outside world. . . .
>
> Indeed, a distinctive and legible environment not only
> offers security but also heightens the potential and intensity
> of human experience.[24]

Perhaps Lynch's claims for what a clear urban image can accomplish
are a little too broad and too optimistic, but his argument is worth considering seriously. Lynch longs for city space that is planned, legible, of
use to its inhabitants, conducive to their needs, representative of their
desires.[25] Although the fascist-built Borgata Gordiani was planned, it was
nonetheless a part of a larger peripheral landscape that is a somber riot
of hopeless contingency. From Rome's walls the borgate—official and
unofficial—spread themselves out in an uneven, tentacular fashion. All
are variations on a theme in the key of mud and pilfered building materials. The spatial distortion of the borgate is echoed appositely by the
impossible shot–reverse shot sequence that renders Accattone's strange
confrontation with the funeral procession. By interpreting the film's
avoidance of point-of-view editing as an eschewal of an interest in character subjectivity, we can see this as a refracted analogue of Roman society's eschewal of responsibility for the borgate and their inhabitants—a
refusal to provide for the subjective needs of these citizens of Rome.
This passage of the film provides us not with an experience of subjective
identification, but of economic subjection. Understood thus, the texture
of the film's manufacture registers the disturbances of the development
of Rome's periphery; its attitude—the film's—we can read, but not
Accattone's.

This tendency to flout or distort the tenets of point-of-view editing
is rehearsed ever more rigorously and relentlessly in Pasolini's second
film, *Mamma Roma,* the subject of chapter 5. But one thing more remains
to be said about this sequence. In it we see Pasolini's resistance to the
codes of classical cinema.[26] Such resistance is what constitutes Pasolini's
peculiar modernism. This film (and all of his others) expresses a pal-
pable obsession with the means of cinematic production and a willing-
ness to rupture the authority of convention. But Pasolini's modernism
seems something bought at the expense of any faith in the modern or

modernity. Indeed, modernism and modernity are split from each other in *Accattone:* modernism is enlisted in an attack waged against modernity. However, Pasolini is not a modernist in the way that, say, Godard is, or Brecht, or Vertov. To understand the nature of Pasolini's modernism, we must first put away the notion that modernism is somehow realism's other, or that realism is the bad object that modernism rejects.[27] Pasolini's is a modernism shot through with realism; his realism is one inflected and informed by modernism. He wants to document experience (often understood as the métier of realism), and so he does, but in a way that forces on us an awareness of the formal, technological means of producing this documentation (often understood as the vocation of modernism). In Pasolini's films the material of the real world is never dissolved in formal complexity. And yet, at the same time, the vision of the world that these films provide us with is a sticky sort of vision in which the materiality of the medium is always felt, almost haptically, sensually.[28] The relationship between realism and modernism in Pasolini's work is one of identity, which is to say, they are the same thing.

In *The Painting of Modern Life,* a book preoccupied with modernism and urban peripheries, T. J. Clark evokes a Van Gogh painting, *The Outskirts of Paris* (1886), a representation of the spatial and visual conditions of what were the borgate of the late nineteenth-century French capital, thus: "neither the dingy line of buildings nor the edges of fields, nor even the five retreating figures on the path, establish much of a sense of scale or demarcation: things are seeping into one another, and the landscape is taking on a single, indiscriminate shape." Clark's notion of the "seeping periphery" is germane to the conditions we sense in the Roman periphery where buildings and forms fail, in Lynch's terms, to cohere as an image. Paragraphs later, in reference to the same painting, Clark makes another observation whose implications might actually reach beyond Paris, Rome, van Gogh, and Pasolini: "The atmosphere of dissolution and misuse seems unmistakable, and the suggestion strong that the modern may add up to not much more than the vague misappropriation of things."[29]

"Misappropriation" strikes me as a productive rubric under which to continue this study of Rome's urban structures, its peripheral neighborhoods, and Pasolini's representations of the same. Of course, the misappropriation of the borgate is in no way "vague." The spatial contours of the borgate's misappropriated landscape might be vague, but the sense of dejection and abuse is all too sharp. The city continues to expel or repel citizens or would-be citizens, an action that curiously results in the endless misappropriation of the countryside for the urban. While what ensues—the periphery with its borgate, high-rise projects, hovels, and shanties—cannot be identified as classically urban, it nonetheless remains a hapless and haphazard form of urbanizing—again, the seeping of the city into the domain of what had been its other (i.e., the countryside). Of course, "seeping" is a poetic way of putting things that fails to express the violence implicit in Rome's peripheral expansion. If we think back to the sventramenti, what begins in the city center with the misappropriation of space via the expulsion of the lower classes results in the appropriation of undeveloped land for the use of the city as poorly urbanized homes for those it has exiled or refused entry. There is double misappropriation at work then: one in the center giving rise to one in the margins. This twinned misappropriation is what gives rise to the sense of the borderless expansion of the periphery.

Thinking of the modern in terms of misappropriation is also suggestive in relation to Pasolini, who, of course, is one of the great (mis)-appropriators. Literary sources, classical music, movie stars, film styles: Pasolini wrests all of these sources (and many more) from their usual habitats and reinserts them into his own cinematic texts. The uneven, unpolished surfaces and jarring sound-image relations of Pasolini's aesthetic clearly demonstrate that he understood the modern (and modernism) to be about disjunction and seepage, parataxis and drift. In an interview that he granted to students at Rome's Centro Sperimentale di Cinematografia,[30] Pasolini described his aesthetic thus:

> The sign under which I work is always contamination. In fact if you read a page of my books you'll notice that contamination is the dominant stylistic factor, because I, who come from a bourgeois world—and not only bourgeois but, at least when I was very young, the most refined sections of that world—I, reader of the most refined decadent writers, etc., have attained this world of mine. Consequently, the "pastiche" had necessarily to be born. . . . Evidently when I deal with a given material I represent it in its real physical brutality; this means that I go to Pigneto and I photograph those walls, that rubbish, that sun, and I take Franco Citti and I photograph him as he is; obviously, however, all this gross . . . physically violent material is then lifted by me to a different linguistic level.[31]

Much can be learned from this ad hoc and off-the-cuff ars poetica. Pasolini's aesthetic is clearly porous, open, and attuned to the stuff of the physical world. Yet he also, like any artificer, is interested in remaking, to an important degree, the world and its objects. We should think back to the discussion of the scene in which Accattone dives from the Ponte Sant'Angelo with its Bernini angels. In that scene Pasolini clearly avails himself of the raw material of Roman topography and the Roman citizenry. He chooses the site for its visual appeal and its historical significance, both of which come to him ready-made and both of which he appropriates merely by photographing them. Similarly, by casting Franco Citti, rough-hewn denizen of the borgate, Pasolini has appropriated another "shred" of reality. Juxtaposing these two together—contaminating Bernini with a borgata dweller by placing them in conspicuous relation to one another inside the same shot—is what Pasolini means when he says he "lifts" his material to "another linguistic level." Of course, taking something from the real world and making it your own is at the very foundation of any artistic practice, so, in a sense, Pasolini is saying little that is new here, though he may say it in compelling terms.

I would like, however, to consider the resonance of the word *contamination* in relation to the subject of the periphery. *Contamination* refers, in its usual sense, to touching something unclean, to the spreading of disease, and, therefore, to the violation of borders. The language we are apt to associate with contamination resonates strongly with the language used so often to describe the borgate. The peripheral borgate exist also under "the sign of contamination." The country catches the city's disease; the city's swollen body pushes itself further out into what had been farmland, or else that same body rejects and expels lower-class Romans as alien matter; immigrants to Rome invade the body of the city and cause the disruption of its functioning; Clark's remark that "things are seeping into one another"—take your pick, it's an attractive metaphorical fit. Given that the borgate already operate under the sign of contamination, there are unmistakable homologies between Pasolini's aesthetic and the periphery itself, its "clusters of hovels . . . expanses of shacks like Bedouin camps, collapsed ruins of mansions and sumptuous cinemas, ex-farmhouses compressed between high-rise buildings, dikes with high walls, narrow muddy alleyways, and sudden empty spaces, empty lots and small fields with a few heads of livestock," and so on. In a very strong sense, we could say that Pasolini actually derived his cinematic aesthetic of contamination from peripheral Rome.[32]

Accattone is heavily contaminated, we might also say, by the legacy of Italian neorealist filmmaking that flourished in the postwar years on into the 1950s. Clearly the film resonates with the neorealist tradition of using nonprofessional actors, choosing "plots" from the misery of contemporary existence, and shooting on location. Pasolini's particularly raw camera technique of opening the lens to create vividly crude contrasts between dark and light also nods in the direction of Rossellini's most unstudied moments in films like *Paisan* (*Paisà,* 1946) and *Rome, Open City.* It was Pasolini's shooting style, in fact, that supposedly soured Fellini on his commitment to finish funding *Accattone* after his production company, Federiz, had financed the earliest stages of filming.[33] In fact, *Accattone* may have, as the biographer Schwartz claims, appeared to Fellini as "a rehash of neo-realism's films of fifteen years before, old-fashioned in its bleak quasi-documentary quality."[34] Certainly Fellini's production was much sleeker in the early 1960s than his earlier work, concerned less with the material squalor of the borgate and more with the moral squalor of the Via Veneto. Fellini might have blanched at *Accattone* not because it seemed merely out of date, but rather because he quite probably recognized that the film was a frontal attack on the legacy of neorealism, the movement in which he played an important role. Fellini himself turned away from neorealism proper by turning to stylistic experimentation and overtly spiritual thematic matter. But then along comes Pasolini, in the era of *La dolce vita,* making a film about pimps, swindlers, and homely whores—none of whom come close to being as lovable as Fellini's Cabiria.

Pasolini's cinema is more of a challenge to the specific history and codes of neorealism than it is to the institutional (internationally observed) codes of narrative film language; his deconstructive impulsive is aimed more locally. His warping of reverse field cutting is not as violent an assault as is the withering attack his first films make on the legacy of Italy's most cherished film movement. This attack—one might want to call it a rereading—is waged through the misappropriation of neorealism's distinguishing characteristics. It is true that no one ever agrees fully on what constitutes neorealism, but several key elements are often generally consented to. The critic and director Luigi Chiarini sketches four identifying points that indicate the "new spirit" shared by the first neorealist films:

> (1) men derived from the audience's own reality replaced the
> pre-conceived characters in conventional narratives of the past;
> (2) the chronicle . . . , events and facts, culled from the daily
> existence of men, replaced the prefabricated adventures of

novels and comedies; (3) the throbbing photographic document replaced pictorial and figurative virtuosity; (4) the cities
and countryside, with people effectively living there, replaced
the papier-maché scenery of the past.[35]

On all four definitional characteristics, *Accattone* might be counted as a
neorealist film. Its actors (with a few notable exceptions) are nonprofes-
sionals; its plot is hardly one at all—merely a loosely connected string
of events that might happen any day in peripheral Rome; the images
are impressive for their unfinished, amateurish, "throbbing" immediacy.
And last, of course, there is no artificial set; there is only Rome itself.
Pasolini, though, adopts the trappings of neorealism in order to push
past what he believed were its sentimental progressive politics and into a
realm in which the ideas of social mobility and personal or collective bet-
terment are negated.[36] Actors, events, locations—Pasolini has appropriated what we should call the mise-en-scène of the neorealism of De Sica
while calling what he regards as the idealism and humanism (perhaps
even sentimentality) of its politics into question.

In a text written in the early 1960s, Pasolini expresses his distrust of
neorealism's politics very precisely:

> It is useless to delude oneself about it: neorealism was not a
> regeneration; it was only a vital crisis, however excessively op-
> timistic and enthusiastic at the beginning. Thus poetic action
> outran thought, formal renewal preceded through its vitality
> (let's not forget the year '45!) the reorganization of the cul-
> ture. Now the sudden withering of neorealism is the necessary
> fate of an improvised, although necessary, superstructure: it is
> the price for a lack of mature thought, of a complete reorga-
> nization of the culture.[37]

Pasolini elsewhere said of neorealism, disparagingly, that it was "subjective and lyricizing" and "still tied to pre-Resistance culture."[38] Pasolini's critique of neorealist aesthetics and neorealist politics (indissolubly
linked) will be the subject of much of the rest of the present chapter
and of chapter 5. In moving in and out of Pasolini's various attacks on
neorealism (waged both in writing and in the films), we must be careful
to remember that Pasolini's take on the movement is complicated. First
we must recognize that he is criticizing a movement that he believes to
have failed in its attempt to assist and promote the "complete reorganization of the culture." As a Marxist (though not an official member
of the PCI), he knew that such a reorganization would have meant only

one thing: a proletarian revolution. But for a relatively politically conservative neorealist filmmaker like Rossellini, who is generally agreed to
be the founding figure of neorealism, such a political revolution would
never have been the aim of neorealism. Rossellini was more comfortable
describing neorealism as expressing "a greater interest in individuals" or
"the artistic form of truth."[39] Part of the history of the reception of neorealism is, in fact, the history of the persistence with which it was judged
a failure, particularly by critics on the left, and Pasolini shows himself
to be writing and thinking in this tradition.[40] And yet neorealism was
too various and diffuse ever to have amounted to a proper movement;
in a sense, insofar as he refers to it as a unitary movement, Pasolini is
attacking something that never existed.[41] This last point brings me to
another important thing that we must note about Pasolini's reading of
neorealism. Neorealism is also, in part, an Oedipal invention of his own,
a fictional father whose faults he must advertise and against whose pro-
ductions he must pit his own work. However, all of this is not to say that
Pasolini's critique of neorealism's putative failure is misplaced, illegiti-
mate, or unfruitful. Whether or not it was neorealism's job to assist in
producing a new, socialist, or at least economically equitable Italy, the
fact remains that such an Italy did not exist in 1961. Neorealism, the
movement that had seemed to promise so much, both politically and
aesthetically, therefore, became for Pasolini an electrifying field of reference, a kind of foil against which his own version of cinematic politics
could take shape.

To understand the differences between neorealism and *Accattone,*
we might consider it in relation to the neorealist social problem film,
the most illustrative examples of which are De Sica's films from the late
1940s and early 1950s. Most of De Sica's films from this period are about
the failure of the social safety net; this is the case in *Shoeshine* (*Sciuscià,*
1946), *Miracle in Milan, Umberto D.,* and *The Roof.* The De Sican social
problem film always implies a solution to its problem even if that solution is not found and therefore is not represented: if only the PCI cell
had helped Ricci buy a new bike; if only Rome had better social welfare
services; if only Umberto D.'s landlady was not such a social climbing
shrew. The failure of society to care for its weakest members—clearly the
theme of De Sican neorealism—suggests by implication that the same
society *might* have behaved itself better, *might* have succeeded under better circumstances. Related to (indeed, undergirding) this tendency in
De Sica's work is the way in which the films frame economic problems

in very personal, characterological terms, so that, for instance, in *Il tetto, The Roof,* the immediate conditions of Luisa and Natale's homelessness are produced either because of their in-laws' selfish obstinacy or a potential landlord's greed. These analyses, I think, fuel Pasolini's charge that neorealism is "subjective" and "lyricizing." Pasolini's conceptualization of neorealism as such will inform *Accattone* and *Mamma Roma,* and I will try in the coming chapters to account for both the usefulness and the shortsightedness of such a willful conceptualization.

Accattone is intended by Pasolini as a critique of neorealism. I believe that it is in the film's form that we sense most acutely Pasolini's criticism: we sense this particularly in the use of the camera and in the editing. There is something either inherently just or else deeply contradictory about the fact that Pasolini would essay his critique of neorealism — whose formal excitement, he believes, outstripped its political theorization — through the agency of film form. To argue this is not simply to rehearse a formalist cliché. Rather, it is to assert that the film's formal elements (rather than, say, its narrative contents or plot) are the products of a willful dilation of the "tenets" of neorealism (e.g., Chiarini's four points). In exaggerating and deploying neorealist formal tendencies in an intentionally misunderstood (i.e., misappropriated) manner, Pasolini mounts a devastating counterargument to neorealism that not only implicitly criticizes what Pasolini believes to be the shortcomings of neorealist filmmaking, but also offers a striking visualization of an altered urban landscape that is itself the victim of the product of a "lack of a reorganization of the culture." While neorealism, and in particular De Sica, must be credited with granting us some of the first cinematic images of the periphery and its injustices, its method of looking at the periphery is what Pasolini is most impatient with. The mode of Pasolini's visualization, in fact, more than its object (which it shares with neorealism), is what will distinguish his cinema from that of a neorealist like De Sica.

This visualization is most strikingly materialized in Pasolini's use of extremely long (in duration) traveling shots in which the camera dollies backward while at least two characters advance toward the direction of the camera. There are two significant instances of this sort of shot in *Accattone* as well as two highly charged examples in *Mamma Roma.* I want to focus in some detail and at length on the first appearance of this type of shot.

In *Accattone* our protagonist has gone to seek out his estranged wife at her work in order to ask her for a loan. She works in a miserable depository where women busy themselves cleaning and sorting glass bottles.

It's the sort of extremely marginalized work one would hardly know existed until one sees it. Accattone asks for his wife's whereabouts from a woman who squawks her name, "Ascensa!" Ascensa does not respond, so Accattone decides to wait out the few minutes until the women get off work. He seats himself against a shack, opposite a young blonde woman who is plunging dirty bottles into water boiling in an old oil drum over a fire of scrap lumber. She is plump, blonde, simple, and sweet; her name is Stella, and she is soon to become Accattone's lover and, later, his whore. But for now Accattone harmlessly flirts with her while waiting for Ascensa. After his colloquy with Stella, Accattone waits by the gate for Ascensa, who, garbed in peasant black with baby slung on hip, marches past him without acknowledging his presence. He follows her. From this last action, the film cuts to a backward dollying full shot, Ascensa on the right in the foreground, Accattone on the left, catching up behind. This shot continues in the same manner for the next minute and forty seconds, a rather fantastic length of time. During that time Ascensa and Accattone never quit their walking or their quarreling. He has come to ask her for money, and she flatly refuses him. They walk on a street cobbled with *sampietrini*—the black basalt stones that pave almost every street in Rome. On screen left appear scrubby trees and tall street-lights that mark the boundaries of empty lots and farms, while on the right a broken succession of forlorn structures and fences unrolls. Atten-tion to the bottom of the screen shows the image shuddering, an effect of the street's unevenness; the boom mike casts an occasional shadow at the bottom of screen left. A couple of stray fellow pedestrians appear from time to time, heading in the opposite direction of the camera, dis-appearing into the deeper planes of the always-receding landscape. The sun is bright and seems to have baked everything into a dusty stillness. The characters' interminable advance, their hardheaded closeness to the camera, and the surface of the image renders the landscape, even just as it has passed, ever so flat and far away. They seem to be no place, but rather moving through a space that exists only to be traversed.

This shot is perhaps an instance of the "uninterrupted observations" that Pasolini imagines, in "The City's True Face," would be necessary to answer or analyze the phenomena of the periphery. But despite how remarkable this cinematography is, it has rarely been discussed by Paso-lini critics and scholars. In fact, Nowell-Smith, who is otherwise incred-ibly sensitive to the nature of Pasolini's form, singles it out for abuse as one of the "more tedious moments in the film."[42] Contrary to this

Accattone and Ascensa's long walk, rendered in a backward dollying long take.

attitude, I would argue that this is one of the most important and fascinating scenes/shots (they are in this case identical) in the film. The argument between Ascensa and Accattone might just as well have been shot with a stationary camera setup; its content ("You've been a terrible father"; "Give me another chance") does not demand that it be shot in this manner. The shot, moreover, puzzles because of the way it combines stylistic excess and stylistic asceticism. It is hyperbolically long, and yet so little happens within it. Its status as a long (or "sequence") shot connects it to the legacy of neorealism, as does its interest in objective observation of people and places. We might remember the celebrated scene in De Sica's *Umberto D.* in which the maid's waking and making coffee is followed for a full three minutes—no dialogue, no "event" other than this diurnal ritual observed by the camera. The impulse (as much ideological as aesthetic) to use film as a tool for observing life in its details—not just the great moments, but the moments in between—ascribes to life an implicit significance. Zavattini, De Sica's creative partner in many of his best films and one of the great neorealist apologists, celebrated "the cinema's overwhelming desire to see, to analyse, its hunger for reality."[43] Zavattini's conception of neorealism tends toward orality; that is, it always wants more—more of what Zavattini calls reality, by which he intends the world in all of its detail and all of its multiplying moments. Zavattini uses an anecdote to explain neorealism's "hunger" for reality. An

American producer, he says, explained to him the difference between Hollywood and neorealism:

> "This is how we would imagine a scene with an aeroplane. The 'plane passes by . . . a machine gun fires . . . the 'plane crash- es. . . . And this is how you would imagine it. The 'plane passes by. . . . The 'plane passes by again . . . the 'plane passes by once more . . ."
>
> He was right. But we have still not gone far enough. It is not enough to make the aeroplane pass by three times; we must make it pass by twenty times.[44]

There is something of this imperative in the shot from *Accattone*. Ascensa and Accattone walk and quarrel . . . they continue to walk and quarrel . . . they walk and quarrel some more. But in Zavattini's further elaboration of his fixation on getting more out of reality, it becomes clear that he was envisioning something else than what we see in Pasolini's very long shot. Zavattini:

> [W]hile the cinema used to make one situation produce an- other situation, and another, and another, again and again, and each scene was thought out and immediately related to the next (the natural result of a mistrust of reality), today, when we have thought out a scene, we feel the need to "remain" in it, because the single scene itself can contain so many echoes and reverberations, can even contain all the situations we may need.[45]

What Zavattini describes is what he and De Sica produced in *Umberto D*. The simple narrative fact—maid wakes and makes coffee—is studied in all its tiny components. As André Bazin says, "[W]e see how the grind- ing of the coffee is divided . . . into a series of independent moments."[46] Instead of this sort of analysis, effected, it is important to note, by the sig- nificant level of editing, Pasolini offers a long, uninterrupted shot, what he would call a "shred" of reality.[47] Zavattini and De Sica burrow inside a scene, animated by curiosity, greedy for how much knowledge they can extract from it. Pasolini's cinema behaves differently. His camera is both respectful, insofar as it maintains a distance from the characters by always receding from them, and intrusive because it does not relent. Implicit in the camera work is a kind of awe for the world of the profilmic, for the world, an awe that is shared by the theorists of neorealism, in particular by Zavattini and Bazin.[48] The attitude that the camera seems to imply is expressed in Pasolini's own film theory. Pasolini believed that reality itself was a natural language and that film translated reality into a written language, what he called "the written language of reality."[49] Putting the enormous interest and the obtuseness of this belief to one side,[50] his theoretical writings again and again evince a radical attachment to the majesty of the phenomenal world and to film's ability to represent it. The following passage expresses this attachment to the reality of the world:

> [O]ne can identify the relationship between my grammatical concept of cinema with what is, or at least I believe to be, my philosophy or my way of life—which does not strike me in the final analysis as being other than a hallucinated, infantile, and pragmatic love for reality. It is religious in that in some way it is fused, by analogy, with a sort of immense sexual fetishism. The world does not seem to me to be other than a totality of fathers and mothers, toward whom I feel an absolute rush of feeling, composed of respectful veneration and of the need to violate said respectful veneration through even violent and scandalous desecrations.[51]

Looked at optimistically, the shot under discussion might be seen to evince such a simple and profound interest in the world and film's mimetic relation to it. The processional aspect of the two characters' and the camera's advance down the forlorn street could be said to conjure a sense of Pasolini's veneration. But there is desecration in this shot, too—desecration aimed at neorealism. By way of a discussion of this desecration I intend to return to a discussion of Pasolini's critique of Rome's peripheral landscape and the injustices embodied therein.

As mentioned before, there are several stylistic affinities between Pasolini and the legacy of neorealist filmmaking. But clearly the profound differences between Pasolini and his neorealist forebears amount to a practice of Oedipal transgression—or desecration—on Pasolini's part. I have mentioned above that Pasolini's understanding of neorealism is, at least to some degree, an Oedipal fantasy. Rossellini, De Sica, et al. must number among the "fathers" that he mentions in the above quotation. The specific nature of Pasolini's desecration (what could just be regarded as a bad case of "the anxiety of influence") can be made clearer by way of a comparison of the ending of *Accattone* to that of De Sica's *Bicycle Thieves*. In the De Sica film, Ricci attempts to steal a bicycle and is stopped by vigilant onlookers. Dejected and ashamed, the son takes the father's hand in what has often been interpreted as a gesture of forgiveness and grace and they begin their walk home, their figures merging with the crowds streaming out of the nearby soccer stadium. Despite the film's overwhelming pessimism and rigorous critique of urban space, the relationship between father and son still expresses some remnant of faith in the restorative power of human affect, in spite of the obstacles presented by a hostile society.[52] At the end of Pasolini's film, Accattone attempts, with two of his companions, the robbery of a salami truck. When the police arrive, he tries to abscond by stealing a motorcycle. The reference to the end of De Sica's film could not be more pointed. Like Ricci, Accattone does not make it too far; he turns a corner and we hear the sound of tires squealing, a collision. Accattone dies on the Ponte Testaccio,[53] his last words, "I'm all right now" ("Mo, sto bene"). Only death brings succor to the underclass, the film seems to say.

This assertion—if, indeed, that is the import of this final scene—rankled critics on the left who had been weaned on the humanist optimism of neorealism. As Naomi Greene writes, Pasolini "underscores, even luxuriates in, the tragic, fatalistic, and even religious elements that constantly threatened to subvert the political thrust of neorealism itself."[54] However, I do not think Pasolini intends to subvert the political thrust of neorealism so much as he intends to improve on it, to extend it. He intends to subvert neorealist ideology, which he finds limiting, but I do not think he intends to subvert politics as a mode of action. Greene is mistaken in going on to claim that the film "proclaims the futility of social or political struggle."[55] Pasolini's close attention to the real geography of his characters' lives, of their spatial and architectural world, is too real, too precisely referential, for *Accattone* to be construed as a decadent abjuration of politics. In fact, the potential fatalism of the film's ending is placed, intentionally and legibly, in tension with its documentation of Roman geography and architecture. Why else have Accattone die just outside Testaccio, the place that was, in a sense, Rome's first borgata, its first periphery? The irony of the scene is this: that Testaccio, as forlorn as it appears in the film, nonetheless exists as a working-class quarter, a place that is meaningfully, if pejoratively, sewn into the economic and social life of the city of Rome. Even here there is no place for Accattone.

I want to pause over a puzzling feature of this last movement of the film. When Accattone steals the motorcycle he is actually *in* Testaccio (just prior to the theft we can spot a plaque on a building reading "Via Beniamino Franklin," even if we do not recognize the landscape), but when we discover him dying on the Ponte Testaccio, he is actually on the other side of the Tiber, and Testaccio is visible in the background. If we are to read this sequence in my accustomed, stubbornly empirical mode, it does not make sense either spatially or temporally. In the few seconds that intervene between the initial theft and the events on the soundtrack that announce his crash, Accattone would not have had the time to reach the other side of the bridge, some four hundred meters away from where this action begins. (That the other characters who remain in Testaccio at the moment the crash is heard could actually hear it from where they stand is similarly improbable.) Furthermore, as the characters run to the site of the crash, they do so moving from screen right to screen left, the camera panning left to follow them, and we see Testaccio, as already mentioned, looming visibly in the background across the river. While a good case may be made for the purely pictorial value of having Testaccio feature in the background of the sequence, I think there are other ways of appreciating the apparent geographical and temporal illogic of the scene. Accattone's last, desperate attempt to improve his situation results in his being hurled (across the invisible space that separates two pieces of film edited together) *outside* Testaccio, across the river, away from the city. While Testaccio is the site of the theft that results in his death, the death itself must happen outside *even this* impoverished neighborhood. In fact, by acting as pictorial background to this death, the apartment buildings of Testaccio figure not only the distance that is elided by the film's editing, but also the distance that Pasolini has traveled from neorealism.[56]

What Pasolini objects to in neorealism and the critical discourse surrounding it is not the belief in film as a meaningful medium for the representation of contemporary reality. Pasolini's attack on neorealism (waged through his films) is premised on a mistrust of what he wants to understand as neorealism's political sentimentality. That Accattone's only chance to feel, in the character's own words, "all right," arrives in the moment of death suggests that this, in fact, was the fate of the subproletariat that had been left out of Italy's economic miracle and pushed to the margins of the urban public sphere. Both left and right would have preferred to forget the existence of the subproletariat, the former because it failed to achieve class solidarity (Accattone is, after all, a pimp and a thief), and the latter because it failed to integrate itself or be integrated into the machinery of capitalism. Neorealism, with its "lack of mature thought," so Pasolini believes, would never be able to digest the stubborn fact of subproletarian existence. At the end of *Bicycle Thieves,* despite the fact that Ricci is still out of job, he is represented as an out-of-work proletarian, not a subproletarian. His apartment (albeit one in the borgate rapidissme) is kept clean by his wife; his family loves him; he wants to work. The distance between this world and the world of *Accattone* is considerable.

Critics and filmmakers who still clung to the promises—or premises—that neorealism embodied blinded themselves to the fact that advanced capitalism's delayed but violent efflorescence in Italy foreclosed a full participation in civic and economic life for an entire class (or subclass) of people. At least this was Pasolini's belief, and it is to this belief that *Accattone* owes its particular look and texture.

To recapitulate, then: *Accattone* figures an Oedipal strike against the heritage of neorealism. *Accattone* and, as we shall see, *Mamma Roma* share certain stylistic and thematic traits with the canon of neorealism. But often the places at which Pasolini's films draw the nearest to their neorealist ancestors are those where they are furthest apart. Such is the case with the long traveling shot that I have been analyzing, and returning to this shot will also return us, at last, to the subject of the spatiality of Rome's urban development and Pasolini's critique of the same.

Interestingly, in an interview published in the late 1960s, Pasolini makes direct reference to the long take in remarks he made about neorealism:

> I always shoot very short takes. . . . [T]his is the essential differ-
> ence between me and the neo-realists. The main feature of the
> neo-realism is the long take; the camera sits in one place and
> films a scene as it would be in real life. Whereas I never use a
> long take (or virtually never). I hate naturalness. I reconstruct
> everything.[57]

What is curious about these comments is how they simultaneously occlude and underscore the use of the long take in Pasolini's own work, while also managing to mischaracterize neorealist shooting style.[58] Certainly the long take and deep focus cinematography were central to Bazin's conceptualization of the achievement of neorealism.[59] Of course, the long take does participate in neorealism's basic animating impulse: to observe reality patiently in all its minute fullness. Understandably, this aspect of the long take informs Pasolini's labeling of it as the *sine qua non* of neorealism. His assertion, however, that he "never" uses the long take, when in fact the long takes in his first two films make up what might be considered the most memorable or formally remarkable scenes in the films is puzzling to say the least.[60] By singling out the long take and by dissociating himself from its use, Pasolini dissociates his use of the long take from how he imagines (or misremembers) it to be deployed in neorealism. His contention is that neorealism employed the long take in the service of naturalism, while in his own cinema the exact opposite is the case. Naturalism, which he identifies with neorealism, is a *bête noire* in Pasolini's discourse; he opposes it to the "realism" that he practices: "I believe deeply in reality, in realism, but I can't stand naturalism."[61] Naturalism for Pasolini means transparency, too-digestible mimesis, a mode in which the materiality of the real and the radical difference of one thing from another are smoothed over by clichéd aesthetic codes. His long takes (though he seems to have forgotten about them!) are obviously not naturalistic.

In another passage from his theoretical writings, Pasolini attacks with vigor the films of the American avant-garde to which he was introduced during a trip to New York in 1966. Although he does not mention him by name, the object of Pasolini's scorn is the filmmaker Andy Warhol:

> To understand what naturalism in cinema is, let us consider an extreme case—which presents itself, or is presented, as an example of avant-garde cinema: in the basements of the New York of the New Cinema, sequence shots which last for hours are shown (for example, a man sleeping). This, then, is cinema in its pure state . . . and as such, as representation of reality from a single visual angle, it is subjective in an insanely naturalistic way: primarily inasmuch as *it also* is *the natural time of* reality. As always, culturally, the new cinema is an extreme consequence of neorealism with its cult of the real and of the documented. But while neorealism cultivated its cult of reality with optimism, common sense, and good nature—with the consequent sequence shots—the new cinema turns things upside down: in its intensified cult of reality and in its interminable sequence shots, rather than having as fundamental proposition "that which is insignificant is," it has as fundamental proposition "that which is is insignificant."[62]

Here Pasolini is thinking of Andy Warhol's film *Sleep* (1963), which is not composed of one long sequence shot, but is, in fact, rather elaborately, if repetitively edited. Furthermore, Pasolini's attitude toward this film (and the filmmaking of which he means it to be representative) is far too polemical to be taken at face value. Anyone who has spent time looking at Warhol's films knows how seductive and engrossing they are, how, in fact, they do seem to valorize the existence of the "insignificant." But putting these objections aside, the passage interests us because of Pasolini's enormous sense of indignation at this cinema's "interminable sequence shots." It seems more than a little strange that neorealism should suddenly count as a good object in opposition to Warhol, and precisely for those attributes ("optimism, common sense, and good nature") that had earlier provoked his scorn. Later in the same paragraph Pasolini goes on to broach the subject of neorealist cinematography:

> The brief, commonsensical, measured, natural, affable sequence shot of neorealism gives us the pleasure of recognizing the reality we live and enjoy daily through an aesthetic comparison with academic conventions; the long, foolish, inordinate, unnatural, mute sequence shot of the new cinema, on the contrary, generates in us a horror of reality, through the aesthetic comparison with neorealistic naturalism understood as a school for life.[63]

What is not being admitted to here is actually a horror of recognition. "Long, foolish, inordinate, unnatural": everything he hates about Warhol we find in that long dollying shot of Accattone and Ascensa, right down to the perceived parody of neorealism. The righteous indignation of the passage reeks of protesting too much.[64]

The visibility of the boom mike's shadow, the shakiness of the frame, and, most important, the simple fact of the shot's monotonous (but enthralling) duration foreground the material processes of the film's manufacture and emphasize the camera's and the characters' movement qua movement. Do we need to know that the characters traveled a certain distance while arguing? In what way is this information important? In terms of the causal chain of narrative events, the distance they walk is unimportant—irrelevant even. But in terms of the historical context of the film it means a great deal. What the long shot impresses on its viewer is a sense of distances and empty expanses between points in space. By literally expressing—materializing—distance through its motion, the shot implies the broader contours of spatial reality as it was experienced by those, like Accattone and Ascensa, living in Rome's peripheral neighborhoods. In this sense, Pasolini demonstrates one version of truth in Godard's contentious declaration that "Tracking shots are a question of morality."[65]

The shot synecdochically graphs the situation of the borgate which Ferruccio Trabalzi explains in the following terms:

> The delicate connection between Romans and their city . . . was
> fully ruptured in the borgate. The small merchant or artisan
> displaced to a borgata found himself several kilometers from
> the nearest transportation depot; the same was true for the
> women who performed domestic work for the upper classes:
> the buses they needed for transportation to work were far away,
> ran infrequently, and were unreliable. The trip to work became
> long and uncomfortable and soon led to the loss of jobs, to
> long hours away from home and family, and to increasing ten-
> sion, which in turn often erupted in violence.[66]

Accattone and Ascensa, of course, do not even work inside Rome's walls. The labor that Ascensa performs can just barely be referred to as a "job," and Accattone does not work at all.[67] Thus, in the borgate they are excommunicated from Rome and excommunicated from meaningful labor. Their lives are defined less by what they do and more by the distances they have to travel, the type of spaces they have to travel through. Urban space has become so distended, so stretched to the limits of the recognizable that it has become something not so much lived or lived in as endured. The shot, like Warhol's *Sleep* (as Pasolini interprets it), generates a "horror of reality." In his constipated, choleric response to Warhol, Pasolini spoke truer than he knew.

Such a "horror of reality" has also been expressed by another theorist of the cinema, a theorist who shared with Pasolini an interest in realism: Siegfried Kracauer. In his *Theory of Film*, Kracauer describes a film project dreamt by Fernand Léger that directly anticipates the cinema of Warhol:

> Like photography, film tends to cover all material phenomena
> virtually within reach of the camera. To express the same other-
> wise, it is as if the medium were animated by the chimerical
> desire to establish the continuum of physical existence. . . .
> This desire is drastically illustrated by a film idea of Fernand
> Léger's. Léger dreamed of a monster film which would have
> to record painstakingly the life of a man and a woman during
> twenty-four consecutive hours: their work, their silence, their
> intimacy. Nothing should be omitted; nor should they ever be
> aware of the presence of the camera. "I think," he observed,
> "this would be so terrible a thing that people would run away
> horrified, calling for help as if caught in a world catastrophe."
> Léger is right. Such a film would not just portray a sample of
> everyday life but, in portraying it, dissolve the familiar contours

of that life and expose what our conventional notions of it
conceal from view—its widely ramified roots in crude existence. We might well shrink, panic-stricken, from these alien
patterns which would denote our ties with nature and claim
recognition as part of the world we live in and are.[68]

Of course, claiming such recognition for the borgate as "part of the world
we live in" is exactly what Pasolini was up to in his extremely long take
of Accattone and Ascensa. The shot exposes the Zavattinian desire of
"remaining in" a scene by exploring the limits of this very idea. However,
in the most famous instance in which Zavattini and De Sica remain in a
scene—again, the coffee-grinding scene from *Umberto D.*—what we have
is not the fierce criticism produced by the historically specific and literal spatiality of *Accattone*'s cinematography. Rather, this famous kitchen
scene, despite its wonderful phenomenological achievement (what Bazin
called its representation of "the succession of concrete instants of life")[69]
arrives finally at the sentimental and the lyrical. It is not historical analysis. In *Accattone* Pasolini managed to do something that neorealism did
not: he managed to analyze a set of social conditions through a specific
cinematic practice, one that was grounded in and achieved through
a political and historical understanding of form. This was a method
of looking at and moving through the spaces of social subjection—an
unflinching, earnest, intense, and exemplary instance of raw, embodied
vision. Though Pasolini could not admit it, De Sica (whose work haunts
and irritates Pasolini most persistently) *did,* in fact, direct his gaze at
the Roman periphery, at the fate of the dispossessed, but despite his
achievement, his mode of vision remained, essentially, picturesque. He
expanded the visual and geographic lexicon of Italian cinema, but did
not extend the formal means with which they might be documented, represented. Pasolini succeeded by exaggerating neorealism's own tenets.
By "remaining in" the scene of Accattone and Ascensa's walk via his
long take, he actually communicates something of the social and spatial
despair that belonged to the borgate. His long take does not illustrate
"poverty." Beyond visualization, *Accattone spatializes* a loathsome social
and historical condition that was predicated on a misuse of space itself.
In short, the traveling shot performs a conflation of *Accattone*'s attack
(and, perhaps, improvement) on neorealism and of the film's critical
attitude toward the spatial, geographic, and architectural abjection of
the postwar Roman periphery.

Not long after the walk with Ascensa that I have spent so much time discussing, Accattone again encounters Stella who briefly comes to figure in his life as a sort of Beatrice—or else a low-rent Monica Vitti. She represents for Accattone a relief or release from the squalor of his life. He manages to buy her new clothes and some cheap jewelry (purchased with money gained from stealing his son's baptismal medal) and begins squiring her around. It is during this segment of the film, dominated by Stella's assimilation into Accattone's life, that we first are given significant, sustained shots in the film of the newer high-rise developments that were built at such a furious pace during the 1950s. So far the camera has foregrounded the hovels of the borgate. Now, towering in the background and thereby laying claim to the action in the foreground, are tall, white, imposing apartment blocks, some inhabited, others in various states of construction. After Stella's makeover is complete, she and Accattone walk along the rubble- and rubbish-strewn perimeter of the construction sites; they are literally at the city's edge. It is here that Stella confesses that she is not as innocent as she seemed, that, in fact, her mother was a prostitute, that she knows the way of the world. Pasolini has not casually chosen this site for Stella's confession. Before Stella and Accattone appear in their walk alongside the new construction, the film offers a pan, from right to left, of the itinerary of their walk. The background is foregrounded, and so we are invited to read the conversation

Accattone and Stella's long walk: no new beginning.

between Stella and Accattone against the image of the apartment building that stand in mute witness to it. Accattone thought he had discovered a way to begin again with Stella. She destroys this illusion by confessing her worldliness. Although Accattone pretends not to care, soon enough Stella is on the streets, working for him, as have all of his women before her. No new beginning. So too with the high-rise construction behind them. Here the city begins again: new public housing for the poor and new luxury apartments for the middle class stand shoulder to shoulder. But, as we shall see in the following chapters, the class division in postwar Rome was left intact, undisturbed by the optimism the new buildings might imply. A few scenes later Stella and Accattone take another walk; it is the same walk, taken in the same place that he took with Ascensa, shot in a continuous dolly, only this time longer, at nearly two and a half minutes' duration. No new beginning. We will take a few more long walks with Pasolini. Most important, we will take one in his poem "The Tears of the Excavator," which finds in the images of the urbanization of the periphery a metaphor for the desolation of political, cultural, and spiritual life of Italy, and another in *Mamma Roma,* a film even more explicit than *Accattone* in its conflated critique of neorealism and the development of the Roman periphery.

Chapter 4

Pasolini, the Peripheral Sublime, and Public Housing

I n the opening lines of an untitled poem written just three years after the production of the poems collected in *Rome 1950, A Diary,* and only published after his death, Pasolini affords us a fragmentary, fleeting, but sensually compelling account of the new construction that was changing the material world of the Roman periphery:

> I would hurry in the dusk's mud
> behind disorderly stairs, around silent scaffolds,
> through the neighborhood drenched
> in the odor of iron and of laundry
> drying, in the fetid dust,
> among shacks made of tin
> and drain pipes, new walls going up,
> with their paint already peeling,
> against a backdrop of a faded metropolis.
>   On the broken asphalt,
> among the blades of grass
> acrid from shit and the black
> plains of mud that the rain
> digs up in infected warmth—
> the crooked lines of cyclists, wheezing
> lumber trucks, all would begin to blur
> in the middle of the suburbs
> where already some bar was casting its circles
> of white lights . . .[1]

The poem describes Pasolini making his way home, back to the house he shared with his mother (and now his father who had since joined his wife and son) in the borgata of Rebibbia, returning from a day of teaching or running the errands necessary to keep his tenuous literary career afloat. The poem, in its headlong succession of images and loose, casual syntax, suggests the inchoate, fluctuating landscape of the periphery in which, among the shacks and humble dwellings of older borgate, new apartment buildings began to be raised here and there. The poem communicates the desultory, "contaminated" nature of the landscape, already familiar to us from the journalistic pieces discussed in chapter 1, and, of course, from *Accattone*.

In the poem there is still the sense of the periphery as a mooncalf territory: neither country nor city, but a place where both seem to overlap one another. To be accurate, the country was not overlapping the city; rather, the city was making its way into what had been country and the sub-urbanized borgate—of both official fascist and improvised varieties. As I have already mentioned, the growing prosperity of the 1950s attracted greater numbers of internal migrants to Rome. Some of these new arrivals were members of the middle classes, arrived in Rome for work in the government's ever-fattening bureaucracy or in the financial institutions or other white-collar institutions that had their seats in Rome. Others of these were desperate peasants who arrived at the city from the south and the Roman countryside with no thought other than to improve, however modestly, the penury of an impoverished rural existence. Both types of immigrants placed enormous strains on Rome's already tight housing market. As explained above, the construction industry—aided by government investment initiatives—set to work to build middle- and lower-class housing, both as a solution to Rome's housing crunch and to absorb the destitute and jobless who arrived every day in great numbers looking for work. Thus, during the 1950s Rome's periphery was one enormous construction site. No wonder, then, that Pasolini should choose to contemplate a construction site as a metaphor for the changes being wrought by Italy's newfound and growing prosperity.

In "The Tears of the Excavator," a long poem published in his most celebrated volume of poetry, *Le ceneri di Gramsci* (*The Ashes of Gramsci*, 1956), Pasolini continues to elaborate his response to Roman urban development with greater self-consciousness than he had done in his earlier poetry. The poem takes its title from one of the machines looming over every construction site throughout the city: the tall, gaunt earth excavator. Pasolini's poetry from this period is consistently written in rhyming or near-rhyming tercets, a poetic form borrowed from Dante's *Divine Comedy,* which, it hardly needs to be said, was written in exactly rhyming and interlocking tercets, a form known as *terza rima.* The implicit Dantean allusion made by this choice of forms suggests that Pasolini shares with Dante the exile's grief and bitterness.[2] Dante, of course, wrote his great poem in exile from his native Florence, a city to which he was never allowed to return. Pasolini, as explained before, moved to Rome as a near refugee from his native Friuli. Although by the time he wrote *Le ceneri di Gramsci,* Pasolini had grown comfortable in Rome and had become a fixture on the Roman scene, he still clung fiercely to the exile's outsider persona. This sense of exile was only compounded by the difficult years in the early 1950s that he spent living in the hinterlands of the Roman periphery. Of course, Pasolini also took great pleasure in living there; the borgate were, after all, home to the ragazzi di vita whom Pasolini knew as friends, as sex partners, as the subjects of his narrative and near ethnographic documentation of their lives and speech. These boys, too, and their families, it might be added, were also in a kind of exile from their own native towns and villages, or else from the center of Rome itself.

Pasolini's decision to write in terza rima (a form to which he returns often in his poetry) also exemplifies his commitment to find a kind of *via media* that would encompass both the techniques of modernism and traditional literary forms in order, in Keala Jewell's words, "to escape a classic fixedness of literary forms and concomitant retrograde representations without resorting to modernism."[3] Rather than read this decision as a means of avoiding modernism, I would prefer to see this poetic syncretism as, instead, an explicit feature of his modernism, a modernism that is engaged in blurring the boundaries between modernism and its binary others—be those realism or, in this case, tradition. This decision is yet again another form of contamination. In Jewell's terms, though, the cross-breeding of two modes is analogous to Pasolini's "distinctive portrayal of a Rome at once ancient and modern."[4] Pasolini regarded the borgate as a symptom of modernity and yet also experienced them as a repository of vitality. As I will argue, his ambiguously complex deployment of poetic forms is congruent with his poetry's oxymoronic description of Rome as both "stupendous" and "miserable." His poetic method is also congruent with the excessive nature of the rhetoric of the sublime mode, which figures significantly in Pasolini's aesthetic in "The Tears of the Excavator" and in the screenplay and film *Mamma Roma,* whose aesthetic extends out of this poem.

"The Tears of the Excavator" begins at dusk, "down here along the curving / river."[5] The river is, of course, the Tiber and its banks were the cruising grounds for small-time hustlers and johns; the location suggests that the poem, perhaps, is postcoital. From this point the poem maps a little urban odyssey: Pasolini's walk from the site of the sexual encounter, through the (then) working-class district of Trastevere, skirting the Janiculum and the grounds of the Villa Doria Pamphili, to land at his home in a middle-class apartment on the Via Fonteina where he had moved in the mid-1950s with his mother and father, released at last from their purgatorial stay in Rebibbia. (Pasolini's apartment building on this street was also the home of the poet Attilio Bertolucci and his son Bernardo, who would become a filmmaker.)[6] As he makes his way home Pasolini catalogs some typically metropolitan visual fragments: "dark marketplaces," "sad streets," young men "on motorbikes, in overalls and workpants," customers lingering in "brightly lit cafés."[7] Were it merely Pasolini's point to gather these impressions and link them poetically, we would have little more than the musings of a standard-issue *flâneur,* staple of Parisian boulevards and Benjamin-inspired urban studies scholarship. Or we might compare the litany of urban images to a typical montage of shots that would function as the establishing images for a film set in Rome, perhaps like the "establishing shot" that we have already looked at in Pasolini's early Testaccio story. But Pasolini offers us these little urban vignettes as a mild prelude to a ferocious pronouncement:

> Stupendous, miserable city,
> you taught me what men learn
> joyously and ferociously as children,
>
> those little things in which we
> discover life's grandeur in peace:
> going tough and ready into crowded
>
> streets, addressing another man
> without trembling, not ashamed
> to check the change counted
>
> by the lazy fingers of the conductor
> sweating along passing façades
> in the eternal red of summer;

to defend myself, to attack, to have
the world before my eyes and not
just in my heart, to understand

that few know the passions
in which I've lived; that they're
not brotherly to me, and yet they are

my brothers because they have
passions of men
who, joyous, unknowing, whole,

live experiences
unknown to me. Stupendous, miserable
city, you made me

experience the unknown
life, you made me discover
what the world was for everyone.[8]

The apostrophe that begins this address carries the aroma of Dante, and the invocation of the metropolis and its teeming hordes has something of T. S. Eliot in it as well. But the "stupendous, miserable city" is not merely a dystopia like Eliot's London[9]—at least not yet; there are still things redeemable living and moving in this landscape. The first five tercets in the quotation above sketch a code of behavior for the proletarian urbanite who must be nimble and callous in order to navigate a hostile city.[10] But Pasolini does not despair over the abrasions of urban life; rather, he takes some sober pleasure in them. Pasolini's fellow citizens are "not brotherly" and yet they are his brothers. This intimacy as impersonality is of a piece with the oxymoronic nature of many of the poem's images and much of its word play. Rome is both "stupendous" and "miserable." *Stupenda* is the wonderful, the marvelous, the excessive, while *misera,* of course, refers to wretchedness, poverty, meanness; Rome encapsulates and epitomizes both of these possibilities in their discreteness and their simultaneity. Furthermore, the words' oxymoronic conflation suggests the work of the mind attempting, through a violent misuse of language, to describe that which cannot be described—the way the poem's title (and central metaphor) yokes two divergent possibilities together: the tears of an excavator—the sentient machine. We see, then, that Pasolini asks us to play with a whole series of oxymoronic or catachrestic tropes. We might note as well that intimate strangeness has often been understood as one of the hallmark contradictions of urban life.

The street, the theater, the tram—all are places where bodies unknown to one another are forced into proximity.[11] (Later in the poem, Pasolini describes his daily commute during which he was "squeezed each day / onto a wheezing bus; / and every trip back and forth / was a calvary of sweat and angst.")[12] As well, the urban sexual pickup, from which, as suggested above, Pasolini may be returning, combines the antinomies of the alien and the intimate. Pasolini moves beyond the fleeting, sensate qualities of this urban contradiction and mines it for philosophical value. What does it mean not to know so many whose bodies one bruises or brushes on a daily basis? The poem skirts this question by short-circuiting the question of knowledge itself altogether—by refusing to settle whether the difficulty of knowing another is a matter of preference or inevitability. The men that he passes on the street (and who would or could have been his sexual partners) Pasolini recognizes as "brothers because they have / passions of men / who, joyous, unknowing, whole, / live experiences unknown to me." "Unknowing" makes its appearance after "joyous" and before "whole"; clearly the term sheds its usual pejorative connotations. Their "unknown" experiences act as a kind of fund of immense value, dear to Pasolini because they are beyond his reckoning and his understanding and his ability to represent them. Passing through this series of oddly unreflective reflections leads him eventually to repeat the oxymoron whose texture he clearly relishes:

> . . . Stupendous, miserable,
> city, you made me
>
> experience that unknown
> life, you made me discover
> what the world was for everyone.

The "unknown life" is not the object of future knowing; it is only an object of "experience" and resists representation. The repetitive stress on "stupendous, miserable, city," coming as close as it does on the heels of the phrase's first enunciation, accumulates something close to the force of anaphoric repetition. In Dante, anaphora seems to appear when representation is at a crisis: "THROUGH ME THE WAY INTO THE SUFFERING CITY, / THROUGH ME THE WAY TO THE ETERNAL PAIN, / THROUGH ME THE WAY THAT RUNS AMONG THE LOST."[13] These are the words written above the gates of hell. Dante's *Comedy* is studded with instances of the "ineffability topos," moments when the poet draws attention to his inability to depict fully or accurately the awesome nature of the object of his representation. Repetition like the sort we see in Pasolini's poem seems to function implicitly as an ineffability topos: the experience cannot be described, only reiterated. Pasolini's repetition of the word "stupendous" to describe Rome, not only in this poem but elsewhere, suggests his inability to represent the vastness of the city and therefore the necessity of resorting to the word "stupendous," which itself expresses an imaginative/representational failure. Pasolini's city is not hell, but neither is it a stranger to the infernal. The importance of linking the city to anaphoric repetition will surface again in discussing Pasolini's cinematic production and its relationship to the sublime.

In the second movement of the poem, Pasolini describes several times the periphery and its borgate that were his home during those early Roman years, "in Rebibbia exile," to borrow Barth David Schwartz's phrase.[14] The descriptions bear at least a cursory analysis if only for the fact that they record vividly the material reality of this landscape:

> Poor as a cat in the Coliseum,
> I lived in a slum of dust clouds
> and limestone, far from the city,
>
> far from the countryside, squeezed each day
> onto a wheezing bus;
> and every trip back and forth
>
> was a calvary of sweat and angst—
> long walks in the heat's haze,
> long dusks in front of my papers
>
> heaped on the table, among muddy streets,
> low walls, small whitewashed
> windowless shacks that had curtains for doors . . .
>
> The olive vendor, the ragman passed by,
> coming from some other slum, with their
> dusty merchandise that looked like
>
> stolen goods . . . with their cruel faces of young
> men aging amid the vices of those
> whose mothers have grown hard in hunger.
>
> Renewed by the new world,
> free—a fiery flare, an indescribable
> breath gave a sense of serene
>
> piety to that humble,
> sordid, confused, immense reality
> swarming in those southern slums.

> . . . I was in the center of the world, in that
>
> world of sad Bedouin slum towns
> and yellow prairies chafed
> by a relentless wind
>
> from the warm sea of Fiumicino
> or the countryside, where the city
> disintegrated among hovels, in that world
>
> which could be dominated only by
> the penitentiary, square ocher
> specter in the ocher haze,
>
> pierced by a thousand identical
> rows of barred windows, amid
> ancient fields and drowsy farmhouses.[15]

This section's opening metaphor is telling: "Poor as a cat in the Coliseum." The metaphor's vehicle is something located in the center of Rome—at the Coliseum. Pasolini is as poor as that cat, but, unlike the cat, he lives far beyond any recognizable Rome, beyond such reassuringly immutable fixtures of the Roman urban fabric. Pasolini's opening gambit in this section of the poem is rather crudely metaphorical. Metaphor, of course, by definition demands the superimposition of two otherwise (outside the structure of the metaphor) unrelated things. Thus, this particular metaphor by its very nature as metaphor (and its force nurtured by its crude obviousness) underscores the dissimilarity between Pasolini's urban geography and that of the Coliseum's cat.

The desperation of Pasolini's situation is further intensified by the machine-gun repetition, within a very few lines at the beginning of the quotation, of hard *c* sounds[16] in the original Italian: Colosseo (Coliseum), calce (limestone), calvario (calvary), camminate (walks), calda caligine (heat's haze), crepuscoli (dusks), carte (papers), and ammucchiatte (heaped). These hard sounds seem to multiply themselves; their breeding consonance and alliteration "swarms"—to use one of Pasolini's favorite words that appears later in this passage. The periphery is that place where the city "disintegrated among the hovels." In Italian, the city literally "loses itself."[17] Swarming, confusing, immense, the periphery's disorder is challenged only by the ocher Rebibbia penitentiary that gives the area its name. A product of the state, the prison's "thousand identical / rows of barred windows" look forward to the regular planes of the housing developments that would eventually come to raise their heads above the peripheral landscape. The "thousand" windows of the prison, of course, is only a number meant to express the building's enormity. While its oppressive architectural order would seem to separate it from the disorder of the borgate, its great size participates in the seeping and seemingly limitless contours of the Roman periphery. But despite—*or because of*—the periphery's squalor, Pasolini is able to say, near the end of this section:

> . . . Those slums, naked
> in the wind, not Roman, not Southern
> not working class, were life
>
> in its most pertinent light:
> life, light of life, full
> of a chaos not yet proletarian
>
> (as the local Cell's rough newspaper
> and the latest waving of the weekly
> magazine claim it is): bone
>
> of daily existence,
> pure because so
> near, absolute because
>
> all too miserably human.[18]

The poem ends finally on the encounter with the excavator whose tears give the poem its title. After an interlude in the comfortable middle-class neighborhood where Pasolini was living at the time he wrote the poem, the setting shifts to the construction sites at the city's periphery; these could be building sites at the edge of his own neighborhood, which at that time was indeed peripheral. The time is morning; we find the construction workers with their shirts "already scorched with sweat."[19] And then, everywhere, above the white noise of construction work, an awful sound:

> But amid the stubborn explosions of the
> rock-crusher, which blindly dismembers, blindly
> crumbles, blindly grabs,
>
> as though without direction
> a sudden human scream is born
> and periodically returns,
>
> so crazed with pain it seems suddenly
> human no longer and becomes once more
> a dead screech. Then slowly it's

reborn in the violent light
among the blinded buildings, a new
steady scream that only someone dying,

in his last moment, could hurl
into this sun, which still cruelly shines
though softened by touches of sea air . . .

The scream is the old excavator's,
tortured by months and years
of morning sweat—accompanied

by silent swarms of stone-
cutters; but it's also the freshly
convulsed earth's, or, within the narrower

limits of the modern horizon,
the whole neighborhood's. . . . It is the city's,
plunged into a festive brilliance

—it is the world's. The crying is for
what ends and begins again—
what was grass and open space and has become

waxy white courtyards
enclosed within a resentful decorum;
what was almost an old fairground

of bright plaster slanting in the sun
and has become a new block, swarming
in an order made of stifled grief.

The crying is for what changes, even if
to become something better.[20]

Metaphor, anthropomorphism, the pathetic fallacy—the poem moves toward its conclusion with a violent flowering of tropes and figures. Not only does Pasolini overload this passage with literariness, he even—like Yeats in "A Prayer for My Daughter"—tells us exactly what his metaphors mean, how we are to read them. The excavator's cry is really Rome's cry, is really the world's. The cry protests against "what ends and begins again." Here, at the city's limit, where hovels commune uneasily with gleaming new high-rise apartments and working-class projects, a machine cries out in imaginary complaint against the products of progress. What ends and begins again? The answer nearest to hand is the city of Rome. At the periphery the city as it was ever known comes to its official end, its borders drawn muddily by the ad-hoc, low-rise, low-grade housing of the borgate. But there also does it begin again. As high-rises thrust their preening shoulders against and above their lowly neighbors, something akin to the city—or an idea of it—resumes. The pain of this beginning again, this urbanization of what had been borderless frontier, is expressed in the excavator's preternatural whine. But even in the apartment block's will to order, there remains some residue of the borgate's abject limitlessness. The new block is "swarming/ in an order made of stifled grief." Earlier in the poem we saw the borgate swarm. Now it is the apartment high-rise that swarms in "order"—another oxymoron, we might note. We cannot tell from the poem whether the building that will be raised on the plot cleared by the plangent excavator will be a public housing project or a middle-class high-rise. The import, for Pasolini, is in either case the same: the swarms of artisanal hovels and one-room mud dwellings that made up the borgate will simply be replaced, their miseries reproduced by swarms of bossy new pretenders. Both swarming bodies embody and enact injustice and oppression. The conclusion the poem draws, we will have noticed by now, bears a strong likeness to Accattone's failed attempt at renewal and reform.

The urbanization and development of the periphery might be "something better," but that doesn't mean we are to trust them. Perhaps, even, they are worse: we can hardly imagine Pasolini calling a newly minted mass housing project by the name of "life," the term by which he calls the borgate. Perhaps the new building will be "something better" in a narrower sense—purely architectural. The phrase "something better" is most likely a tip-off that the site Pasolini observes is probably a public housing project and not a luxury or middle-class building. But both types of construction only add to the formless peripheral swarm whose misery cannot be calculated, or if it can be calculated, then it cannot be properly represented, just as he warned it could not in his essay "The Shantytowns of Rome." Instead, the poetic language and poetic metaphors that are strained and stretched, the words like "swarm" that are depended on a bit too heavily—these things suggest the resistance that the awesome scale of the periphery presents to Pasolini's representational practice. We could, if we wanted to arrive at this lesson more easily, simply look at any number of the aerial photographs taken of the periphery during the late 1950s to see how even photography with its automatic mimetic capacities fails to provide an image of the periphery: large blocky buildings, chalk white due to the black-and-white film stock, buildings crowd in on one another, seem to overlap, to hum in nervous proximity while extending in every direction, beyond the photograph's frame, the arbitrariness of whose border—slicing straight through the buildings along its four edges—testifies to the absence of borders in the periphery and the photograph's failure to capture, to represent this same overbuilt, borderless landscape.

So much discussion of the teeming and seemingly limitless peripheral landscape suggests that this landscape and the aesthetic means by which Pasolini evokes it participate in the nature of the sublime, that order of experience that encompasses the too large, the monumental, the intimidating, the unquantifiable. Immanuel Kant, whose *Critique of Judgment* contains the fullest interrogation of the subject, says that the sublime refers to that category of experience "to be found in a formless object, so far as in it or by occasion of it *boundlessness* is represented."[21] Because the growth of the periphery is so tied, in Pasolini's way of understanding and representing it, to notions of swarming boundlessness, I will digress here for a moment to consider Kant's definition of the sublime since he so firmly locates it in the realms of the boundless and formless. Whether Pasolini would have appreciated being forced into proximity to Kant I cannot guess. I make this move, though, in order to find a means of accounting for the effect of Pasolini's insistent reference, in "The Tears of the Excavator" and in the screenplay of *Mamma Roma* (which we shall come to shortly), to the Roman periphery as enormous, boundless, and cruel, terms that if they resonate anywhere, resonate in the register of the sublime.

According to Kant, the sublime is a category identifiable in large part due to its difference from the beautiful. In many ways, the sublime is a thus a negative concept: it is that which the beautiful is not. Kant begins to explain their difference:

> The Beautiful in nature is connected with the form of the object which consists in having [definite] boundaries. The Sublime, on the other hand, is to be found in a formless object, so far as in it of by occasion of it *boundlessness* is represented, and yet its totality is also present to thought.[22]

Form and formless, the bound and the boundless—these are the terms that Kant conjoins, respectively, to the beautiful and the sublime. One of the most intriguing aspects of Kant's theory is his idea that the immensity of the formless (and therefore sublime) object "is also present to thought." Boundlessness describes one of the many "formal" or material features of the sublime: things great in size, great in number, great in power—a mountain, a crowd, an ocean. The material dimension of the sublime is the channel through which we recognize it as such. But the intellectual dimension, that it be "present to thought," is the channel through which we chart its effects. So what, then, does Kant mean by the sublime being "present to thought"?

To understand Kant's meaning, we must first attend to what he calls "the most important distinction" between the beautiful and the sublime, which is this:

> Natural beauty (which is independent) brings with it a pur-
> posiveness in its form by which the object seems to be, as it
> were, pre-adapted to our Judgment, and thus constitutes in
> itself an object of satisfaction. On the other hand, that which
> excites in us, without any reasoning about it, but in the mere
> apprehension of it, the feeling of the sublime, may appear as
> regards its form to violate purpose in respect of the Judgment,
> to be unsuited to our presentative faculty, and, as it were to do
> violence to the Imagination; and yet it is judged to be only the
> more sublime.[23]

According to Kant's understanding of beauty, we recognize the beautiful as such because it (the beautiful object) conforms to an *a priori* concept already present in consciousness. Beauty is familiar, reassuring, already there. The sublime, however, by being unfamiliar, seems to violate purpose,[24] and even though we are witness to it, we can't quite represent it to ourselves: it is "unsuited to our presentative faculty." Having said this, Kant makes the initially enigmatic point that "in general we express ourselves incorrectly if we call any *object of nature* sublime."[25] This is the case because it is impossible for an object of nature to violate its own purpose. So how then can we call a mountain or an ocean sublime? We can't actually, at least not properly, for the sublime exists not in nature or in the external world, but rather in the mind, which projects the concept of sublimity onto certain objects of its perception. Kant uses the example of the ocean:

> Thus the wide ocean, disturbed by the storm, cannot be called
> sublime. Its aspect is horrible; and the mind must be already
> filled with manifold Ideas if it is to be determined by such an
> intuition to a feeling itself sublime, as it is incited to aban-
> don sensibility and to busy itself with Ideas that involve higher
> purposiveness.[26]

We see here, then, that the object itself is not sublime, but rather its confusion and magnitude "incite" the viewer to distort the sense data of the object and then to project onto the object *ideas of* the sublime, which in themselves do possess purposiveness. The sublime, unlike the beautiful, does not belong to the world but rather to the mind that perceives the world. We might further say that the sublime arises from a disturbance, usually a disturbance in the field of the vision, so acute that the mind must rush in to assist in giving some shape to the experience. Paradoxically, though, the mind gives shape to the experience by calling it shapeless and, therefore, sublime. To illustrate by way of a rather banal example: suppose I encounter a mountain of enormous size, so large that my eyes cannot take in its shape comfortably, so large that I cannot *visualize,* even in my imagination, what the dimensions of the mountain are, what it might look in its fullness. I may be so awed by the size of the mountain that I am led to call it immeasurable, limitless. Of course, there could also exist a marker detailing the precise height and geographical area of the mountain, which would allow me to *know* the mountain's size, and yet this knowledge would not produce in me the ability to visualize imaginatively its enormous size. I will persist in saying that it is immeasurable, because according to my practical ability to perceive it or conceive of it, *it is.* This experience of the insufficiency of the senses and the imagination in the face of the empirical experience of the world and the knowledge available to the reason is, for Kant, the experience of the sublime.

To recapitulate, then, the sublime is an effect of our reason outstripping our imagination which "exhibits its own limits and inadequacy" in the face of the sublime object.[27] Whereas the beautiful is repose, poise, ease, the sublime is discomfiture:

> The feeling of the Sublime is therefore a feeling of pain, arising from the want of accordance between the aesthetical estimation of magnitude formed by the Imagination and the estimation of the same formed by Reason.[28]

The reason's estimation is greater than that of the imagination. We can conceive the imagination sensing its own humiliation in front of the sublime object, while reason enjoys this defeat of its rival and partner:

> There is at the same time a pleasure thus excited, arising from the correspondence with rational Ideas of this very judgment of the inadequacy of our greatest faculty of Sense.[29]

Which is to say that consciousness—that amalgam of reason and imagination—enjoys its feeling of being overwhelmed in one area and rising to the occasion in another. Jean-François Lyotard has summarized the sublime's admixture of pleasure and pain more elegantly than I am able to:

> . . . a pleasure mixed with pain, a pleasure that comes from pain. In the event of an absolutely large object—the desert, a mountain, a pyramid—or one that is absolutely powerful—a storm at sea, an erupting volcano—which like all absolutes can only be thought, without any sensible/sensory intuition, as an Idea of reason, the faculty of presentation, the imagination, fails to provide a representation corresponding to this Idea. This failure of expression gives rise to a pain, a kind of cleavage within the subject between what can be conceived and what can be imagined or presented. But this pain in turn engenders a pleasure, in fact a double pleasure: the impotence of the imagination attests *a contrario* to an imagination striving to figure even that which cannot be figured, and that imagination thus aims to harmonize its object with that of reason—and that furthermore the inadequacy of the images is a negative sign of the immense power of ideas. This dislocation of the faculties [of imagination and reason] gives rise to an extreme tension (Kant calls it agitation) that characterizes the pathos of the sublime, as opposed to the calm feeling of beauty.[30]

I quote the passage at length to avail myself of the elegance of Lyotard's summary of the relationship of the imagination and reason in the context of the sublime. The agitation, or tension of the sublime, is also described by Kant in terms of mobility:

> The mind feels itself *moved* in the representation of the Sublime in nature; whilst in aesthetical judgments about the Beautiful it is in *restful* contemplation. This movement may (especially in its beginnings) be compared to a vibration, *i.e.,* to a quickly alternating attraction towards, and repulsion from, the same Object.[31]

So the sublime is movement from and toward; it is attraction and repulsion.

Its restlessness, its painful pleasure, its self-consciousness and implicit sense of representational defeat, but also the compliment it pays to the powers of the human intellect: all these traits of the sublime are very clearly at work in Pasolini's poetry, and, as we shall see, in his cinema, and thus their presence suggests the usefulness of linking Pasolini's work to the concept of the sublime.

In fact, one of Pasolini's privileged memories (perhaps a screen memory, but what of that?) of his aesthetic development provides a sharply delineated textbook example of the dilemma of sublime poetics:

> Once I had entered puberty, drawing acquired a new meaning; the "average" aspirations inspired by my family upbringing and by my teachers, mingling with those ardently fantastic ones drawn from the reading of Homer and Verne, gave me a whole world, another world, which I desperately sought to set down in the horrid pages of my drawing album. Here the discourse should focus on the shield of Achilles; how much that tremendous shield made me suffer would take too long and be too difficult to tell. It was then that I experienced my first anguish when confronted with the relationship between two extensions—so different, one from the other, as are reality and representation. . . .
>
> I remember that I subdivided the page into ten or so segments and drew in them the creation of the world; I had just turned thirteen and we were living in Cremona. . . . I saw myself bending over the page, constantly urged on by the pure problem of the relationship between the real and the imaginary. At that time the fact of representation seemed something terrible and primordial, precisely because it was in a state of purity: the equivalent had to be definitive. Faced by the problem of reproducing a maddening meadow, the question for me was this: did I have to draw each blade of grass? I did not know at that time that by filling in a whole area with green pastel I would have achieved the movement of the meadow and that this would have been sufficient excuse to neglect the blades of grass. Such hypocrisies were still very remote from me and it was with real suffering that I submitted to colouring in a green background which was supposed to be the meadow on which God breathed life into Adam.[32]

The individuality of countless blades of grass cannot be represented or translated onto Pasolini's "horrid pages." They resist—defy—his efforts to represent them, which is to say that their infinite number resists the imagination, the faculty of presentation. His reason, though, keeps throwing in his face the reality of each little blade. The compromise he arrives at, the green background, only alludes to what is unrepresentable about the meadow (countless number of blades of grass); in other words, to return to Lyotard's formulation of the problem, "the faculty of presentation, the imagination, fails to provide a representation corresponding to this Idea." And the result is pain, or in Pasolini's Italian, "*sofferenza*." The situation presents itself quite clearly as one in which the sublime is at stake, but it also demonstrates that sublimity is an effect of the reason's cleavage from the imagination, reality's distance from representation, and that, as such, it is a disturbance in consciousness that the mind produces.

Pasolini was not attempting to draw a storm-swept ocean or the pyramids at Giza, or any of the other stereotypical subjects that normally suggest themselves as breeding grounds for sublime emotions. The curiosity of the memory of this experience, occurring as it does in so early and so innocuous a context, suggests that the rhetoric of the sublime may be endemic to Pasolini's artistic production—that Pasolini will often conceive of representation as an agonistic exercise of its impossibility because the world to be represented is itself essentially beyond being represented. In this sense, an understanding of peripheral Rome as the progenitor of sublime experience would be more an effect of Pasolini's desire and less that of the nature of the periphery itself. Furthermore, resort to the rhetoric of the sublime risks erasing the material, geographic, and architectural specificity of the peripheral landscape risks turning this landscape into just another exercise in the unrepresentable. However, Pasolini still clings to the specific and particular experience of the Roman periphery in his poetic descriptions and in his films. There seems to have been a striking coincidence between Pasolini's ongoing, overarching aesthetic concerns and the reality of Rome's rapid and immense growth, which was his subject.

There exists, as well, a venerable tradition of conceiving of Rome as a matrix of sublime sensation—a tradition that Pasolini would have been familiar with and in which he seems self-consciously to insert his own understanding of peripheral Rome.[33] This tradition belongs most to the English Romantic poets who made much of the notion of Rome as evocative of the sublime. Of course, the Romantics received their sublime impressions from the ruins of the ancient city and from Rome's fantastic accretion of layer after layer of history—all visible and yet somehow incomprehensible. Shelley, for instance, claims to have written his verse drama "Prometheus Unbound"

> upon the mountainous ruins of the Baths of Caracalla, among
> the flowery glades, and thickets of odiferous blossoming trees
> which are extended in ever winding labyrinths upon its im-
> mense platforms and dizzy arches suspended in the air. The
> bright blue sky of Rome, and the effect of the vigorous awak-
> ening of spring in that divinest climate, and the new life with

> which it drenches the spirits even to intoxication, were the
> inspiration of this drama.[34]

Although the city inspired his "Prometheus," Shelley offers us a clearer picture of what this inspiration amounts to in his letter to Thomas Love Peacock of March 23, 1819. I quote below several passages:

> —At Albano we arrived again in sight of Rome—arches after
> arches in unending lines stretching across the uninhabited wil-
> derness . . . masses of nameless ruins standing like rocks out of
> the plain. . . .
>
> There are in addition a number of towers and labyrin-
> thine recesses hidden & woven over by the wild growth of weeds
> and ivy. Never was any desolation more sublime & lovely. . . .
>
> Come to Rome. It is a scene by which expression is over-
> powered: which words cannot convey.[35]

The challenge that Rome presents to the poetic imagination is experienced as a kind of ecstasy. Lord Byron, Shelley's countryman and contemporary, responds in a similar vein to Rome. In his "Childe Harold's Pilgrimage" the city elicits this apostrophe:

> O Rome, my country! city of the soul!

Not too many lines later, Rome's chaotic magnitude forces Byron to seek refuge in the ineffability topos:

> Chaos of ruins! who shall trace the void,
> O'er the dim fragments cast a lunar light,
> And say, 'her was, or is,' where all is doubly night?[36]

Both Shelley's and Byron's ecstasies over Rome's magnitude are echoed in Pasolini's evocation of the Roman periphery as an indecipherable "swarming" mass of architecture. Pasolini also shares with Shelley and Byron the fact that all three came to Rome as exiles; perhaps the perception of Rome as sublime is particularly acute for the outsider.[37]

Another outsider, but this one an Italian, the poet Giacomo Leopardi, left his home in the north of Italy and visited Rome for several months in 1822. Interesting is Leopardi's being underwhelmed by Rome's overwhelming size. He recognizes in Rome an incipient version of the plague that would so afflict it in Pasolini's day, almost a century and half later: the expansion of the city to dimensions unsuitable for use by its inhabitants. Here is Leopardi in a letter home to his family, dated December 3, 1822:

All the population of Rome would not be enough to fill the piazza of Saint Peter's. I saw the cupola, even with my short-sightedness, from five miles away while traveling, and I saw it with its ball and cross, very distinctly, the way you see the Apennines from where you are. All the grandeur of Rome serves only to multiply distances, and the number of steps you have to climb to find someone you want. These immense buildings and hence the interminable streets are so many spaces flung out to separate men instead of spaces which contain men. I do not see the beauty in placing ordinary chess pieces on a board as long as the Piazza della Madonna. I am not saying that Rome seems uninhabited, but I do say that if men really needed as much space to live and walk as they do in these palazzi, these avenues, squares, churches—the entire globe could not contain the human race.[38]

Pasolini adopts the rhetoric of the Romantic Roman sublime—immensity, confusion, ineffability—and applies it to the Roman periphery. This move is perhaps willfully perverse, but not without reason. The periphery had indeed grown to such a size in so short a time—had become so thick with architecture both mean and modern—that we can easily see how he might quite naturally resort to the rhetoric of the sublime in his attempt to account for its enormity. The sublime, after all, is explicitly not the beautiful; therefore, the Roman periphery's squalor actually affirms the legitimacy of considering it in terms of the sublime. The sublime is a restless category of experience: unsettled, mobile, jarring and jarred, inflamed with images of unfathomable totalities, and yet fragmentary, incomplete. In contemplating the sublime, one thinks of Pasolini in "The Tears of the Excavator," grappling with a host of opaque philosophical complexities, all the while making his way through suburban Rome, saddened, enthralled, and stupefied by a city that "swarms" in its seemingly infinite expanse. My intention in making the connection between Pasolini's production and an aesthetic of the sublime is not merely to show that the work can be claimed for the sublime, but that the sublime mode opens up a way of understanding what is both compelling and disturbing about Pasolini's representation of and relationship to Rome and its stupendous, miserable periphery. The concept of the sublime illuminates "The Tears of the Excavator," but it also sheds light on *Mamma Roma,* both the published screenplay and the film, which I turn to analyze in the next chapter. As we shall see, *Mamma Roma*'s look at the world of the Roman periphery is rigorous and repetitive. It proposes no solutions to the problems it puts forward, choosing instead to insist on the unrepresentable nature of that which it obstinately endeavors to represent.

Before, however, turning directly to *Mamma Roma,* one more context needs to plumbed: that of the film's location. This film is not generically set in the "howling wilderness" (again, Eleanor Clark's compelling phrase) of apartment buildings in the Roman periphery. It is set very concretely in a particular state-sponsored housing project of architectural and historical note. The project is called the Tuscolano II and it was built as a part of the INA Casa housing initiative, a successful and highly publicized effort to generate both jobs and housing for low-income Roman citizens.

INA Casa's successes and failures were debated vigorously in the architectural journals of the period. Some of its constructions still stand out in the history of postwar architecture as admirable examples of building sensitively for the poor and dispossessed—examples counter to much of the anonymous and brutal public housing built in Italy (and elsewhere) before, during, and after this period. Italian society of the 1950s could point to the INA Casa projects in order to congratulate itself on its economic development, its humane attitude toward the poor, its modernity. But the picture that Pasolini gives us of INA Casa in *Mamma Roma* departs from this self-congratulatory view. A thorough understanding of the INA Casa program and its reception should be essayed in order to appreciate more fully Pasolini's take on it in *Mamma Roma.* Moreover, the consideration of the significance of INA Casa in relation to Pasolini's filmmaking is consonant with a contemporary interest among Italian architects and architectural historians in reconsidering the INA Casa buildings both architecturally and historically. These buildings, according to one recent account, "number among the most important monuments of the Roman postwar period."[39]

INA Casa was instituted by what came to be known as the "Fanfani plan" or the "Fanfani law." This law was passed by the Italian parliament on February 28, 1949, and was named after the relatively progressive (for a member of the conservative Christian Democratic party, at least) Minister of Labor Amintore Fanfani. The plan was a joint effort of private and public interests, financed by a payroll tax levied on employers and employees, and by existing state monies and philanthropic donations.[40] The plan was designed to accomplish two primary goals: first, to create much-needed housing in cities whose populations were growing geometrically, and, second, to create jobs for a proletarian and even subproletarian workforce that was both unemployed and un- or under-housed. The plan also sought to employ and rehouse workers in rural areas. In 1948, one year before the institution of the Fanfani plan, the number of unemployed workers in Italy had risen above two million (equivalent to the entire population of Rome at that time). A 1951 census (even already two years into the INA Casa plan) revealed that almost 7 percent of Romans lived in grottoes, shacks, or in stairwells, while nearly 22 percent lived in conditions of severe overcrowding.[41] Clearly, INA Casa addressed itself to a pressing need.

The law's title states its intentions forthrightly: "Provisions for increasing worker employment, facilitating the construction of labor housing."[42] Almost all of the literature on INA Casa explains that the projects were designed to create demand for preindustrial materials, such as tile and wood, which were already in production in Italy. Similarly, building designs were kept to a fairly simple technological level so that unskilled laborers could be put to work at building sites with little or no training. Manfredo Tafuri sums up the foregoing in terms unmistakably tinged with skepticism:

> The aims of the plan were clear: to stem the increasing rate of unemployment; to place housing in a subordinate role relative to sluggish sectors, holding it to a preindustrial level and tying it to the development of small business; to keep stable for as long as possible a fluctuating sector of the working class that could be blackmailed but never organized; and to make public intervention a support for private intervention.[43]

Tafuri's meaning may be a bit unclear to a reader unacquainted with the literature on the subject. "To place housing in a subordinate role relative to sluggish sectors" simply means that the projects were to shy away from employing technologically advanced construction methods; the construction industry should not aim to outstrip the relatively low levels of industrial technology already in use in other areas of the Italian economy. Furthermore, we should note especially Tafuri's description of the employment opportunities created by INA Casa as, in fact, a means of stabilizing (i.e., containing, in Tafuri's understanding) a working class that could be politically dangerous as long as it remained unemployed. This attitude is very close to Pasolini's attitude in *Mamma Roma*.

The official view, published in *I 14 Anni del Piano INA Casa* (The fourteen years of the INA Casa plan), is expressed in rather more positive and positivistic terms:

> The choice of the construction sector for a massive interven-
> tion against unemployment seemed opportune for a num-
> ber of reasons. First of all because investments in this field,
> more than any other, allowed for the immediate absorption
> of laborers. . . .
>
> Moreover, construction allowed for the widescale employ-
> ment of untrained labor, which accounted for the better part
> of unemployed workers.[44]

These are the arguments for why INA Casa made good economic sense.
But the text waxes rhetorical and ideological when it seeks to articulate
the overarching vision of INA Casa:

> What characterizes a social experiment like INA Casa is its con-
> stant objective, its final goal, which is always man, the defense
> of the interests of the family, the continual concern to assure
> its recipients the fullness of its benefits.[45]

The note of paternalism struck here becomes slightly more ominous
in a later passage that follows a description of the public services and
recreational spaces (putatively) designed into each project:

> But services and public space are not enough. It was also nec-
> essary to teach the new assignees [of INA Casa homes] to take
> care of their homes without ruining them, to teach them to
> live collectively, to facilitate public meetings.[46]

This passage gives us evidence of INA Casa as an ideological project
above and beyond its material goals of alleviating unemployment and
the housing shortage, and so Tafuri is at least partially justified in his
belief that one of INA Casa's aims was the "stabilization" of a sector of
the working class. People were not only being housed and employed;
they were also being turned into proper citizens of the Italian state. The
creation of good citizens is later elaborated as one of the "three essential
aspects" of the INA Casa plan:[47]

> The Plan intended to give to all workers a human and suitable
> house, not to consign them to barracks. To this end the Plan
> sought to insert itself in the Italian architectural tradition, so
> rich in the variety of its history and of its landscape. The Plan
> did not impose designs, but rather chose designers to whom
> it suggested schematic types (functional and affordable) for
> projects that could easily be inserted into the environments
> where they were to be built.

> The workers were to feel themselves, as much as possible,
> the owners of these houses. The Plan wanted to educate the
> assignees to administer the housing projects responsibly, in
> an autonomous mode and . . . to turn the new neighborhoods
> into serene and modern communities.[48]

These few excerpts alert us to the state's (unfortunately unsurprising) attitude of high-handedness toward the beneficiaries of its plan. The anxiety over the unruliness of the new INA Casa tenants is such that it is felt they must be taught not to "ruin" their own homes. In effect, by stressing the need to make the tenants feel themselves "proprietors" of the new houses, the plan inducts them into the world of private property ownership to the same degree that it encourages the establishment of "modern communities." INA Casa's own official discourse also points implicitly to the crucial role that space, architecture, and habitation all play in the construction of a civic identity—a construction carried out cooperatively by the state and the citizen subject. To argue for this slightly contentious take on the INA Casa plan is not to dismiss its serious contribution to alleviating joblessness and homelessness, but to illumine those aspects of the plan that would have most attracted Pasolini's Marxist-inflected suspicion.

INA Casa never provided for all the housing needs of Italy's underclass, but what it did accomplish is impressive, if only in sheer numbers. Ten years after the commencement of the plan, INA Casa had constructed in Rome alone 110,953 apartments, or 7.33 percent of the available apartments in the city of Rome.[49] Furthermore, as mentioned before, some of the projects stand as architectural landmarks of the period, not only in Italy, but in the context of worldwide postwar architecture. The most famous and certainly the most frequently studied INA Casa project is the Tiburtino Quarter, designed by a team headed by Mario Ridolfi and Ludovico Quaroni and built on the southern periphery of Rome. The generous attention the Tiburtino Quarter has received from architectural critics and historians is due mostly to its deployment of a regional vernacular style, and this style is what led critics at the time to label the project "neorealist," borrowing this muddled term from the world of film. This intersection of film history and architectural history begs analysis.[50]

Neorealism in Italian architecture might partially trace its origins to the movement for organic architecture, the progenitor of which was Frank Lloyd Wright whose influence was imported into Italy by Bruno

Zevi, Wright's disciple in Italy who had studied and worked with the master in the United States during the interwar period. Zevi arrived on the Italian scene just after the war and quickly began disseminating the organic credo, which wanted architecture built for humans and real human conditions on a human scale.[51] Other architects sympathetic to this project banded together in 1945 to form the Associazione per l'Architettura Organica (APAO). The two directors of the Tiburtino project, Ridolfi and Quaroni, both were associated with APAO. They and a group of younger architects and former students of theirs, all of whom worked on the Tiburtino, came in time to be known as the "Roman school" of Italian architecture, and it is this school that is most closely associated with architectural neorealism.[52]

Tafuri and Dal Co almost dismissively call the Tiburtino "a veritable manifesto of architectural Neo-Realism."[53] Certainly, in almost any discussion of architectural neorealism, this neighborhood is looked to as a kind of *ur* text—the *Rome, Open City* of architectural neorealism. But what the term *neorealist* might refer to in the context of architecture is not immediately obvious. Architectural historian Maristella Casciato offers a set of identifying principles, obviously borrowed from the definitions of neorealist literature and cinema:

> The adjective "neorealist," when applied to architecture, indicates neither a style nor even an established vocabulary. It rather connoted a vigorously anti-abstract attitude, opposed to the monumental and academic approach of the Fascist years and open to an architecture of daily life, modeled directly on the material and psychological needs of the people who were to use it—common people who were seen in a lyrical but not mythical light. "Neorealist" is vernacular architecture, rural and bucolic, though sometimes also marked by the influence of Scandinavian residential types. Neorealist design showed a concern with artisan detailing and traditional construction techniques. It was realistic architecture because it followed local culture, emphasizing aspects of local color and respecting local spatial characteristics but never lapsing into simplistic imitation.[54]

This is the rosy view of architectural neorealism, and it seems mostly derived from empirical observation (i.e., what the buildings look like). There was never any manifesto of architectural neorealism, but the close match between Casciato's definition and the design of the Tiburtino project would suggest that Tafuri is correct in labeling it the neorealist "manifesto."

The neighborhood was one of the two very first INA Casa projects built in Rome, the Valco San Paolo project being the other.[55] Both were begun in 1950. The Tiburtino Quarter occupied 8.8 hectares of land and comprised 771 apartments built to house 4,000 inhabitants. Three building types were used: apartment towers of seven stories, apartment houses of three and four stories, and rowhouses. This last type is perhaps the one most often used to illustrate what is characteristic about the quarter.[56] The townhouses give the project its much-discussed village-like atmosphere. Street patterns were drawn in slightly irregular fashion and facade abutments were staggered and varied so as to give, in Peter G. Rowe's assessment, the impression of "an incremental, discontinuous process of development" and to impart "a distinctly picturesque quality reminiscent of much older and rural towns."[57] The combined anxieties of building in the periphery of the city, in the *non-città*, and building to house migrants from rural villages seem to have conspired to produce the quaint morphology of the Tiburtino. The neighborhood was replete with shuttered windows, grillwork, steeply pitched roofs, and tufa facades plastered over and painted in warm tones traditionally associated with Roman architecture.

We might pause now to consider how this architectural program could be considered under the rubric of neorealism; what justifies the

The Tiburtino Quarter. The project's irregular rooflines were intended to suggest the haphazard, organic development of an Italian village. Photograph by the author.

appropriation of a term used originally and most famously to designate a school of filmmaking? If, for the moment, we think of cinematic neorealism in terms of the urban bleakness of *Bicycle Thieves* or the paratactic and the reticent episodes of Rossellini's *Paisan,* then the rather sunny disposition of the Tiburtino project would seem to make it an odd candidate for inclusion under the neorealist umbrella. But the same folkloristic elements of the project that seem to inspire its being referred to as neorealist have their precedents in neorealist filmmaking and film theory. As was discussed in the previous chapter, neorealism eschewed the use of professional actors. Film actors, instead, were to be found on the street—"real" people who would alchemically impart to the screen the gravity of their "real" problems. Likewise, the fictional screenplay was to be rejected in favor of plots taken from the events one could read about in newspapers. Real locations were to be favored over the sets of Cinecittà. These precepts were followed with little rigor or consistency by most of the films that have come to be understood as constituting the core of the neorealist canon (chiefly these are works produced by Rossellini, Visconti, De Sica, Fellini, and Giuseppe De Santis in the late 1940s and early 1950s).[58] Nevertheless, the myth of the "real" has clung to neorealism. There is, then, a structural parallel between cinematic neorealism's appropriation of real life and concomitant rejection of the paradigms of classical filmmaking and architectural neorealism's appropriation of the look of real villages and concomitant rejection of abstract architectural solutions of the sort favored by rationalist fascist building styles.[59] Visconti, for example, extols the use of nonactors because of their "fascinating simplicity,"[60] while Chiarini, as quoted above, insists on "the chronicle . . . , events and facts, culled from the daily existence of men."

In the same way that Tiburtino's village-like atmosphere mimes the small towns that its inhabitants had left behind, cinematic neorealism valorizes the landscape of everyday life. Writing in 1941, De Santis, who began directing his own movies after the war, championed the centrality of the Italian landscape to future Italian filmmaking in order to offer a coded critique of the supposed artificiality of fascist film culture:

> How would it be possible to understand and interpret man
> if he were to be separated from those elements in which he
> lives everyday, and with which he is in constant communica-
> tion? These elements are: (1) Either the walls of his house,
> which must show the marks of his hands, his taste, his nature,

> and so on, or (2) the streets of his town, in which he meets
> other men (such meetings must not be occasional, but must be
> underscored by the special character that such an act carries
> with it).... Or (3) his timid profession and his identification
> with the nature which surrounds him, on which he depends
> so much that he becomes moulded in its image.[61]

De Santis's argument that landscape and man mirror one another, *mise en abîme,* certainly seems to have been put into practice at the Tiburtino. The neighborhood projects back to its inhabitants an image of their own supposed desires.[62] Furthermore, the picturesque design of the Tiburtino project—its production, *ex novo,* of local color—can also be linked to neorealist filmmakers' and theorists' choice of Sicilian writer Giovanni Verga as a model for neorealist filmmaking. Verga was a realist fiction writer of the late nineteenth century whose *I malavoglia*[63] was loosely used as a source for Visconti's *La terra trema.* Verga's milieu is decidedly that of rural village life, and his fiction, "miraculously stark and real," was taken as a model for neorealism because it "offers us both the human experience and a concrete experience."[64] From the foregoing we see, then, that the Tiburtino Quarter was indeed firmly linked to certain established neorealist tendencies. Its sympathetic critics, though, would tend to see it less in the despairing tradition of *Bicycle Thieves* and more akin to the scenes of Silvana Mangano with her skirt suggestively hiked above her knees in *Bitter Rice* (*Riso amaro,* 1949), a film directed by De Santis and generally considered to be one of neorealism's less aesthetically and politically committed artifacts, an example of what has been called "rosy" or "pink" neorealism (pink being a paler shade of red, of course).

Shortly after its completion, the Tiburtino Quarter was subjected to intense criticism, often by architects who had worked on the project. A dossier of materials on the project was published in 1957 in *Casabella.* The dossier included drawings, plans, maps, photographs, and essays by several of the key contributors to the project. Carlo Aymonino, one of the key architects of the Tiburtino, contributed the lead essay, "Storia e cronaca del Quartiere Tiburtino" (History and chronicle of the Tiburtino Quarter), in which he both criticizes and defends the project's shortcomings and achievements.[65] His tone is one of benevolent reproof:

> Influenced by a renewed interest in traditional materials as elements of the language of strict economy, and prideful of this
> renunciation as being realistic (today, considering the period

as a whole we might jokingly say "neo-realistic") we reached
the absurd level of appropriating pieces of seventeenth-
century Rome, composing facades according to a scenographic rhythm—witness the windows with railings only on
the top floor, the little external staircase that begins at the
second floor only to reach a single apartment in the building
on the piazza, the balconies only on two or three floors of one
house . . . the underpasses and overpasses, up through to the
obsessive division of enclosures. . . . Sure we avoided the possibility of tenants not being able to recognize their own houses,
but this psychological goal became the paradox of having to
"invent" a story told in dialect, which would act as the surro-
gate for what was impossible: the construction of those houses
directly by those who would inhabit them.[66]

Quaroni also hones in on the dangerous picturesqueness of the project.
In his more playful but more acerbic assessment, "Il paese dei barocchi,"
which translates as "The Village of the Baroques," the project which he
and Ridolfi had organized together looks, only three years after its completion, like a quaint failure: "In our push toward the 'city' we ended
up at the 'village.'" This comment also points to the oft-repeated criticism that the Tiburtino project did not properly integrate itself into the
fraying fabric of the city's periphery. Tafuri aphoristically describes this
shortcoming: "Exiled from the city, the Tiburtino scornfully turned its
back on it." The Tiburtino was built where it was because the land there
was cheap. Economic forces had drawn INA Casa's tenants to the city,
but economic forces would also keep them at the city's edge. Even the
Tiburtino's visual and spatial design might be seen as itself as kind of
country-come-to-town, or, in Tafuri's words, "a regressive utopia with
nostalgic accents." Commenting on the class segregation implicit in far-
flung public housing, Giovanni Astengo, a prominent urbanist and the
editor of *Urbanistica,* pointed to the unavoidable "sensation of not participating in the life of the city" that pervaded the INA Casa complexes.
Despite the good intentions of a project like the Tiburtino, "the privilege of having a nice house can also in the end turn into a neurosis."[67]

　　But only to find fault with the Tiburtino Quarter seems too easy. More
recently scholars in Italy and elsewhere have begun a critical reappraisal
of the project and other INA Casa projects that express the neorealist
impulse; generally they find as much to praise as to blame. As Piero
Ostilio Rossi judiciously observes in his note on the project, despite its
limitations, "Tiburtino is, however, a testament to a generous attempt to

illustrate, in architectural and urbanist terms, the aspirations of those social classes that . . . were beginning to make themselves visible with a new dignity in the life of the country." And Casciato's aside that the project's complex style amounted to a "heterodox bazaar of fantasy solutions," seems to offer some a model of understanding its village eclecticism outside the context of cloying picturesqueness. Bruno Reichlin understands "Tiburtino's triumph of simple parataxis" and "apparent absence of compositional hierarchies and structural order" as "an antimodernist revolt against the supposed logical and formal necessity that had been taken on symbolically as an expression of the most radical rationalism." Reichlin clearly means to imply that he interprets Quaroni and Ridolfi as intending the Tiburtino to rebel against the modernism of fascist architecture, often identified as rationalist. Reichlin's interpretation of the project as a "revolt" testifies to its claim to be taken seriously. Even Tafuri, perhaps the project's most incisive detractor, claims that "[i]n spite of everything, the Tiburtino remained a slap in the face of petit-bourgeois respectability. Neither a city nor a suburb, the complex, strictly speaking, was also not a 'town,' but rather an affirmation of both rage and hope."[68]

Even Pasolini might be called on to give evidence in support of the project. In his novel *A Violent Life*, the main character, Tommaso Puzzilli, a child of the borgate, returns from a stint in prison to find that his family has been granted an INA Casa apartment in the Tiburtino Quarter. The narrator describes the quarter's construction:

> But then one day they started flinging together new buildings around there, along the Tiburtina a bit above the Fort. It was an enterprise of government-sponsored INA-Case, and the blocks of housing began to sprout on the fields, on the little hills. They had strange shapes, pointed roofs, little balconies, skylights, round and oval windows: the people began to call those buildings Alice in Wonderland, Magic Village, or the New Jerusalem, and everybody laughed, but all the people who lived in those slums began to think: ''Aaaah, at last they're gonna give me a palace!'' And there wasn't one of the refugees, the shanty dwellers, who hadn't tried presenting an application to get out of the miserable heaps of junk they lived in.[69]

Here the attitude seems akin to Tafuri's: the Tiburtino may amount to little more than "regressive utopia." But when Tommaso arrives in the Tiburtino for the first time after his release, his reaction has nothing in it of skepticism:

> When Tommaso was let out, it was a fine May sunset. This was the first time Tommaso had seen the INA-Case development finished: when he was picked up, it was just a pile of bricks and scaffoldings that people looked at with irony, knowing what was going to come of it. Now it was there, all nice and completed, with a little wall around it, on the fields that had remained what they were before, full of filth. The brand new streets curved in among the pink, red, yellow houses, also curved with lots of balconies and skylights and rows of railings. Arriving with the bus, looking at it, you really thought that quarter was Jerusalem. . . .
>
> . . . He came to apartment twenty-nine. Here another lovely surprise was waiting for him: on the door there was a card with Puzzilli written on it: PUZZILLI, in big letters, elaborately painted. "Jeezus!" Tommaso muttered, laughing, red in the face, his eyes glistening with emotion.[70]

Of course, the narration here, despite its being in the third person, is mimetic of Tommaso's consciousness. His excitement over the new INA Casa apartment should not be identified *ipso facto* as Pasolini's.[71] But the real improvement in the lives of Tommaso and his family and their real-life counterparts is indisputable. We should not wonder if they prefer the regressive utopia of the Tiburtino to the aggressive dystopia of the borgate.

Tommaso's moistened eyes, however, might not have moved Pasolini, who was rarely seduced by anything handed down by the Italian state, no matter how well intentioned. It is curious, though, that when he made *Mamma Roma,* a film about life and death in an INA Casa project, he chose not to set the narrative events in the Tiburtino, but in another INA Casa neighborhood off of the Via Tuscolana at its far southeastern reaches, the Tuscolano II Quarter.[72] I do not have concrete, biographical evidence of why this production choice was made. However, the nature of the neighborhood's design and the nature of *Mamma Roma,* I think, answer this question for us. First, to the neighborhood.

Much larger than the Tiburtino, the Tuscolano II covers 35.5 hectares of land and comprises 3,150 apartments built to house some 18,000 people. Certain features of its design are much more rigorously modern than those of the village-like Tiburtino; its central building is rather abstract in composition. Though it was built during the same period as the Tiburtino, the Tuscolano II, for better or worse, did not generate quite as much publicity and has not been studied as closely by architectural historians, a state of affairs explained, I think, by the fact that the project is not as elaborately or obviously neorealist as the Tiburtino. The project, whose design leaders were Mario De Renzi and Saverio Muratori, is a bit closer to the rationalist architecture of the fascist period, much more typically modernist than the Tiburtino. Its most impressive, or at least imposing, structure is a long, V-shaped apartment building with six floors. Muratori is most responsible for the design of this building, and the structure testifies to the "rigor . . . unity and legibility" that, according to Tafuri, characterize much of this architect's work.[73] This is the building that Mamma Roma and Ettore move to, and that Pasolini's camera depicts as an immutable, engulfing presence, alien to the needs and suffering of the film's central characters.

Pasolini, as we shall see, approaches the Tuscolano II with hostile skepticism. He quite possibly is unfair. Peter G. Rowe, unlike Pasolini, is sympathetic toward the project, and sees it as a kind of reserved cousin to Tiburtino—like a more assimilated migrant, whose rural rough edges have been smoothed away. His description of the building:

> Muratori's extension of the V-shaped apartment building creates an urban space that is at once familiar and commonplace like a traditional town piazza, as well as modern and functional for use as a bus stop and general-purpose open area. The architecture of the apartment building is clearly defined by a rational framework of vertical concrete columns and horizontal slabs, whereas the side profile is faced in *tufo* stone and features a pitched gable with a multitude of village-like chimneys. Panels within the concrete facade framework also feature *tufo* infill in a manner similar to local villages, together with shuttered windows and traditional balconies. Again a double reading of modern and vernacular is apparent.[74]

Rowe's reading of the building exaggerates the vernacular qualities of the building. The balconies and the rhythm of infill and framework do convey the humility of rural vernacular architecture.[75] Tufo is native to the region of Lazio, the region that contains Rome, and many villages in northern Lazio appear to be carved out of a single block of the porous, brown stone. Undoubtedly, some of the Tuscolano project's first tenants would have emigrated from rural Lazio and might have been welcomed visually by the tufo's familiarity. But viewed from a modest distance, it is difficult, if not impossible, to distinguish the tufo, while the balconies and their thin iron railings disappear into the shuttered windows. Instead, the concrete vertical and horizontal elements that visually demarcate the separation between floors and individual apartments create a pronounced grid that gives a fairly severe unity to the facade's gestalt. And the "piazza" that receives Rowe's compliments is a piazza in name alone. More recently it serves as nothing more than a vast parking lot.

Rowe's vernacular reading is, therefore, generous, perhaps to a fault. Emphasizing, however, the building's more modernist qualities, as I do here, is not intended to undermine his reading completely. Neither the vernacular nor the modernist tradition would have been necessarily more appropriate for a Roman housing project in the postwar period. But my emphasis on the building's modernist elements helps to clarify, I think, why Pasolini films it in such an unrelenting manner: his unrelenting camera work seems to be a response triggered by his understanding of the building itself as unrelenting. This will become clearer when, shortly, we will turn to an analysis of the film.

Unlike the Tiburtino, the Tuscolano project does not exactly, to paraphrase Tafuri, "turn its back on the city." The V-shaped building (the building that will serve as the location of Mamma Roma and Ettore's house) is open toward its surrounding environment. Its arms extend toward the neighborhood between itself and the Via Tuscolana (though not toward the center of Rome). But the gesture of opening out toward the city would have been purely formal in any case, considering the neighborhood's distance from the center, a distance that would have seemed greater in the early 1950s before the city grew out to meet it in the following years.

Central to an understanding of the project's architecture is the function of the arched entrance to the neighborhood that is made by an underpassage that is carved out of the center of the V-shaped building. The entrance, which offers communication between the piazza/parking lot and the rest of the development, is not exactly in the center of the building. It spans the width of two apartment bays and begins from the eastern half of the V. Its downward-sloping, less-than horizontal elements intersect with a vertical pier or column; the intersection forms a cross of sorts, much to the apparent interest of Pasolini who returns to the suggestive nature of this element repeatedly. The entrance is the most modernist feature of the building. Rowe offers a mixed reading of it, calling it "clearly traditional in its location and prominence, and yet highly technological in its specific form and substance."[76] Paolo Angeletti claims for this entrance a privileged function in negotiating the Tuscolano II's relationship to the surrounding city, "with which

A view of the Tuscolano II's central V-shaped building, designed by Muratori. Note the infill that suggests tufo and the traditional balconies; these putatively neorealist elements are organized and contained within the structure's overall grid. Photograph by the author.

A view of the Muratori building's central arch, which Pasolini will focus on in *Mamma Roma*. Photograph by the author.

the only rapport is through the doorway."[77] As will shortly be apparent, both Rowe's and Angeletti's descriptions of this doorway resonate with Pasolini's attitude toward the project as a whole. In short, the choice of location better suited Pasolini's notion of the obsolescence of the neorealist project, in film as well as in architecture and other cultural forms. Even Rowe, who tends to see the Tuscolano project from a positive and positivist neorealist point of view, argues that "the neorealist tide that had buoyed Italian architecture after the war began to recede at Tuscolano."[78]

As a single architectural statement, the Muratori building is far more imposing than anything found at the Tiburtino. But more imposing than the building itself is its surrounding neighborhood. The principal arterial street of this neighborhood is the Via Tuscolana. This area was home to the most massive development in all of 1950s Rome. The neighborhood was built on lands aggressively divided and sold for development by the aristocratic families Gerini and Lancelotti who profited enormously from boom-economy real-estate speculation. Most of the buildings constructed in this zone were very large apartment buildings; development of this sort caused the population density levels to exceed 1,200 inhabitants per hectare.[79]

We can only imagine that the scale and density of development of this neighborhood helped to play a determining role in influencing Pasolini's decision to set *Mamma Roma* there. The development around the Tuscolano II is much denser than that around the Tiburtino Quarter. Thus, as a location the neighborhood embodies more dramatically the sense of Rome as a city that had wildly overgrown its borders. Here the Roman periphery was at its most swarmingly sublime. Here most glaring was the gap between the (perhaps) well-meaning intentions of neorealist architecture and the rapacious land speculation that hemmed it in and of which, in Tafuri's analysis, it was, in fact, a subspecies. Obviously the landscape appealed to Pasolini's filmmaker's vision and Pasolini's polemicist's sense of rhetoric. Here he would shoot *Mamma Roma*.

Chapter 5

Mamma Roma and Pasolini's Oedipal (Housing) Complex

Mamma *Roma* much more self-consciously declares itself as an urbanist text than does its predecessor, *Accattone*. An actual public-housing project is used as both allegorical matrix and physical-historical setting for the events of the narrative. The eponymous central character, played with self-conscious abandonment by Anna Magnani, reclaims her son after leaving her life as a prostitute and brings him to live in her apartment in a dilapidated Liberty-style[1] building in the periphery. Things seem to brighten later when they move into a new development, where, according to Mamma Roma, "i signori" (the gentle-folk) live. Mamma Roma sells produce in the new neighborhood's market; Ettore gets a job waiting tables in Trastevere, and his mother buys him a motorcycle. It's la dolce vita, subproletarian style. But Mamma Roma's pimp, Carmine, returns to force her back on the streets, and when Ettore finds out the nature of his mother's profession, he is traumatized and turns to a career in petty thievery. He ends up in jail where he falls ill and dies; Pasolini's camera figures the boy's death quite literally as a crucifixion. Mamma Roma is destroyed, and the film ends with a forbidding shot of the peripheral cityscape that has, so the film seems to say, betrayed her.

This is a skeletal outline of the plot. Its subproletarian characters, its setting in Rome's periphery, its ending in death, its starkly brusque shooting style—all these things link the film quite strongly to *Accattone*, of which it seems, in many ways, a natural continuation.[2] But the film is at once more bland and more bitter. As vital and seductive as is her portrayal of Mamma Roma, Anna Magnani's star persona imparts a comfortable familiarity to the film that *Accattone* utterly lacks. Her character and the character's name function as obvious allusions to Rossellini's *Rome, Open City,* which *Mamma Roma* invokes as an organizing intertext at several key moments. Magnani's lovable theatrics ensure the film at least some measure of palatability to sensitive stomachs sorely tested by *Accattone*'s menu of strange, unknown faces. But Accattone's death at the end is less obviously a result of social forces than Ettore's in *Mamma Roma.* Ettore dies in prison, without receiving proper medical care, having been jailed for a very minor offense. The film's final images, in which Mamma Roma's distraught face is intercut with an image of the peripheral cityscape, project the cause of her grief onto the image of the city. Furthermore, the film's setting in one of Rome's shiniest new public-housing projects would seem to promise some alleviation of bleakness. Not so. As I will argue, the housing project itself and the liberal belief in progress which it expresses (or which is literally expressed through it— which it embodies) receive Pasolini's scorn and blame, as if they were the actual agents of Ettore's death and Mamma Roma's grief. The film derives its polemical power through the evocation—via the aforementioned insistence on the landscape—on peripheral Rome as brutal, immense, and unassimilable, in a register which we might call the sublime.

Certainly Pasolini's choleric attitude in preparing *Mamma Roma* would have been informed by the events surrounding *Accattone*'s initial reception. *Accattone* was threatened with censorship, admission to it was restricted to those over eighteen, and the film was temporarily pulled from screens on phony grounds of obscenity. Of course, it was also the object of much abuse by the mainstream (and right-leaning) newspapers.[3] Furthermore, in *Mamma Roma* Pasolini explicitly tuned in to the implications of the economic miracle, the effects of which (visualized neatly by Pasolini in images of modern public-housing projects) were reaching the lowest levels of society, the subproletariat, allowing it, in the director's words "to become petit bourgeois and therefore perhaps fascist, conformist, etc."[4] Pasolini's growing sense of estrangement from the currents of contemporary Italian culture and daily life certainly find expression in the inexorable downward trajectory of Mamma Roma's characters. As Barth David Schwartz epigrammatically puts it:

> If *Accattone* is Pasolini's borgata as a sealed, airless, and airtight
> system whose inhabitants must die when their values collapse
> on contact with a harsher, outside reality, then *Mamma Roma* is
> its coda: Any of the subproletarian people who try to struggle
> up and out will be pulled, or pushed, back and under. Accat-
> tone never imagines a way out; for Mamma Roma, that road
> exists but has been mined by "the system."[5]

As mentioned above, that "system" is represented—both synecdochically and, perhaps, metaphorically—in the film by the structures that
house its characters. When Mamma Roma first brings Ettore to her
house, the one they will move from, she apologizes for its squalor and
for the class of people who live there with her. The tenants of the building where they are moving are of another class—they go to school and
get jobs, or so she explains to Ettore. Everything hinges on this move
out of a massive and forlorn Liberty apartment building and into a newly
built INA Casa project, the Tuscolano II.

Early in the film, when Mamma Roma is retrieving Ettore from the
country, she reprimands him for his lack of respect for her efforts to take
him home: "I've waited sixteen years for this moment," she says. "You
don't know how cruel this world can be." These words spoken, the film
cuts, as if offering evidence of her claim, to a long shot of the mammoth
apartment building that is Mamma Roma's home. The building is located
on the Piazza Tommaso de Cristoforis in Casal Bertone, a working-class
neighborhood almost due east of San Lorenzo Outside the Walls, one
of Rome's principal pilgrimage churches. The building, facing a large,
desolate piazza, is a six-storied affair, comprised of two wings joined by a
large entrance arch whose opening is almost four stories tall. The total
effect of the building is one of sham grandiosity—an empty exercise in
urban set design. From a vantage point in the piazza (where the shot is
taken) the two wings of the building suggest an orthogonal divergence
away from the central arch where they meet. The arch and the perspec-
tivally derived scenic effect of the extending wings link the building
to the iconography of Renaissance ideal city views and stage design in
which, most often, buildings appear to converge orthogonally toward a
central arch.[6] Noting Pasolini's deep connection to Italian art history is
a critical commonplace in Pasolini studies. In Bologna Pasolini studied
with the most prominent of all Italian art historians, Roberto Longhi, to
whom, not incidentally, *Mamma Roma* is dedicated. It seems fairly safe,
therefore, to read this shot of Mamma Roma's apartment building as a

loose allusion to Renaissance ideal city views. The point in making this connection, of course, is rather obvious: Pasolini's allusion is an ironic one. The neighborhood of Casal Bertone and this building's overlarge arched entrances hardly constitute an ideal city, but rather an anti-ideal. This neighborhood is a slightly more refined cousin of the borgate rapdissime. It is a lumbering, disconsolate affair, whose few architectural flourishes (i.e., the "grand" entrance arch, the top of which is actually flanked by two ornamental statuary deer) mean to distract attention from the neighborhood's more or less crummy material reality. Mamma Roma doesn't think much of this apartment herself. She apologizes for it, in fact, and assures Ettore that they will be relocating in a few days' time. Shortly they will live, she says, "in a neighborhood belonging to another class." By this she means the Tuscolano II INA Casa project.

As they walk toward the building, Ettore's and Mamma Roma's movement is filmed by a backward dolly, while the shots of the building are taken on a forward dolly. The shot of the building that begins the sequence is taken from a considerable distance, so that the entirety of the structure can be grasped as a visual unity. This is the shot, as explained above, that creates the impression of the anti-ideal city. When Mamma Roma first points out the building to Ettore, the succeeding dolly shot of the building, appearing just ten seconds after the opening shot, is much closer. This cannot be a spatially accurate subjective point-of-view shot in the strict sense because the characters cannot have traversed the distance implied by the differing camera set-ups in so short a time. The film next cuts back to Mamma Roma for a shot of four seconds' length in which she continues to explain their living arrangements and moving plans. Then the film cuts back to a dolly shot of the building, only this time the camera is already entering the arched entrance, which seems to swallow it like some devouring maw. The camera dollies forward, smoothly, implacably, offering finally a view of the building's enclosed courtyard. The effects of this sequence are manifold. As in *Accattone,* the shot/reverse-shot editing does not function according to the normative codes of subjective point-of-view editing. The shots of the building possess an autonomy similar to the shots of the nighttime peripheral cityscape that interrupt the sequence in *Accattone* in which the Neapolitan thugs attack Maddalena. The building and its gaudy entrance dwarf Mamma Roma and Ettore. Even though she dismisses the building highhandedly, the film does not offer her a real point of view of it. Instead, the building absorbs her criticism and continues menacingly to loom.

Later, inside the apartment, depressed by the reappearance of her pimp, Mamma Roma takes Ettore to look out their window, out over the Campo Verano, the cemetery that extends away from San Lorenzo. Framed by the camera and by the window from which they look, the two stand in a medium close-up. Mamma Roma says, "Look how ugly it is here, with the view of the cemetery." The film cuts to a shot of the cemetery—marked by a whitewashed gate and a copse of umbrella pines—then cuts back to the shot of Mamma Roma and Ettore. The cemetery does not seem particularly ugly, but it is an obvious and depressing image of mortality. Without revealing the nature of her exchange with Carmine, Mamma Roma explains that it will be a little while before she and Ettore can move into their new house. The film cuts back to the shot of the cemetery, the shot that closes the scene, over which Mamma Roma says with halfhearted optimism, "That's okay. We'll laugh later." The shot pattern accords with what we expect from point-of-view editing: a shot of characters looking, a shot of what they look at, the characters looking again, and so on. The same pattern of point-of-view editing in which we see characters looking out a window, followed by a reverse shot of a landscape, returns later in the film. However, in those sequences, as we shall see, the characters are denied a point of view.

The scene that immediately follows this occurs some weeks later in the film's chronology, after Mamma Roma has earned enough money to pay off Carmine again and can now leave the streets. It is nighttime. Mamma Roma sits laughing amid a little parliament of hookers and pimps. The scene is starkly lit, the background cloaked in a blackness punctuated by white coronas of light seeming to float in the pitch—the haloes of streetlights. They are somewhere on the outskirts of town— the kind of marginal place where Roman prostitutes would wait to meet johns who arrived on foot, in car, or on motorcycle. Mamma Roma stands, takes leave of the group—she is finally escaping the life of the streetwalker—and begins to walk toward the camera, which begins to dolly backwards. The scene, from this point on, is shot in a manner similar to the scenes in *Accattone* analyzed in chapter 3. The difference here is that Mamma Roma's walk sinuously twists and turns, unlike the rigid, unidirectional trajectories of Accattone and Ascenza and Accattone and Stella. As Mamma Roma moves, she never stops talking. Various friends and acquaintances enter the frame, walk awhile with her, and then veer off into offscreen space. She seems to move in a kind of vast parking lot. The streetlights that stud the background increase in number, creating abstract patterns and perspectival reference points for a space that cannot really be measured. The scene creates the same sense of the dilation of space at the periphery, but here space, which is barely discernible from the black night sky and shimmering streetlights, has become literally abstract—meaningless and infinite. Even though she is supposedly walking home, her passage through black, indeterminate space seems to have no destination. And as she walks, laughing and gesticulating *alla* Magnani, she tells a story to those who listen while briefly strolling beside her. Its theme? Fascist public housing:

> In front of my house there was this rich old guy who had so much money he couldn't even count it. He dressed like Robespierre—mustache, walking stick—like the king of Santa Calla. . . . Y'know how he made his money? During Fascism, Mussolini came to him and said, "Make me a neighborhood for the people"—now it's Pietrarancio. This guy makes the first house—beautiful—all the walls perfectly done, with bathrooms so clean and beautiful you could use them for dining rooms. Mussolini came and said, "Great, it's exactly what I wanted." Sonuvabitch, as soon as Mussolini's gone, he starts only building bathrooms and stops building houses. Now they call it Toilet Town. It's all just a long line of dead buildings.

Should the earlier scenes and dialogue fail to convince on this point, then this speech clearly signals the subject of public housing as centrally and unavoidably important to the film's meaning. Mamma Roma's discourse directs our attention to the issues of failed public-housing schemes, the hapless interventionism of the Italian state, the brutality of economic injustice, the segregation of classes along geographic lines, and the visual monotony of the Roman periphery. As hilarious and absurd as is this story's telling, it functions seriously as a kind of Rosetta stone for reading the rest of the film.

The abstract nocturne of this scene is immediately followed by a blindingly white establishing shot—a cityscape—of what we come to learn is Mamma Roma and Ettore's new neighborhood: gleaming apartment buildings stacked on top of one another with a rotund church dome bulging out in the middle of the flat rooftops. What we are looking at is the neighborhood of Cecafumo that flanks either side of the Via Tuscolano on its far southeastern end, before it reaches Cinecittà. The church whose dome we see is San Giovanni Bosco, an odd, modern ecclesiastical structure, consisting of a square basilica crowned by an exaggeratedly tall drum on top of which sits a shiny round dome:

The establishing shot of the Cecafumo neighborhood, off the Via
Tuscolana, where Mamma Roma and Ettore move. This shot, or versions
of it, will be repeated several times across the film, most significantly at
the end as the film's last image.

St. Peter's crossed with the Palazzo del Lavoro at EUR.[7] The next scene
shows Mamma Roma inside the church with Ettore.[8] She points out their
significant "neighbors"—a bigwig in the Monarchist party, a restaura-
teur, though it's unlikely these people live in Mamma Roma's actual
building. From a dolly medium close-up of Mamma Roma and Ettore
leaving the church, the film cuts to a dolly shot, beginning at a distance
of some one hundred meters, of the Muratori building at the center of
the Tuscolano II—its modernist arched entrance at the center of the
shot, the buildings leading up to it and flanking it acting as perspectival
orthogonals—yet another ideal city. The shot and the sequence that follows rhyme with (or recapitulate) the sequence at Casal Bertone. Following this first "ideal city shot," there is a static long shot and a succeeding
medium close-up dolly of Mamma Roma and Ettore walking toward the
building. "It's pretty, isn't it, our new house? Just like your mother said,"
she suggests to Ettore. The two shots of them walking in the direction of
the building last ten seconds altogether.

Next, the film cuts to another dolly, only now the camera is already
gliding under the arched entrance and toward the cruciform slab pier
that serves as the visual centerpiece of the building, the architectural element that Rowe describes as "clearly traditional in its location and prominence, and yet highly technological in its specific form and substance."
Again, there is a corruption of the shot/reverse-shot structure's usual
relationship to subjective point of view. The camera's dolly shots do not
represent or give access to character point of view. It would be impossible

for Mamma Roma and Ettore to have reached the arched entrance in so brief a span of time (again, only ten seconds). This method of shooting and editing seems to express an indifferent autonomy that belongs to the building and, perhaps, by extension, to all large-scale development of the periphery. Although built for "the people," when looked at through Pasolini's camera, the Tuscolano project seems to belong only to itself. Based on his rhyming shooting style—we might also wish to call it anaphoric—Pasolini refuses to see any difference between this building and the one his characters left in Casal Bertone.

If we look at the notes for the published screenplay, we find this description of the Muratori building, Mamma Roma's "pretty" new house:

> The new apartment isn't much different from the old one: only instead of being lost in a huge Liberty building, it's lost in a huge modern one, of a dark red hue, full of windows, brand new. In any case, it's true that beneath it there's grass, as fresh and green as it was during the era of Augustus.[9]

The language here clearly echoes the understanding of the INA Casa project Villa Gordiani that Pasolini articulates in "The Concentration Camps": "They are the same as before. This is still a concentration camp." Given the trajectory from this earlier journalistic polemic to the present film, we might suspect that there could be something overdetermined in Pasolini's response to this location. We should also pause to recall the gaps between screenplay and film text that exist in any film project and that are of special interest in regards to Pasolini. As we have seen in *Accattone,* Pasolini conceived of the screenplay as a literary genre, and each of his own screenplays as literary works unto themselves. With *Mamma Roma* Pasolini even went back after filming to revise the screenplay to render it, in his own words, more coherent "from a literary standpoint."[10] Thus, although the screenplay may visualize things that do not appear in the film, as happens between the screenplay and film of *Accattone,* the screenplay can act to tutor our understanding of the film, especially in relation to the film's discourse on the urban. Thus, the directions for the scene immediately following the one above interest us:

> Pink, yellow, like tin, like sugar, the infinite lines of public housing projects extend themselves in an oblique zig-zag, bursting out in all directions. Some shoot straight up, some are squat, sinking into the summer horizon, blinded by the sun, swarming like clouds.[11]

The long shot, performed with a forward dolly, of the Muratori building, arch visible at center.

The reverse field, medium close-up backward dolly shot of Mamma Roma and Ettore: "It's pretty, isn't it, our new house?"

The forward dolly toward the central arch, suddenly too close.

The film does not, in fact, give us quite such a detailed view of the land-scape in this scene, although these words could perhaps describe the several shots of the area like the one described above that punctuate the actual film from this point on.[12] Pasolini's language in the screenplay rehearses the imagery of "The Tears of the Excavator":

> . . . what was
> grass and open space and has become
>
> waxy white courtyards
> enclosed within a resentful decorum;
> what was almost an old fairground
>
> of bright plaster slanting in the sun
> and has become a new block, swarming
> in an order made of stifled grief.

This is not an affectionate view of the new development that has sur-rounded and supplanted the lowliness of the borgate. Of course, Paso-lini is not merely nostalgic for the borgate's squalor; rather he holds out a space of critical negativity, the right to dissent from INA Casa's and Mamma Roma's desire, in the words of his poem, "to become something better." This negativity is expressed through the evocation of the neigh-borhood in terms of sublime boundlessness. The buildings are "infinite" in number and are "bursting out in all directions"; they exhibit a diver-sity of formal features ("Some shoot straight up, some are squat") so disparate and great in number that they actually resist being seen: they sink into the horizon and swarm like clouds.

Although the film does not offer us the shot described in the screen-play, what it does give us is the establishing shot of the Cecafumo cityscape that preceded the first scene inside the church, a shot that will be repeated obsessively as the narrative progresses. The shot is inserted each time Mamma Roma or Ettore begins or concludes a line of action meant to improve his or her social position. It opens and closes a sequence in which Ettore buys his "girlfriend" Bruna a medallion on a chain. A shot of the necklace against her bosom is immediately followed by a shot of the cityscape. The shot punctuates the scenes of Mamma Roma's schem-ing to land Ettore a job as a waiter in Trastevere; it precedes the scene in which she wakes Ettore to give him his motorcycle. It will appear finally as the last image of the film. In all this shot appears eight times in the film. It is the visual translation of those anaphoric lines from "The Tears of the Excavator," "stupendous, miserable city." The mere fact of its mute repetitiveness resists interpretation. It is something not so much understood as suffered. Because it is so often inserted into a pattern that suggests but ultimately confounds and negates character point of view, the image creates a sense of the city's periphery as something beyond comprehension, an excess that cannot be properly digested, consumed, or even represented. Another of the screenplay's descriptions of this same repeated shot reads thus:

> Under the scorching noonday sun, or else the softer sun of the
> afternoon, the panorama of the Roman periphery appears,
> brown, whitewashed, immense, formless.[13]

This quite clearly is yet another instance of the language of the sublime. The image that we actually see in the film corresponds to some degree to the screenplay's prescriptions: the prospect is a jumble of rooflines, buildings nearly stacked on top of one another. Yet to what extent can we say that the image itself emits of the sublime?

To be certain, the image communicates the hostility and the architectural alienness of the newly overurbanized peripheral landscape. The very strangeness implicit in the shot of this chalky white, busy, and yet ghostly still cityscape could, perhaps, be considered under the rubric of the sublime. However, it would be just as important to conceive of the landscape not only in terms of the Kantian sublime, but also in the terms Lyotard sets up: the "pain" of a "failure of expression." The shot's power derives as much from what it lacks as from what it possesses. Its power resides in its strangeness. Given the title of the film, we, as spectators, might feel entitled to be given something of Rome that we might actually recognize. The title and Anna Magnani's performance point us straight back to the neorealism of Rossellini's *Rome, Open City*. That film's memorable last shot is, of course, a wide panorama of the cityscape of Rome: a sea of tiled rooftops and the dome of St. Peter's presiding with confidence over all—in Millicent Marcus's words, a "symbol of regeneration."[14] Clearly the Cecafumo cityscape in *Mamma Roma* should be interpreted as a corrosive allusion to *Rome, Open City*'s last image. Here is a dome, yes, and here is Rome, but what dome and what Rome? And what meaning do we make of this dome and this Rome? The shot establishes with great severity that this place exists, and yet we, as viewers, may be in some doubt as to what this place is. We will admit that it is Rome—some Rome, somewhere. But the very fact that this image and the buildings pictured in it do not correspond to familiar, comforting images of the city must be registered as a source of discomfort—at least cognitive, if not aesthetic. Furthermore, the shot's power extends out of its own indeterminate functioning in regards to the narrative. Again, its muteness and repetition and detachment from the characters' point of view all contribute to make the shot ever more strange. Meanwhile, it brushes so close to familiarity (it "recalls" neorealism; it *almost* suggests subjectivity grounded in point of view; it keeps returning) that it maddeningly seems to solicit and refuse comprehension through the simple fact of its mute, insistent reappearance. This shimmering opacity induces a restless, uncertain experience that draws us into the register of the sublime. However, the film flirts with the register of the sublime in another very significant way.

Behind the Tuscolano II, in fields that spread out toward the train tracks running north-south to and from Naples, there stand, isolated and immense, the ruins of ancient Roman aqueducts. Some of the ruins are larger and consist of passages of arches beginning and ending abruptly. Others are even more rude, consisting of odd, indecipherable fragments. Were the Roman reticulate masonry not visible, we might believe them to be not the product of human labor, but boulders deposited on Italian soil by some errant glacier. This landscape of ruins skirts the entire backside of Tuscolano II. It is a park of sorts. In the immediate postwar period immigrants to Rome made houses under the larger ruins—the ones with complete arches that could be used as roofs. Entire borgate were built among these ruins. Pasolini even describes them in his aforementioned essay, "The Shantytowns of Rome,"[15] and we have encountered them before in Zavattini's *Amore in città.* This landscape that Pasolini uses in *Mamma Roma* is as burdened with potential meaning as is the Tuscolano II and its surrounding overbuilt neighborhood.

The aqueduct ruins are first seen in the film in a scene that follows shortly after the scene of Mamma Roma and Ettore's walk home from church. In front of the Muratori building Ettore and Mamma Roma are met by a group of boys, all properly *endimanchés,* like Ettore, in cheap, tight, new clothes. Mamma Roma gives Ettore some spending money, and he departs with his new friends. Following this scene, the film cuts to a wide shot of the boys scrambling across a field, the white buildings of Cecafumo sitting in the distance. Next the film offers an extremely wide and long panning shot, moving slowly from left to right, in which are visible, in the far background, the neighborhood skyline,[16] and before it, running from the nearest plane of the image back toward the edge of the buildings, an expanse of scorched, uneven meadow. As the camera pans, there come into view, slowly, the ruins of the aqueducts, scattered about. The single moving image contains in its field of vision both the newly minted apartment buildings and the ruins: the too new and the too old, side by side. After this pan the film cuts to find the boys moving through the ruins, weaving in and out of their brooding and broken massiveness; occasionally a boy is framed by a complete arch. They seem to take the strange landscape for granted. The ancient ruins might as well be piles of discarded building materials. In fact, in some of the shots we can see recently excavated piles of earth adjacent to some of the ruins—most probably evidence of some construction going on nearby. In a scene occurring just a bit later we see Ettore walking alone in this same landscape. One shot from this scene stands apart as the most impressive of those in the film to combine views of the peripheral neighborhood and the ruins. It is another exceptionally long and wide shot, again with the buildings stretching across the entire horizon in the distance, the plain before them and, slightly to the right of the image's center, one tall, lonely, monolithic fragment of the aqueducts standing in the middle distance. Its height stretches almost across the entire height of the film frame. Ettore approaches it, circles it, stands next to it, and then seats himself next to it on the ground. The strange coexistence of old and new is at its most stark in this image.

Although we cannot resist enjoying the striking juxtaposition of the ruin and the peripheral cityscape, the shot (and the others like it in the film) would seem to deploy a fairly obvious visual rhetoric of old and new. Rome is thick with such awkward historical intimacies. We see

Ettore amid the ruins of the aqueducts, with towers belonging to the Tuscolano II in the background: two versions of the sublime.

in the screenplay written evocations of the shots I have tried to evoke above. The following quotation immediately follows the above passage in which are described "the infinite lines of public housing": "And in the middle of the field, some old brown ruins, crumbling on a hillock of dirt. Against a background of an aqueduct encrusted with little shacks and lean-to's, these ruins raise their still-extant forms: half arches, half-remembered vaults, fragments of arcades."[17] I think Pasolini, however, is up to something more interesting here than merely documenting for our pleasure the historical montage already embedded in the Roman landscape. Rather, he offers us self-consciously the familiar landscape of the Romantic sublime—of Byron and Shelley, of "arches after arches in unending lines stretching across the uninhabited wilderness . . . masses of nameless ruins standing like rocks out of the plain"—set side by side with the "swarming" (perhaps anti-Romantic) sublime of the peripheral cityscape. But this Romantic landscape of aqueducts—as faithfully suggestive of the sublime as it is—is not the one that ultimately interests Pasolini. The Roman ruins elicit the sublime of the fragmentary, the missing whole, of poetic loss, of the historical imagination's sense of noble humiliation in failing to picture what has been. Pasolini, though, is interested in the sublime of the too-much, the excessive, of the horrible and uncountable abundance that stuns contemporary social and visual imagination. The Romantic sublime (that of Shelley, Byron, and Roman ruins) is most often an arena of personal, interior creative struggle. Pasolini summons the lexicon—the *mise en scène*—of this mode only to abandon it in favor of the sublime of the Roman periphery—"brown, whitewashed, immense, formless." Of course, the desire to understand the periphery in terms of the sublime may be as much an effect of personal desire as anything we might find in Byron or Shelley. Nonetheless, understanding the periphery as evocative of the sublime could be understood as carrying a political charge. As expressive of the sublime, the periphery cannot be dismissed as merely ugly, or beneath contempt. Instead, we begin to see it as something awesome, of great importance, impossible to understand, perhaps, but also impossible to ignore. That we not ignore this huge and hostile territory and the people living within its borderless confines: this is Pasolini's desire.

The only scene in the entire film in which the action unfolds in Rome's city center occurs when Mamma Roma and her fellow prostitute and sidekick Biancofiore visit the piazza in Trastevere where Ettore is working at a restaurant. The two women press themselves up against a wall, spectators of the life in the piazza: people making their leisurely *passeggiate,* strolling musicians, and in the midst of all this, young Ettore, clearly relishing his job as a waiter, ferrying plates of pasta to waiting tables with an air of innocent theatricality. This scene deserves at least a passing mention because it so clearly demonstrates the class segregation inscribed by the working-class housing developments in the periphery. Residents of INA Casa have two roles to play in the city center: the laborer or the touristic consumer. Ettore has a job, but it is a job won by Mamma Roma's blackmailing the owner of the restaurant. And the only role Mamma Roma can play is that of the spectator/consumer. The irony of a character called Mamma Roma (and played by Anna Magnani, who embodied all the smart-ass, wisecracking earthiness of the *popolo romano*) being reduced to a mere tourist in the city whose name she bears should not escape our attention.

The last several sequences of scenes in the film conclude its urban studies sermon with a brutal flourish. By this time Ettore has discovered the nature of his mother's profession and has rejected her and quit his job. He is arrested attempting to steal a radio from a bedridden patient in an indigents' hospital. The patient he steals from is played by Lamberto Maggiorani, the same actor who played Antonio Ricci, the protagonist of *Bicycle Thieves.* Maggiorani's character wakes just in time to see Ettore pluck his radio from the nightstand and yells, "Ladro, ladro," the same words yelled to interrupt Ricci's similarly inept theft of a bicycle. This obvious allusion—part homage, part parody—is yet another move in Pasolini's withering take on neorealism. Thrown into jail for his crime, Ettore is next seen lying moaning and feverish on his prison bed—evidently suffering from tuberculosis or some other similar malady.[18] After a fit of fever-induced rage, he is placed in solitary confinement, fastened to a bed, his arms splayed out at his side, immobilized by leather straps. Pasolini pointedly photographs Ettore's body to allude to Mantegna's "Dead Christ" (c. 1500): his death will be nothing less than a crucifixion. A shot of Ettore's face in extreme close-up, muttering, half consciously, "Mamma, I'm freezing to death. I feel terrible. Tell them to cut me loose. Mamma . . . ," is immediately followed by the familiar and, by now, ominous shot of the peripheral cityscape that has been repeated across the film.

Next we see Mamma Roma making herself breakfast, obviously inconsolable, though unaware of Ettore's death; she rehearses to herself the injustice of Ettore's imprisonment. She pulls her cart to the market, unable to answer inquiries after Ettore made by her fellow market vendors. At the market she is told of her son's death in prison. She becomes hysterical and bolts from the market. The film cuts and returns us once more to a forward dolly long shot—its pace brisker than ever before—of the Muratori building at the Tuscolano project. Next, a backward dolly of Mamma Roma running in the direction of the camera's retreat, toward the building. Then a cut to the crowd running behind her. Finally, cut to another forward dolly, the camera once again moving under the arched entrance toward the "found" crucifix of the arch's slab-like supports.

The movement toward this architectural crucifix suggests that Ettore and Mamma Roma have been hung on the cross of class segregation and false dreams of class mobility—dreams fostered by the INA Casa Tuscolano project's masquerade of progress and social equality. The sequence opens itself up to symbolic interpretation. In a poem, one of a diaristic series, published at the end of the screenplay, the Tuscolano is described in similarly religious terms: "I see / clouds tear themselves to rags on the roofs / of the six-storied altars of Cecafumo."[19] And in another of these poems: "They're altars, / these INA Casa stage sets."[20] But apart from the obvious religious allegory at work, we should not lose sight of the sequence's phenomenological power. The camera's hastening glide toward the impassive building has a force all its own that resists paraphrase while still contributing mightily to the overwhelming sense of tragedy. Furthermore, we need not read the arch as a crucifix in order to reach the conclusion that the building and the forces and discourses (governmental, economic, architectural, urban) that it metonymically embodies are in no way kindly disposed to the lives of the building's inhabitants. Ultimately, however, the impossibility of paraphrasing these shots (the moving shots toward the building) makes them breathtaking and moving. Their resistance to paraphrase suggests that they, too, are aimed at the evocation of sublime emotion.

Mamma Roma makes her frantic way into her apartment where she flings herself onto Ettore's bed and holds his clothes to her body. She looks to the window, leaps up and toward it, flinging it open as if to fling herself from it, but she is stopped by the neighbors who have followed her from the market. Four shots close the film: 1) Mamma Roma, her face wild with grief, struggling but restrained on either side by her friends from the market, gazing out of the window, toward the camera in a medium close-up; 2) the mute, impassive Cecafumo cityscape, the

The last two shots of the film, suggesting but denying point-of-view editing.

vision of which now recalls nothing so much as a cluster of whitewashed sepulchres; 3) Mamma Roma, staring, no longer struggling; and 4) again, the cityscape. The film ends.

As ever, the shot sequence, which alternates a looking subject with a landscape, might initially suggest that we share Mamma Roma's point of view as she gazes inconsolably at the peripheral neighborhood: an incoherent jumble of white apartment buildings whose competing rooflines are presided over by the dome of San Giovanni Bosco. But we would be wrong to ascribe the landscape image to Mamma Roma's point of view. First, this shot has been repeated too often at too many different moments following too many different types of shots for us legitimately to believe that it belongs to any character's point of view. It has established its own autonomous functioning. Lino Miccichè and Maurizio Viano are two of the only critics who have tried to understand this sequence's resistance to being understood as an exercise in subjective point-of-view editing. Citing the shot's "lack of a correspondence to a strong and completed narrative nucleus" and its "discontinuity" within "the diegetic fabric of the film," Micciché argues energetically that the shot is decisively not a "subjective image," but rather an "ideological image."[21] Thus the image's logic and its message belong to the organizing intelligence of the film, to *Mamma Roma,* if you will, but not to Mamma Roma.[22] The shot's anaphoric intonation is that of "The Tears of the Excavator" "stupendous, miserable city . . . stupendous, miserable city." Again, the anaphoric repetition suggests—through its mere repetitiveness—that the object to be represented, in this case the peripheral cityscape, cannot be represented properly, just as, clearly, the character's subjective interaction with it (via point-of-view editing) cannot be represented properly either. Not just, or not even so much, is it the periphery's sprawling size that resists representation; so does the immense injustice it inflicts on its inhabitants. Both things seem to be understood by Pasolini as operating under the sign of the sublime in its manifestation as formless boundlessness. Because such boundlessness cannot be represented, Pasolini resigns himself to repeating the cityscape's image obsessively, to rehearse this failure, while at the same time to reiterate with vigor and terse eloquence the tragedy embodied by the periphery.

I want to linger a bit longer on the issue of subjective point of view and character identification in the film's finale. Micciché performs an exhaustive analysis not only of this sequence, but of several passages in the film, focusing intense scrutiny on the cityscape's every appearance. He argues forcefully, and I agree, that the shot "is never—*not even when it seems to be*—a *subjective image* but is instead always an *ideological image,* and it does not function within the film as a *diegetic surplus* (which would enrich the *story*) but rather an *ideological surplus* (which enriches the *meaning* of the film)."[23] I want to add to Micciché's analysis the further consideration that the work of this shot sequence (shot/countershot, character looking/putative object of vision) is precisely to solicit our identification of the sequence *as* point of view. Furthermore, an identification of the sequence as such solicits our identification *with* Mamma Roma. These solicitations, however, are lures, ideological snares. We are meant to understand that such a pursuit of identification (of shot with character's vision, of our emotions with those of Mamma Roma) is exactly what this film means to disrupt, to interrogate. Of course we are meant to be moved by Mamma Roma's fate, but the film's form—if we are willing to pay attention to all it wants to tell us—displays to us the facile phoniness of cinema's inducement of spectator identification via point-of-view editing.

The shot sequence is therefore profoundly antisubjective and is in many ways a more radical experimentation with *Accattone*'s antisubjective editing that I analyze in chapter 3. Not only does the shot sequence point to the insufficiency of spectator sympathy and the means of producing it, it also suggests that subjectivity itself—sheer psychic survival—may be a difficult enterprise to maintain for a figure like Mamma Roma—someone living in the periphery, defeated by it as well. The film demonstrates that neither we as spectators nor Mamma Roma can lay claim, subjectively, to that closing shot of the peripheral cityscape. So, too, it suggests that the basic daily enterprise of survival (again, both psychic and material) in the periphery is a challenge of enormous proportions, not least because, as Pasolini envisions (but does not "see") it in his mode of the sublime, the Roman periphery resists not only its representation on film, but also its representation in the minds of its inhabitants. It is not, in Kevin Lynch's words, a place that "can be organized into a coherent pattern."[24]

The Rome of the neorealists, of De Sica, in particular, is a different Rome. The citizens of cinematic neorealist Rome, though they were often treated as refuse, could still offer their subjectivities to be shared with spectators, who, in turn, were moved by their identification with these characters onscreen. We sense this sympathetic condition very acutely in *Umberto D.*, in the famous scene in which the eponymous main character, a pensioner who is in the process of being turned out of his flat (significantly, this is yet another film about housing), contemplates suicide as he looks from his bedroom window at the street below. As Viano has cleverly pointed out, the last sequence of *Mamma Roma* recapitulates (only to eviscerate) this scene from the De Sica film.[25] In *Umberto D.* we are yoked into spectator identification via the usual shot/reverse-shot point-of-view editing; such identificatory processes are amplified (nearly enforced), in fact, by the use of a dramatic point-of-view zoom shot: Umberto's vision rushes toward the Roman pavement onto which he *just* manages *not* to throw himself.

Such a scene is another instance of what Pasolini would have called neorealism's sentimentality and lyricism. The final sequence of *Mamma Roma* stages the historical impossibility and the personal abjuration of such a mode of cinematic representation. The solutions of neorealism, in other words, are judged to be insufficient. Moreover, and more at the heart of the urban historical thrust of this book, whereas *Umberto*

D. describes and creates within the spectator's mind a feeling for the spatial proximity of Umberto's body and the Roman street below, in *Mamma Roma*[26] no such proximity exists. We should ask, in other words: If Mamma Roma had managed to throw herself out of the window, where would she have landed?

Not to make too fine a point of things, or to insist on a too-rigid geographic-documentary reading of the film, but an actual visit to the Tuscolano II project reveals even greater evidence of the way in which

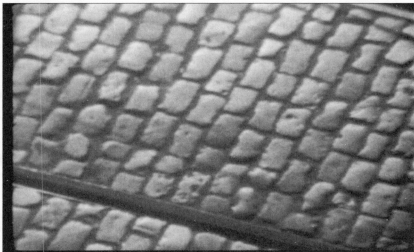

Subjective point of view at the window, looking down, near the end of *Umberto D.*

Pasolini's critique of neorealism and its traditional (sentimental, lyrical) editing strategies is identical to his critique of peripheral urban space. From the Muratori building from which Mamma Roma gazes, no panoramic view of the larger neighborhood is possible. The Muratori building lies to the west and slightly to the south of San Giovanni Bosco; the V-shaped facade roughly faces toward the direction of the church. But between the Tuscolano II project and the church and its surrounding buildings there was (and is) no open field, as we see in the shot in the film. Instead there were (and are) more high-rise apartment buildings and the busy Via Tuscolana itself. The landscape is a view of the neighborhood *inside of which* Mamma Roma's apartment in the Muratori building is located. But I would argue that an understanding of the unbridgeable gulf between looking subject and urban panorama is insisted on already and implicitly through the mere repetition of the cityscape shot throughout the film. Empirical evidence gathered from actually visiting the Tuscolano II only confirms what is available in the film itself.

To enrich our appreciation of the devastating ironies of this film, we should return to the work of the last chapter in which I emphasized the significance of the film's location as itself an instance of neorealist aesthetic culture. The interrogation (relentless and bitter) that Pasolini performs on the body of neorealism—particularly on the work of De Sica—is essayed not only through sharply defined cinematic allusions (i.e., the casting of Magnani and Lamberto Maggiorani, the recapitulation of narrative sequences, shot set-ups, editing strategies). It is also materialized through its location. *Mamma Roma* declares Pasolini's belief in the failure of neorealist ideology as it took shape in both cinema and architecture. Anna Magnani, herself very nearly a sacred, eucharistic embodiment of neorealist filmmaking, is degraded, deluded, and destroyed by neorealist architecture and city planning.[27] Pasolini has not been alone in making this critique. Witness Manfredo Tafuri making a similar argument:

> INA-Casa's urban policy immediately struck the most informed as antithetical to sound urban planning. The INA-Casa complexes, moved to areas far from the urban centers in order to benefit from low-cost land, spawned further planning, stimulating the land and building speculation that, profiting from the infrastructures created by the public sector, progressively reached and encircled them.[28]

That is, not only did the INA Casa projects segregate their inhabitants from Rome's center, but their far-flung locations also encouraged (perhaps even intentionally) further wanton growth of the periphery fed by a speculation economy. Pasolini uses Muratori's apartment building in the Tuscolano II project as a location that makes perspicaciously visible the project's failure—as social engineering and urban intervention. Such a use of location matches at every point his corrosive appropriation and redeployment of the techniques, tropes, thematics, and literal bodies of neorealist cinema.

Pasolini would have been perfectly aware of the noble intentions—economic, urbanist, architectural—of the neorealist Tuscolano II project, but he refuses to entertain them, just as he refuses to entertain the good intentions of neorealist filmmaking. INA Casa's and Muratori's architectural neorealism is just as guilty of the "lack of mature thought" with which Pasolini charges cinematic neorealism. Pasolini reads architectural neorealism against its grain of populism and class uplift. Where some (i.e., Rowe) see a progressive-modernist twist on Renaissance town planning, Pasolini sees visual monotony and class oppression. Where some see an impressive postmodern arch—"clearly traditional . . . and yet highly technological" (Rowe's phrase)—Pasolini sees a crucifix—a crucifix attached to a building that he also identifies as an altar. Pasolini willfully misreads, misappropriates the legacy of neorealist architecture that so vividly expressed the optimism of the INA Casa program. His misappropriation of INA Casa criticizes the program and the neorealist architecture it inspired for *their* facile misappropriation of the urban morphology and architectural language of the Italian city—formal gestures that did not address the causes of social and economic inequality.

After grasping the complexity of this political argument waged through the histories of two aesthetic media (film and architecture), one must sit back and wonder whether or in what way Pasolini is right, is justified in this marvelous act of Oedipal aggression—this murder of his neorealist fathers. I find myself at this point thinking back to De Sica's rather unassuming film *The Roof*. Did not this film show its spectators something very real and very true about the lives of peripheral Romans, people forced to steal bricks and lumber and work through the night so as to insure they would have a place to live? In fact, in preparation for the production of *The Roof* De Sica and Zavattini undertook quasi-ethnographic research in the periphery to understand and to document the lives of its inhabitants so that their film would be witness to and document of their impossible living conditions.[29] *Il tetto* was probably the first fiction film to offer filmgoers the chance to see an INA Casa project, one associated with architectural neorealism, integrated into the diegetic world of a cinematic fiction. In the film's last image, as Luisa and Natale stand before their newly completed hovel, in the background of the image there loom over them the high-rise Viale Etiopia Towers, an INA Casa undertaking designed by Mario Ridolfi and Wolfgang Frankl.[30] Earlier in the film we even see Natale actually working on the construction site of the Viale Etiopia Towers. These buildings are even more rigorously modernist, built for higher density inhabitation, less obviously "neorealist" than Muratori's V-shaped building at the Tuscolano II. The disparity between the Etiopia Towers and the mean little house that Natale and his friends manage to build overnight (and from materials stolen from the Etiopia construction site itself) could not be greater. Bruno Reichlin argues that the film's last image in which the towers dominate the background is meant to multiply, metonymically, the fate of people like Luisa and Natale, to suggest De Sica's and Zavattini's concern for "the alienated and the disinherited . . . the people as the sum of a multitude of histories and individual destinies that they fear will be annihilated in the mass."[31] If Reichlin is correct in this reading, then there is something fairly conservative at work in this last image (the fear of the dissolution of the individual in the body of the mass), but the image would also offer a skepticism about mass housing not dissimilar to Pasolini's. Contrary to Reichlin's reading, the final shot might also suggest the world of decent working-class housing from which Natale and Luisa are barred.[32]

Pasolini, as I have suggested at various moments, chooses to see what he wants in neorealism; this is part of the way he clears space for his own practice: he repudiates his forebears. He is wrong, we understand, in maintaining that neorealism never actually ventured out into the "real" shantytowns of peripheral Rome. But despite *The Roof*'s documentation of the actual conditions of housing in the periphery, the visual construction of this last scene is extremely picturesque, familiar, assimilable. Whatever meaning we are likely to ascribe to the presence of the Viale Etiopia Towers in the background, it is there that they will remain: *in the background*. De Sica's method of shooting them allows them to recede into a generic skyline. Only by way of recovering a knowledge of what those buildings actually were (and are) can we reverse a process by which the image's meaning is reified as generic.

The last shot of *Il tetto*. The towers of the INA Casa Viale Etiopia Towers are those with the hipped roofs, just to the left of the center of the background.

Of course, the entire project of this book is predicated on the activity of hauling Pasolini's films into the archive, forcing them to breed and mingle again with other historical artifacts and representations from the 1950s and 1960s that constituted the discursive field out of which these films emerged. This book is, in other words, a recovery act. And yet . . . and yet . . . There is still in Pasolini's filmmaking the ongoing hermeneutic problem of understanding his modernist realism, of coming to terms with his realism-*as*-modernism (a term that could be inverted). His cinema is radically preoccupied with documenting the real as real *and* with defamiliarizing both the real and the methods of its documentation. This mutually implicating obsession is what makes it possible for those of us who have never heard of architectural neorealism, of Muratori or Quaroni or Ridolfi, who have never even seen *Bicycle Thieves,* or who have never been to Rome, much less its periphery, to say, upon seeing *Mamma Roma:* "There's something not right about this place, these buildings, this world." Pasolini's methods of shooting and editing produce in the spectator's mind both the impression that this place exists and the conviction that its existence as such is unacceptable. When I saw *Mamma Roma* for the first time, knowing nothing then of the contexts I have been at pains to describe in these chapters, I thought to myself, He doesn't like these buildings. In other words, Pasolini's mode of vision (one that is skeptical of vision itself) constitutes the substance of his difference from neorealism, his politics, if you will. And that same mode of vision is what catches us—off guard perhaps—and pulls us into an exploration of the political meaning of these films.

In the introduction I made reference to Debord's notion of the spectacle and its conversion of all of reality into commodified images. And in chapter 3 I discussed Kevin Lynch's notion of "the image of the city" in relation to the periphery's relative lack of imageable structures that would make its inhabitants feel at home. *Mamma Roma* figures the convergence of Debord's concerns with Lynch's. If in *Accattone* the distension of spatial coordinates in the periphery seemed to render the landscape as something misshapen, dilated, and uneven, then things have certainly changed in *Mamma Roma*. We have moved from the borgate in all their desolate tawdriness, to the gleaming world of the Tuscolano II, clearly a place that, in Lynch's words, "can be organized into a coherent pattern." The Tuscolano II is an image and gives itself over to imageability; *Mamma Roma*'s camerawork clearly demonstrates its success as an image—or rather, to use Debord's term, as spectacle. Certainly the living conditions of the INA Casa project were an improvement over the borgate we see in *Accattone*. But Pasolini distrusts this improvement, and this distrust is founded on his recognition of the project's spectacular nature. INA Casa projects like the Tuscolano II were experiments in state paternalism, semisocialized economic and urban planning, and nominally populist ideology. But as well they were spectacles that, in their formal resemblance to historic ideas of the city, were meant to dazzle their inhabitants into adopting the false-consciousness of private ownership and bourgeois respectability. We might recall Mamma Roma's words to Ettore as they approach the Muratori building on their way home from church: "It's pretty, isn't it, our new house?" This new house, though, never proves to be a means of active and productive participation in the social and economic life of the city. Instead, it behaves like Debord's spectacle whose "function in society is the concrete manufacture of alienation."[33] The full import of social and economic alienation would seem to invite a turn toward the mode of the sublime: Mamma Roma's and Ettore's fate is horrible, unimaginable, impossible to represent.

The Tuscolano II is much more an index of alienation than it is an expression of a just and equitable society. Clearly Pasolini, at least, envisions the housing project in this light; I am convinced by his vision. The image of the peripheral landscape that is so obsessively repeated throughout the film is no less a spectacle (although less coherent) than the Muratori apartment building. Responding to both the building and the landscape, Pasolini's cinematography emphasizes their spectacularity. By alienating his characters from owning any vision of them and by alienating the spectator from any too-comfortable reading of them (as innocuous settings, as simple establishing shots, as subjective points of view), he reveals them to be, quite literally, the "concrete manufacture of alienation."

Pasolini's willful misreading of neorealist cinema and neorealist architecture reveals itself, through its allusions, appropriations, and repetitions, as both an aesthetic practice and a political polemic intended to dislodge its viewers from any comfortable acceptance of modern urban—and therefore economic and social—reality. It is a reality too immense, too various, too complex to be represented accurately, or perhaps, at all. Sensing this representational crisis, Pasolini adopts an aesthetic rhetoric of the sublime in order to force an awareness on his viewers of the awful sublimity that he experienced in the Roman periphery. But Pasolini does not give us the pat answers of the sociologist or the despairing fairytales of a De Sica and his Milanese homeless who ride brooms into the sunset. Rather he forces us to witness his own stubborn struggle to do what he insists is impossible: to give voice and vision to the experience of life in the Roman periphery. These films, which must by necessity fail in the representation of their object, still succeed in bearing witness to their maker's commitment to posing the question of that representation through a rigorous engagement with aesthetics, an engagement with form that, in turn, thrusts the viewer back into the realm of the political. After watching these films we are sent out into the world limping and chastened, but invigorated and enraged—harried into our own dark forest of tall white buildings at Rome's far edge.

Conclusion

The Allegorical Autostrada

The end of *Mamma Roma* would seem to leave us and Pasolini without anywhere to go, really. If image-making, representation, indeed vision itself and our ability to empathize with others have all been radically thrown into question, what cinematic enterprise, what act of poeisis could follow these fierce refusals?

Rome as location and as subject exceeds the grasp of film. But a rhetoric of the sublime can only suffice for so long as a means of framing or legitimizing a representation of that which cannot be represented. As rigorous and challenging as *Mamma Roma* is, both aesthetically and ideologically, it is not a place where one can stay for long. The film's negativity pushes us, pushes Pasolini out of Rome.

Of course, Pasolini never quitted Rome entirely. He remained, until his death, a citizen of the city. The last several years of his life were spent, it's true, in one of Rome's most ambiguous suburbs—in EUR, the ideal city first designed by the fascists and which, by the time he had moved there, was just another bourgeois suburb. When asked why he had chosen to live in EUR, he usually mentioned his mother's comfort as an excuse. At their EUR home there was room enough for her to cultivate a small garden and also, for her enjoyment, a view that looked out toward the sea, toward Ostia, ironically the place where he was murdered in 1975. We might take him at his word and leave it at that, but it is tempting to play with other possible explanations of this choice of neighborhood, one chosen out of the infinite number of other places in Rome where Pasolini could have afforded to live by this point in his life. Might Pasolini have been perversely amused by the rather ludicrous urban pomposity of EUR's hypertrophied piazzas, its modernist evocations of romanità, its pristine obsolescence? Might he well have taken pleasure in living at—even beyond—the periphery, yet, unlike the time of his "Rebibbian exile," this time in bourgeois comfort? Might he have enjoyed EUR's easy proximity to the borgate and to Ostia, places where he continued to frequent the company of teenage boys—i ragazzi di vita—up until the very moment of his murder? Of course, these are idle questions to which there is no real answer.

Though Pasolini himself never left Rome, we can certainly trace a slow process of leave-taking in his films, one that happened gradually and was pursued, curiously, through a turn to allegory. I say a "turn to" allegory as if he were not already working in such a mode. Quite clearly *Mamma Roma* can be read as allegorical. Indeed, the title announces the film as such, in the same way as do Maxim Gorky's *Mother* and Bertolt Brecht's *Mother Courage*. Anna Magnani's fate clearly stands in for the fate of the Roman underclasses; a building stands in for a cultural and aesthetic movement. Such analogues and transparencies, such multiplications of meaning are the stuff of allegory. A vision of Cecafumo as sublime landscape, the apprehension of the INA Casa housing project as a sacrificial altar: these are the moves—willed into being—of the allegorist. But Pasolini's allegory is also one in which there is no allegorical transparency: rather the bodies, buildings, and places that are posed as allegorical vehicles continue to assert their own irreducible specificity: *this* body, *this* building, *this* place. This tension between metaphorical flight and documentary weight is at the heart of Pasolini's practice.

I began this book in an effort to privilege the material, the archival, and the historically specific in Pasolini's work over and above his use of metaphor. The experience of *Mamma Roma,* however, discloses the folly it would be, finally, to keep these two potential heuristics apart for too long. My analysis of *Accattone* in chapter 3, even in its attempt to focus attention on the film's relation to a historically specific set of conditions, opens onto the level of a larger allegorical significance: Accattone's fate can be read as symbolic of the fate of all of subproletarian Rome. But what these analyses also demonstrate is that we cannot reach the metaphorical, the allegorical, without first attending carefully, even minutely to the documentary—the literal, material, and actual. Pasolini's allegories can't loose themselves of their synecdochic anchors in the real.

In this last chapter I want to trace, very briefly, the trajectory that Pasolini's career takes after his explosive entry into filmmaking with *Accattone* and *Mamma Roma*. In doing so I mean more to open things up rather than conclude or settle them; to begin again rather than to end.

Pasolini followed *Mamma Roma* with *La ricotta* (1962), a short work that was part of an anthology film called *RoGoPaG*, its name an acronym of the directors who contributed to it: Rossellini, Godard, Pasolini, and Ugo Gregoretti. The film was produced by Alfredo Bini, Pasolini's producer throughout most of the 1960s. Pasolini's film is the most interesting of the bunch. Whereas the other contributions seem to figure only small episodes in the careers of Rossellini and Godard, Pasolini's film occupies a place at the very center of his oeuvre.

La ricotta takes the form of an extended self-reflexive joke. Its setting is the production set of a biblical (New Testament) epic film. The set is somewhere out in the fields of the Roman periphery; the peripheral cityscape is visible in the distance, not unlike our vision of the Cecafumo cityscape in *Mamma Roma,* but at a further remove. The film-within-the-film's director is played by none other than Orson Welles, who mouths lines of Pasolini's own poetry in response to questions posed to him by a reporter visiting the set. The scene that is being shot at the beginning of *La ricotta* is the crucifixion. One of the thieves to be hung on the cross next to Christ is played by a borgataro named Stracci, meaning "rags" in Italian—a reference nodding in two directions: to the cheap clothes worn by the real Roman poor and to the rags that Stracci wears as his costume.[1]

Stracci is starving throughout most of the film. Every time he is about to avail himself of the on-set catering, he is called back for shooting. Finally he manages to sneak away from the set for a few moments and in that time buys a large quantity of ricotta cheese which he devours madly, along with a load of other foodstuffs that the other cast members mockingly toss at him: loaves of bread, watermelons, raw eggs. Immediately after this manic last supper, Stracci is called back to set. There he is hoisted onto the cross. As the production team squabbles over various petty concerns, no one notices that Stracci, high on his cross in the Roman periphery, has become ill from indigestion, and has died; his fictional crucifixion has become literal. The director says, in the film's final words: "Poor Stracci. He had to die to remind us he was alive."

Despite its apparent simplicity and surface frivolity (jokes abound, strippers perform), *La ricotta* is a strange and complicated film. It is absurd and given to moments of "mannerist" excess. Twice the action of the film (shot almost entirely in black and white) is intercut with scenes (shot in color) of the film-within-the-film's characters posing in awkward tableaux vivants; one imitates Rosso Fiorentino's "Descent from the Cross" (1521), the other Pontormo's "Entombment" (1525–28). These meta-representational interludes are consonant with *La ricotta*'s fundamental premise of reflexivity. Welles, himself the very picture of the director as self-besotted auteur, appears flesh-heavy, garbed in black with thick black glasses; both body and clothes allude unmistakably to the physical presence of another director, Federico Fellini. Thus *La ricotta* is also a parody of Fellini's reflexive, Cinecittà-obsessed film practice (see *8½* [1963], the obvious intertextual object of abuse here).[2] At one point the reporter asks the Welles/Director character, "What do you think of the director Federico Fellini?," to which he answers, "He dances."

There are probably several explanations for Pasolini's parody of Fellini. One might be Pasolini's abiding bitterness over the flap surrounding Fellini's refusal to fund *Accattone*. Pasolini, however, submits himself to the film's parodic scorn as well by, as mentioned before, having Welles read his (Pasolini's) own poetry. The poem he reads was published with the screenplay for *Mamma Roma;* we can see the title on the book cover as Welles holds up the book to read from it.[3] All of the self-reflexive gestures suggest the disjunction between the practice of filmmaking— whether Fellini's or Pasolini's, or anyone's—and the social and historical realities that surround it and on which it feeds. Stracci's crucifixion is noticed too late by the members of the production crew, all too busy staging the simulacral crucifixion to realize they have effected an actual, contemporary one.

The shot that epitomizes the film's meaning occurs in the scene, toward the beginning, when Welles calls for "la corona" (the crown). A series of shots follows in which other members of the production crew derisorily echo the call. Finally, a shot of a cardboard box, a pair of hands reaching into it from screen left, lifting out of the box the crown (of course) of thorns. The camera tilts up as the hands raise the crown aloft. Behind and through the circle described by the crown, we see in the background the chalk-white cityscape of peripheral Rome, not unlike the way we are made to see it in *Mamma Roma,* only this time the metaphorical element is foregrounded, literally, while the material density of the periphery acts as scenographic support. The figure-ground relations in this shot are invertible; that would be the shot's import. But here the

La corona, the crown: the metaphor is foregrounded, and the peripheral landscape is in the background.

allegorical content comes to the fore baldly. In *Mamma Roma,* by contrast, crucifixes still had to be fashioned, cinematographically, from what were essentially found architectural objects.

La ricotta can be read as purgative rite for Pasolini, who was then going into production for his own biblical epic, *The Gospel According to Matthew* (*Il vangelo secondo Matteo,* 1964); as mentioned above, this is his *8½.* Perhaps Pasolini sensed some danger in turning his lens away from the misery of contemporary existence and training it on, instead, the representation of the life of Christ. *La ricotta* might therefore be seen to function as a pre-emptive exculpation of his own practice activated through the admission of his awareness of the dangers inherent in the mode of the historical epic. Understood thus, *La ricotta* functions as a type of metadiscursive and autobiographical allegory. The Roman borgate are being left behind as Pasolini begins to look elsewhere for cinematic material. They appear only in the background, while Stracci, who comes from the borgate, is exterminated by the film. But Stracci's death, of course, also allegorizes the position of the Roman subproletariat, whose lives and deaths exist beneath and beyond the notice of bourgeois culture.

However, if we only think of Pasolini's *Gospel* as a period film, so to speak, one that does not represent contemporary existence, we would miss the richness of its production history and its meaning. The passage from *La ricotta* to *The Gospel* is not entirely a passage from contemporary reference to mythohistoric spectacle. We can understand *The Gospel*'s attachment to contemporary history by understanding its use of locations.

After scouting for locations in Palestine, footage from which he made into a film called *Sopraluoghi in Palestina* (Location scouting in Palestine,

1963–64), Pasolini decided that contemporary Palestine[4] was too modern, its landscape too corrupted by recent construction to serve as a location. Instead he would settle on a strategy of "analogy" in which he would set *The Gospel* in southern Italy, which would then stand in for the Holy Land.[5] The areas in which Pasolini filmed were notorious for being some of the most abjectly poor areas in Italy. For Jerusalem, Pasolini chose Matera, an impoverished town in the region of Basilicata. Matera was infamous for its "Sassi," literally "rocks"—caves that had served for generations and up until the middle of the century as miserable habitations for the citizens of the town. This would be a Jerusalem more ancient and therefore more accurate than the one in Palestine.

Matera is memorably evoked in Carlo Levi's magnificent memoir, *Christ Stopped at Eboli,* one of the central monuments of neorealist literature. Pasolini's analogical strategy makes of Matera—a place most Italians might have preferred not to think about—a holy land. Its poor and its poor landscape must be seen as vessels of grace, as divine. Allegory's analogies are predicated, as in *Mamma Roma,* on the specific history of a place. We might see this as yet another of Pasolini's instances of correcting the neorealist tradition. Levi, who was sent into exile in Matera by the fascist government, borrowed his book title from a local saying that suggested that Christ never made it to Matera; he stopped at Eboli, not wanting to venture any further into the miserable area. Whereas the Christ in the saying never made it to Matera, perhaps Pasolini is saying his Christ will. His Christ will not shrink from the sight of abject poverty like the Christ of neorealism.

However, Pasolini's understanding of Matera as something left behind by progress was not actually correct. Matera actually had been the site of a public housing project almost as famous as either the Tiburtino Quarter or the Tuscolano II. This was La Martella, a project that has been called neorealist architecture's "finest realization."[6] The project brought together architects, planners, geographers, sociologists, anthropologists, and other specialists, all of whom collaborated in the goal of creating a livable, communitarian and working environment, *ex novo,* for the inhabitants of the Sassi who were relocated to La Martella en masse. Whether it was a success (architectural or political) is not my concern here.[7] What interests me is how issues of contemporary public housing and economic privation stand just outside the frame of Pasolini's *Gospel.* Given the thoroughness of Pasolini's location scouting and, as we have seen, his interest in contemporary mass housing, it seems rather unlikely that he would have known nothing of La Martella. In fact, he would have *had* to have known of it because he could not have missed the great numbers of people who had been located from the Sassi to the new development. But Pasolini ignores La Martella's recent history of liberal modernity (we can imagine by now what he thought of it) in order to draw attention to its longer history of impoverished squalor and to beatify those who lived in it.

In the years following the production of these first four films, Pasolini begins to draw political connections between the fate of the Roman subproletariat living in the periphery and the subproletarian cultures of other cities. In an article written to accompany a photo essay published in an Italian newspaper in 1966, Pasolini places the subject of the Roman borgate and their inhabitants in direct relation to similar neighborhoods and peoples the world over:

> I would not be writing yet again on the subject of the slums and shantytowns of Rome if I did not feel that the problem today has changed radically, so much that it requires a new study in order to be understood.
>
> The innocent reader should not fear that he is sitting before yet another paragraph of the "*cahiers de doléance*" on bitter human condition.
>
> Chosen from thousands of possibilities, these images which you have before your eyes and that I am commenting [on] as an "informal expert," are not images of Rome; they belong to Rome only in their secondary, non-essential characteristics.
>
> Here we are on the outskirts of Mexico City . . .
>
> Here we are in Partinico, outside Palermo . . .
>
> Here we are in Calcutta, or outside of Lagos.
>
> Here we are in Sakara outside of Cairo, or in the camps of Beja at Porto Sudan.
>
> Here we are in the villages of Turkey, Greece, Morocco, in Cochin, in Madras, in the little towns around Tripoli, Jordan.
>
> Here we are in all of South America.
>
> He we are in Harlem and the black ghettos of the United States.
>
> In one word, these are not images of Rome but of the entire Third World . . .
>
> Even though these things are here and evident, these images, in today's Italy risk being *unseeable*. I can imagine eyes skimming over these images without looking at them, without realizing what they are. These are the eyes of those who

Architectural drawings of La Martella, neorealist architecture's "finest realization."

"believe" that the slums are not their problem. They are so convinced of the extraneousness and untimeliness of this sub-proletarian, underdeveloped world that they would be unable to see it if it were in front of their eyes.[8]

So speaks the political allegorist. We have witnessed a similar argument before, in "The Tears of the Excavator": "The scream is the old excavator's. . . . It is the city's . . . it is the world's." We now see retrospectively the consistency of Pasolini's thought. However, this latter conflation of the Roman periphery with the rest of the world's slums marks a shift in Pasolini's thinking and filmmaking: he begins to think and act on a global scale. To pursue a description and critique of the forces of global capitalism that are responsible for the existence of these slums (for this does seem to become more and more Pasolini's objective), it will no longer suffice to document the Roman periphery alone. And yet, how would one filmmaker go about documenting the misery of the slums of Mexico City, Palermo, Calcutta, Cairo, Turkey, Greece, Morocco, Madras, Tripoli, Jordan, South America, and New York? The answer seems to be to turn to the mode of allegory that will permit all of these places to be spoken of at once. In an allegorical mode, one may actually be looking at images of the Roman slums, but one is seeing through them the slums of Madras and Mexico City, Cairo and Calcutta.[9]

Hawks and Sparrows was Pasolini's fourth full-length feature fiction film. The film stars Totò, the celebrated Neapolitan comedic star, then nearing the end of his illustrious career, and Ninetto Davoli, a ragazzo di vita whom Pasolini first met while shooting *La ricotta,* and who remained one of Pasolini's closest companions until the filmmaker's death. These two play father and son. We first see them on the road in the middle, it seems, of nowhere. They walk and talk, share philosophical bromides and off-color jokes. They stop for a drink at an isolated bar somewhere on the outskirts of Rome. Outside, in front of the bar, Ninetto engages in a little Godardian group dance with some other boys, while inside Totò insults the *baristà*'s hair (asking him if he does it with a vacuum cleaner).

They continue on down the road a bit, into a sordid borgata of multi-story houses and apartment buildings at various stages of shoddy incompletion. There is a crowd mulling about outside someone's home. Totò and Ninetto stop to ask what is wrong; someone seems to have died. This scene is intercut, mysteriously, with a series of several shots of buildings in the neighborhood. The shots are still and they frame the buildings rather dramatically: the structures are fragmented by the photographic frame, made abstract, brusquely aestheticized in a rather "modernist" manner. The series of shots could be read as an odd visual introduction to the setting of this segment of the film. Totò and Ninetto leave this place almost as soon as they arrive; the mystery as to why the film bothers to introduce several of these buildings with such intentional aestheticism goes unexplained.

The answer may lie in the shots' similarity to one of the most famous sequences in film—certainly in Italian film: those shots of the EUR landscape, completely divested of the film's protagonists, that make up the final moments of Michelangelo Antonioni's *The Eclipse* (*L'eclisse,* 1962). If one watches those notorious last moments of Antonioni's film and then turns to these shots in *Hawks and Sparrows,* the connection is obvious.

This corrosive appropriation, as I interpret it, has to do with the fact that Antonioni's film, set as it is almost exclusively in EUR, was at the time and has ever since been widely (I think mistakenly) understood as a demonstration of the dehumanizing nature of modern architecture.[10] Antonioni is often understood to have essayed a treatise on the poverty of the modern not only in *The Eclipse,* but also in *L'avventura* (1960) and *La notte* (1961), all films that foreground issues pertaining to architecture and urban space.[11] Why does Pasolini parody Antonioni's critical architectural-cinematic discourse?

The sequence in *Hawks and Sparrows* seems to foreclose the viability or efficacy of a cinematic practice like Antonioni's that attempts to investigate the nature of the city through elegantly obtuse photography. Antonioni's method in *The Eclipse,* and here I am referring primarily to the film's famous ending, is to frame typically "unattractive"[12] structures in such a way so as to reveal their hidden or ignored abstract aesthetic dimension. The sequence could be understood as a meditation on the (aesthetically, at least) redemptive potential of the fragment as a figure that could renew or reorient our perception. Pasolini applies this practice to the half-made and homely architecture of this miserable area. This allusion, of course, might or must have more than one level of signification. The meaning that seems most obvious and pertinent to the present work is this: Pasolini believes Antonionian architectural and urban discourse to be a lost object, a practice as obsolete as the determined optimism we sense at the end of *Rome, Open City.* Contemplating the aesthetic potential of the isolated architectural fragment will not, Pasolini seems to say, cut it. The problems of peripheral Rome—its expansion and the subjection of its inhabitants—resist interpretation or analysis by Antonioni's methods. The borgate and the periphery are too big for this. Suggesting that they might be aesthetically redeemed through an aestheticizing gaze is not an answer to the problem they pose. As we have noted already, in Pasolini's understanding, they resist

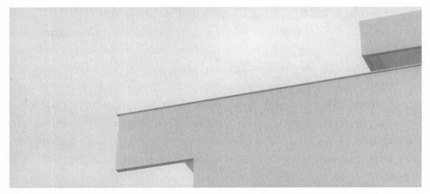

Shot from the famous final sequence of Antonioni's *The Eclipse:* the privileging of the architectural fragment.

Pasolini's corrosive allusion to *The Eclipse* in *Hawks and Sparrows*.

representation by their very nature. Looking at them or *only* at them will not suffice. Thus, the problems they embody—in short, the ruin of the world and the subjugation of subaltern classes by the forces of late twentieth-century capitalism—must be responded to in the mode of the allegorical metaphor.

Thus after this stop, we next see Totò and Ninetto walking down a desolate road, the skyline of the Roman periphery behind them. As the characters walk and the camera dollies backwards[13] a sign comes into view: "Istanbul 4253 km." Pasolini makes the same point in this shot as he makes in his above-quoted catalog of the world's slums. Very shortly after the sign comes into view, the film cuts to a shot of the two characters walking on an elevated ramp of the Tangenziale Est, an elevated highway that connects the center of Rome to the Autostrada running to the north and south.

The initial 755-kilometer length of the Autostrada had only been completed in 1964.[14] It is, and was, certainly, for Pasolini, a nonplace—or rather a structure that threatened to dissolve the very experience and possibility of (specific, regional) place itself into what Henri Lefebvre would call "abstract space," a space that "tends towards homogeneity, towards the elimination of existing differences or peculiarities," a space that exerts "awesome reductionist force vis-à-vis 'lived' experience."[15] The modern highway, which facilitates the easy transport of people and commodities over long distances, breaks down the historical geographic distances that separated distinct places, and re-creates every place as just yet another place to travel through, another place to see. By traveling the Autostrada, the characters leave the city of Rome quite behind them, quite literally.

Rome as the embodiment of a set of specific urban histories and urban practices is no longer of the same interest to Pasolini that it once was. This loss of interest is due to the fact that Rome's specificity has been superseded, swallowed by the homogenizing forces of capitalism, forces of which the Autostrada is a profound and concrete expression. These are Pasolini's words, given in reply to an interviewer who asked him in 1973 to comment on the homogenization of Italian culture:

> . . . this process of acculturation, of the transformation of particular and marginal cultures into a centralized culture that homogenizes everything, occurred more or less simultaneously all over Italy. Several elements came together. The development of motorization, for example. When the diaphragm of distance is eliminated, certain social models also disappear.[16]

Automobile culture, which has reshaped the Italian city and countryside,[17] is but one index of the forces of capitalism that are really responsible for the reshaping of the city and its periphery. In an essay entitled "New Linguistic Questions," Pasolini angrily denounces the process by which the standardized Italian disseminated by newspapers and television strangled the richness and diversity of dialects in Italy. Pasolini actually (and not incidentally) uses the speech by Aldo Moro that inaugurated the Autostrada as an example of this devolution of the variety of Italian linguistic usage into colorless, technocratic "functionality."[18] Pasolini quotes Moro's speech, which follows:

> The productivity of investments in the highway plan thus depends on their coordination in a programming of the infrastructures of transportation that tends to resolve disequilibriums, eliminate obstructions, reduce the waste of competition among the different means of transportation, and, in a word, give life to an integrated system on a national scale.[19]

Pasolini's analysis (which I have summarized above but will not go into in depth) begins thus:

> That sentence is taken from a speech by Moro [delivered] in the meaningful moment of the *Autostrada del Sole* (meaningful insofar as that "infrastructure" is certainly a typical and new moment of linguistic unification) . . .[20]

The Autostrada, for Pasolini, is an embodiment and a representation of the forces that have undermined the vitality of human life—something not unlike the borgate rapidissime or the Tuscolano II.[21]

With the autostrada and other concomitant changes, the city recedes, literally and figuratively from view in Pasolini's cinema—almost like something disappearing in a rearview mirror. This disappearance is both an effect of the acceleration of actual historic forces and a (consonant) change in Pasolini's perspective, which, like late capitalism, goes global in the late 1960s and early 1970s.

The late 1960s saw Pasolini produce a number of works that shuttled back and forth between allegory and myth. *La terra vista dalla luna* (The earth seen from the moon, 1967) and *Che cose sone le nuvole?* (What are clouds?, 1968) are short allegorical films. *La terra vista dalla luna,* the more interesting of the two, is mostly set in and around a shantytown in Fiumicino and in nearby Ostia, as well as in the center of Rome—at the Coliseum, in fact. The film tells the story of Cianciato Miao (Totò), his son Basciù Miao (Davoli), and Assurda (Silvano Mangano), the woman with whom Cianciato replaces his wife and Basciù's mother; together the three constitute a family unit of an unusual kind. The film bears comparison to *Mamma Roma* in that its characters are undone by a desire to ascend the property and class ladder. In *La terra,* however, this is all played out in a grimly comic key. In a stunt they devise to make money to buy a new house, Assurda, perched in one of the many arches high up on the Coliseum, pretends to be driven to suicide on account of her poverty.[22] Cianciato and Basciù ask for donations from the crowd that gathers below. Two tourists played by Laura Betti and Luigi Leone in cross-gendered drag are touring the Coliseum at the same time, on a level above Assurda. Betti's character carelessly drops a banana peel that Assurda slips on to fall to her death. It's another version of upwardly mobile aspiration as a kind of death wish. The center of Rome is seen here as little more than a stage set that serves only to cancel the fate of these lower-class (admittedly absurd) characters. The film's moral, announced on a title card: "To be dead or alive is the same thing."

In 1967 Pasolini made his version of *Oedipus Rex (Edipo Re),* beginning a cycle of films interested in remaking classical tragedy (the other films in this vein are *Medea* [1969] and *Notes for an African Orestes* [*Appunti per una Orestiade Africana,* 1970]). These adaptations of classical, mythic texts were also conceived of and spoken about by Pasolini as allegorical treatments of the present. *Appunti per un film sull'India* (Notes for a film on India, 1967–68), was based on an Indian fable. *Theorem* (*Teorema,* 1968), a film concerning a bourgeois Milanese family undone by the sexually charged visit of a stranger, is wildly allegorical, as is *Pigsty* (*Porcile,*

1969). Clearly the shift to allegory is dramatic, elaborate, and complete. And in each case the resort to myth and allegory stems from an indefatigable desire to criticize the forces of capitalist progress and modernity.

Pasolini shot *Medea* in Italy, Turkey, and Syria. His *African Orestes* moves between Rome, Uganda, and Tanzania. These are stops on the roads leading from Rome that he enumerates in his itinerary of third world misery. Whereas in the *African Orestes* we see postcolonial modernity in the film's several sequences shot at the brand new University of Dar es Salaam (pictured as some version of *Mamma Roma*'s Cecafumo), in *Medea* the idea is to give nothing of modernity and instead to point to a world as yet uncorrupted. What saves this political aestheticization of underdevelopment from becoming merely or only apolitical and condescendingly aesthetic is the fact that these places are being offered to view at all. Sending Greek tragedy into Africa is an allegorical method of meditating on the crisis of modernity and the scandal of third world poverty by *not* representing those same things. *Medea,* in all its strange muteness and exoticizing locales, might be understood as one of those works of art to which, according to Adorno, "has fallen the burden of wordlessly asserting what is barred to politics."[23]

Sandwiched in between these several projects was a small film called *La sequenza del fiore di carta* (The paper flower sequence, 1969), part of an omnibus film entitled *Love and Anger (Amore e rabbia),* with episodes by Bertolucci, Jean-Luc Godard, Carlo Lizzani, and Marco Bellocchio. The film is very simple: it consists of several long, dollying sequence shots of Ninetto Davoli walking down the Via Nazionale on a summer's day, a large red paper flower in his hand. The film begins in the Piazza della Repubblica and continues through a long reverse dolly recording Ninetto's casual progress down Via Nazionale. This street we have encountered before in the discussion of Moravia's *The Woman of Rome* in chapter 2 and this technique of shooting, of course, bears a direct resemblance to those shots in *Accattone* and *Mamma Roma* analyzed in chapters 3 and 5. However, Pasolini makes this footage strange by using the optical printer to overlay the long take of Ninetto with newsreel images that testify to the horrors of the twentieth century. It's an exercise in montage, managed, in the beginning of the film, at least, not so much through editing as through the overlay (onto the Via Nazionale) of various sources of news footage. The soundtrack is also a source of montage: snatches of Bach's *St. Matthews Passion* that were used in *Accattone,* of a voice reading snippets from *The Ragazzi,* of Pasolini's poetry, of pop music. Toward the end a voice intones: "Innocence is guilt" repeatedly, following a long discourse on the subject of innocence and ignorance. The film is the probably the closest Pasolini ever came to making an avant-garde film of the sort that he was so suspicious of in "Is Being Natural?"

The film figures a kind of return and/or farewell to Rome. It does so by recapitulating a formal technique, the peripatetic long take—a technique that, as mentioned earlier in regards to *Accattone,* is born out of the spatiality and geography of Rome. This long take is then overlaid (literally) by a bombardment of information about the world beyond Rome. Toward the end of the film the sequence shot is increasingly interrupted by cuts away to short, low-angle moving shots of the tram lines that overhang the Via Nazionale—perhaps a hint that for Pasolini and his cinematic relationship with Rome, this was the end of the line. In the film's last seconds we hear the sound of falling bombs and gunfire. The image track cuts to newsreel footage of dead bodies (they seem to be Vietnamese bodies—obviously the Vietnam War is the major informing world event here), then back to an image of Ninetto, splayed out on the street in an attitude of death, the paper flower lying at his side. While most obviously the film is an argument against political naïveté or neutrality in the era of Vietnam (whatever the sunny conditions on the Via Nazionale), it is also an interesting comment on Pasolini's own film practice and its relationship to the city in which it first took shape. The recapitulation of the long sequence shot, the film implies, is as insufficient to the task of addressing contemporary (now global) political exigencies as Ninetto's blithe innocence. In other words, Pasolini is dismissing his own former formal mannerisms in the same way he does Antonioni's in *Hawks and Sparrows.* The location of Via Nazionale is particularly apposite, given that it was, in Manfredo Tafuri's terms, "the first street of modern Rome"[24]—a major thoroughfare that, in its late nineteenth-century attempt to graft onto Rome a half-digested urban modernity, inaugurated the misuse of Roman urban space whose eventual effects are the Roman periphery, its borgate, its INA Casa projects. Thus, in a sense, it is the street that leads to the corruption of the present. The film seems to suggest that now it is not so much the case that all roads lead to Rome, as Rome being the place from which the road to political engagement *must* leave, *must* depart.

The films that would follow in the early 1970s—*The Decameron* (*Il decamerone,* 1971), *The Canterbury Tales* (*I racconti di Canterbury,* 1972), *Arabian Nights* (*Il fiore delle mille e una notte,* 1974)—the so-called Trilogy of Life—were attempts to foreground an erotics of innocence, demonstrations of Pasolini's initial (rather unreasonable) hope that the films would make visible "the last bulwark of reality" which were the "'innocent' bodies with the archaic, dark, vital violence of their sexual organs."[25] It was not just the sex that would enable these films, so Pasolini hoped, to resist "the unreality of the sub-culture of the mass media";[26] it was also their setting in a precapitalist world. Such a setting could mean the fictional temporal setting of medieval Italy or England, or it could mean the geographical remove to Yemen, Persia, Nepal, Ethiopia, India.

In 1974 Pasolini edited together some extra footage left over from *The Decameron* that he had shot of the city of Sana'a in Yemen, an ancient walled city. Sana'a had also been used as a location in *Arabian Nights*. Pasolini called the city "a savage Venice in the dust."[27] The film that resulted is *Le mura di Sana'a* (The walls of Sana'a), a documentary-cum-elegiac complaint about the modernization that was threatening to destroy the city's walls and its unique architectural and urban form that had been preserved intact for some five hundred years. Pasolini sent the film to UNESCO as an appeal for an intervention that would save the city and its heritage. Toward ites end (it is only fourteen minutes long) the film moves back to Italy, just outside the city of Orte, where Pasolini speaks (from offscreen) to several Ortani (all men) about the encroachment of modern construction on what had been a pristine medieval walled city. Some of the men express disgust at the landscape's alteration, others shrug; one says he likes the new buildings because he grew up there.[28] The film then moves back to Sana'a and into its most striking passage: several repetitive, long, sweeping pans take in the expanses of the city's ancient walls. The pans move from screen right to screen left. Each pan moves across the surface of the wall, but each must end on an eyesore of recent construction. Pasolini intones this voiceover:

> For Italy it is all over. But Yemen can be saved entirely.
>
> We appeal to UNESCO—Help Yemen save itself from destruction, begun with the destruction of the walls of Sana'a.
>
> We appeal to UNESCO—Help Yemen to become aware of its identity and of what a precious country it is.
>
> We appeal to UNESCO—Help stop this pitiful destruction of national patrimony in a country where no one denounces it.
>
> We appeal to UNESCO—Find the possibility of giving this nation the awareness of being a common good for mankind, one which must protect itself to remain so

> We appeal to UNESCO—Intervene, while there is still
> time, to convince an ingenuous ruling class that Yemen's only
> wealth is its beauty, and that preserving that beauty means pos-
> sessing an economic resource that costs nothing. Yemen is still
> in time to avoid the errors of other countries.
>
> We appeal to UNESCO—In the name of the true, unex-
> pressed wish of the Yemenite people, in the name of the simple
> men whom poverty has kept pure, in the name of the grace of
> obscure centuries, in the name of the scandalous, revolution-
> ary force of the past.[29]

Maurizio Viano takes issue with the "privileged position" that Pasolini
grants himself as the arbiter of what would be best for Yemen.[30] There is
no escaping an awareness of Pasolini's romanticizing of Sana'a as a kind
of colonialist fantasy. But to write the film off would be to miss some of
the most interesting things the film has to tell us—perhaps even in spite
of itself.

The sheer obdurate hokeyness of the voice-over soundtrack threat-
ens to liquidate the gravity of the images and turn Sana'a itself into only
an image, a spectacle of pure difference. But Pasolini, I think, practices an
exemplary hokeyness. This is, after all, a director who framed his version
of the Oedipus myth as autobiography; the actors who played Jocasta and
Creon in his *Oedipus Rex,* according to legend, wore Pasolini's parents
very own clothes from the early 1920s, the period of his birth. If Yemen
were to become a spectacle, it would be so only or most importantly in

A frame from one of the several pans of the walls of Sana'a, the ancient
walls in the background and the threatening new construction in the
foreground.

the eyes of the Western beholder, so acculturated to the consumption of exotic images—one as digestible, as assimilable as the next. What blocks this too-easy, too-quick accession to the spectacular, however, is the way in which the production of these images—their form—returns us to Pasolini's cinematography in *Accattone,* to the "sacred" movement of the pan, to a practice that was borne out of a specific set of historical conditions: the Roman periphery, circa 1961. This same formal gesture, while it sought repetitively, hard-headedly to describe (by documenting) a condition of social and material degradation, also, repetitively, enacted its own representational and (therefore) political insufficiency. Thus, a historicist awareness of Pasolini's formal practice acts (however subtly) as a criticizing agent of the naïveté and condescension of the voiceover.

But the naïveté itself might also be worth considering before we toss it aside. We cannot talk any more about other cultures, even out of sympathy, the way that Pasolini speaks about Yemen in the voiceover in *Le mura di Sana'a.* We lack that innocence. (One wonders if Pasolini actually lacked it as well.) I think, however, that the discomfort we feel with this film and with others of Pasolini's that privilege "primitive" societies over "advanced" ones could be instructive. For one thing, the unease we feel is a measurement of how far we have come in developing languages, modes of engagement and speech with which to address those whom the West creates as "other." But to use the films as a sort of a yardstick is still to insist on them as bad objects. I also think there might be a way of seeing that the very unfashionable and insensitive things that Pasolini says force us, nonetheless, into an encounter with the process of global modernization about which we should feel uncomfortable, if not miserable. There is a utopian wrongness about Pasolini's voiceover: though we must recognize its "orientalizing," "othering," and "essentializing" activity, we must also, I believe, mourn with him the loss of the walls of Sana'a—all that they are and all that they stand for. In a sense, we sit in relation to Pasolini's experiments in third world allegory as he positioned the West in relation to the third world: its "backwardness" instructs our progress.

The anaphoric incantation of the appeal to UNESCO married to the anaphoric movement of the pan across the city walls: as I have said, these things return us to the aesthetic and political nexus of film style and urban periphery that we saw in *Accattone.* Rome remains analogically, allegorically present: we see it in and through Yemen, just as, so Pasolini seems to hope, something of Yemen's fast-disappearing precapitalist innocence would allow Italy to see in Yemen a better, earlier version of itself. What I want to make clear is that it is the consistency of Pasolini's vision (as it is articulated formally vis-à-vis an urban landscape) that allows us to see, more clearly and more disturbingly, the allegorical but all-too-real mutual impingements of first worlds on third worlds and vice versa. As Fredric Jameson has written: "On the global scale, allegory allows the most random, minute, or isolated landscapes to function as a figurative machinery in which questions about the system and its control over the local ceaselessly rise and fall."[31] If Pasolini's third world allegories can at least continue to proliferate such questions, then perhaps their naïveté is an irritant we can tolerate in order to benefit from it: grit in an oyster.

That Pasolini chose increasingly to operate within a mode of allegory as his political analysis grew ever more urgent and ever more gloomy is consonant with the nature of allegory itself, which is, as Michael Murrin has formulated, "a specialized form of discourse" that demands "an unusual mode of thought." This mode of thought is usually moral. Allegory implies, by its very nature, a system or systems of value; it is an ethical call to reflection, a call to arms. It emerges or is resorted to at moments of crisis—personal and political. And yet, as a mode, it "depends on the wealth of language as well as upon its poverty."[32] We hardly wonder that allegory is the path that leads Pasolini out of his troubling engagement with Rome.

The political situation that Pasolini deplores in Yemen is, of course, not the same as the situation he criticized in Rome in the early 1960s. But as the pathetic western commodities that we see desultorily decorating the windows of Sana'a's shops will attest, there is much that they also have in common. Despite its too-precious tendency toward a patronizing connoisseurship of exotic and unspoiled locations, Pasolini's allegorical mode was—and perhaps can still be experienced as—a mode of stitching Yemen to Italy and the west, of forcing their interpenetration, just as his earliest films were methods of reincorporating the lives of peripheral Romans into the consciousness of modern Italy.

Our ability to understand how Pasolini's later films function as allegories depends on our reaching out toward the specificity, the history, the materiality of the places he documents and then offers to us through his disquieting mode of vision. And to understand all of this, we must first understand the *place* from which this mode of vision originates. That is to say: it emerges from Rome, from an encounter with a city—an encounter from which Pasolini would never recover.

Acknowledgments

I suppose one definition of the word *book* might be "the accumulation of debts."

I want first to thank Brian Price, who has read every word I have ever written and who has done more than anyone to encourage my work, correct my imprecisions, and offer support when I might have otherwise given up. I owe enormous thanks to Noa Steimatsky, whose work has fed into my own and who intervened at a timely moment when this book was still a doctoral dissertation and helped me to restructure radically its argument. Noa understands better than anyone Pasolini's vision; always I see his images, in part, through her eyes. I thank Annette Michelson, my teacher, dissertation supervisor, and friend, whose elegant scholarship I hope I bear decent witness to. I also thank the other members of my dissertation committee, Richard Allen, Antonia Lant, and Bill Simon, all of whom were my teachers at New York University and whose influence may be felt in this book in manifold ways.

As the book neared its final stages, I received important advice from Laura Rascaroli, who forced me to think harder about neorealism. Ita MacCarthy offered valuable criticism and translation assistance. I owe thanks as well to David Attwell, Jane Elliott, Frances Guerin, Karen Pinkus, Leslie Richardson, and Eduardo Saccone, all of whom have given me advice and support at various moments. I also thank Sharon Willis, who acted as an anonymous reader for the manuscript and offered a wonderfully sympathetic and critical response to the project.

I thank Derek Attridge, head of the Department of English and Related Literature at the University of York, who made sure I received research leave to finish the manuscript and who has been otherwise incredibly supportive.

In Rome, I owe huge thanks to my Roman family: Judy Harris (to whom this book is dedicated), David Willey, Gwendelina Ajello, and Marco Ajello. All have let me come and go from their place in Piazza Collegio Romano as if it were my own home, and they have made me know Rome more intimately than I might ever have hoped to otherwise. To Judy I owe special thanks for feeding me exquisitely—not to mention for each day's cappuccino at Remo. To Gwen, thanks for sharpening my sense of Roman architecture and urban space, whether trecento or novecento. I thank Nicola Brandt and Martina Fiorentino, who showed me their Romes and were generally available for drinks.

I thank the staff at the Istituto Nazionale di Urbanistica in the Piazza Farnese, and Roberto Chiesi and the staff at the Archivio Pier Paolo Pasolini in Bologna.

I would like to thank my editor at the University of Minnesota Press, Jason Weidemann, who has been enthusiastic about this book since it landed on his desk, and Adam Brunner, also at Minnesota, who has been extremely kind, patient, and helpful.

For help with illustrations, I thank Stephen Gran and Huw Llewellyn-Jones.

Thanks to friends who have participated indirectly in the production of this book, mostly by making life bearable as it was being written, on and off, during the past years: Alex Auder, Laura Chrisman, Pat Crowley, Brian Donnelly, Christine Egan, Ezra Feinberg, Hugh Haughton, Jane Irvin, Hillary Irvin, Mik Larson, Michael Lawrence, Amanda Lillie, Siobhan Mullally, Nick Nehez, Val Nehez, Pat Palmer, Amanda Phillips, Bess Rattray, Byron Suber, Meghan Sutherland, and Mark Turner. And to my uncles, Greg Vernice and Damien Boisvert.

Last, I thank my parents, Bill and Rosalind, and my brother, Stephen, who have supported me in ways that cannot be properly tallied or spoken.

A tutti: ancora, grazie.

Notes

Introduction

1. A note on how I will refer to film titles: I will use English translations for films when such a translation is in conventional use (*Hawks and Sparrows,* for instance). Some films (Michelangelo Antonioni's *L'avventura* [1960], for instance) are conventionally referred to by their original Italian titles, and so I will stick to that usage. When films have no conventional English translation (*La sequenza del fiore di carta,* for instance), I will refer to them by their original Italian titles but I will also provide an English translation in parentheses.

2. Pier Paolo Pasolini, "Studies on the Life of Testaccio," in *Roman Nights and Other Stories,* trans. John Shepley (Marlboro, Vt.: Marlboro Press, 1986), 69–70. This story was written in 1951. It was collected in Pasolini's *Alì dagli occhi azzurri* (Milan: Aldo Garzanti Editore, 1965), 80–88.

3. For some examples of these several types of scholarship, see James Donald, *Imagining the Modern City* (London: Athlone Press, 1999); Sabine Hake, "Urban Spectacle in Walter Ruttman's *Berlin, Symphony of the Big City,*" in *Dancing on the Volcano: Essays on the Culture of the Weimar Republic,* ed. Thomas Kniesche and Stephen Brockman (Columbia, S.C.: Camden House, 1994), 127–62; Annette Michelson, "Dr. Crase and Mr. Clair," *October* 11 (1979): 30–53. Michael Minden, "The City in Early Cinema: Metropolis, *Berlin,* and *October,*" in *Unreal City: Urban Experience in Modern Literature, European Literature, and Art,* ed. Edward Timms and David Kelley (New York: St. Martin's Press, 1985), 193–213; Anton Kaes, "Sites of Desire: The Weimar Street Film," in *Film Architecture: Set Designs from Metropolis to Blade Runner,* ed. Dietrich Neumann (Munich: Prestel, 1996); David B. Clarke, ed., *The Cinematic City* (London: Routledge, 1997); Mark Shiel and Tony Fitzmaurice, eds., *Cinema and the City: Film and Urban Societies in a Global Context* (Oxford: Blackwell, 2001); Linda Krause and Patrice Petro, eds., *Global Cities: Cinema, Architecture, and Urbanism in a Digital Age* (New Brunswick, N.J.: Rutgers University Press, 2003); Paula J. Massood, *Black City Cinema: African American*

Urban Experiences in Film (Philadelphia: Temple University Press, 2003). This is only a very partial list of works in this field; it could go on and on.

4. A recent book that accounts brilliantly for the complexity and specificity of the interrelationships between films and cities is Edward Dimendberg's excellent study, *Film Noir and the Spaces of Modernity* (Cambridge: Harvard University Press, 2004). This book came out as I was completing the first draft of this book.

5. Sam Rohdie, *The Passion of Pier Paolo Pasolini* (London: BFI Publishing, 1995), 109.

6. Henre Lefebvre, "Right to the City," in *Writings on Cities*, ed. and trans. Eleonore Kofman and Elizabeth Lebas (Oxford: Blackwell, 1996), 66.

7. T. J. Clark, *The Painting of Modern Life: Paris in the Art of Manet and His Followers* (Princeton, N.J.: Princeton University Press, 1984), 15.

8. Guy Debord, *The Society of the Spectacle*, trans. Donald Nicholson-Smith (New York: Zone Books, 1995), 29.

9. In many ways industrial urban modernity never came to Rome, as Rome has never been an industrial center in the manner of Milan or Turin (or Paris or London). This problem is explained in chapter 1.

10. Debord, *Society of the Spectacle*, 12–13.

11. Rome's center is, of course, also home to the Italian state and the Vatican. Sociologist Georg Simmel makes the interesting claim that "[t]he principle of the church [Simmel intends here the Roman Catholic Church] is non-spatial," meaning that the church is everywhere at once. Simmel goes on to say that Rome is "absolutely unique, the most incomparable historical-geographical creation and, by virtue of the fact that 'all roads lead to Rome,' its position is fixed as if by a system of countless coordinates. Yet, on the other hand, it has completely lost the limitation of localization at one point by virtue of the enormous extent and substance of its past, and of the fact that it appears as a geometrical site for all the changes and contrasts in history, whose traces and significance have grown together in it, or into it, both spiritually and visibly"; Georg Simmel, "The Sociology of Space," *Simmel on Culture*, ed. David Frisby and Mike Featherstone (London: Sage, 1997), 140, 150. This description of Rome suggests several intriguing avenues of research that cannot be pursued here. We might note, however, that the Catholic Church's nonspatiality bears a striking resemblance to the way that capital, because it can be disembodied, can be everywhere at once. To return to the immediate subject of Rome as a (secular) capital city, we might also note that in a period in which the borders of the national are constantly being redefined in terms of economic exchange (i.e., the new Europe of the Euro, to cite only the most obvious of evidence), Rome's claim to being a seat of power seems rather tenuous.

12. On this episode in Fellini's filmmaking, see Hollis Alpert, *Fellini: A Life* (New York: Marlowe and Company, 1988), 136–37.

13. The work by Benjamin that I am thinking of here is primarily *The Arcades Project*, trans. Howard Eiland and Kevin McLaughlin (Cambridge: The Belknap

Press of Harvard University Press, 1999), as well as *Charles Baudelaire: A Lyric Poet in the Era of High Capitalism* (London: Verso, 1997).

14. Benjamin, *The Arcades Project,* esp. 3–5, 15–17, 31–61.

15. Denis Mack Smith, *Modern Italy: A Political History* (Ann Arbor: University of Michigan Press, 1997), 96.

16. Anthony Vidler, *Warped Space: Art, Architecture, and Anxiety in Modern Culture* (Cambridge: MIT Press, 2000), 67. Subsequent page references appear in the text.

17. Marco Bertozzi, "The Gaze and the Ruins: Notes for a Roman Film Itinerary," *Rome in Cinema: Between Reality and Fiction,* ed. Elisabetta Bruscolini (Rome: Fondazione Scuola Nazionale di Cinema, 2001), 15.

18. Keala Jewell, *The Poeisis of History: Experimenting with Genre in Postwar Italy* (Ithaca, N.Y.: Cornell University Press, 1992), 24. Another fairly recent addition to this scholarship, again focusing primarily on Pasolini's literary production, though with some reference to his filmmaking, is Gianni Biondillo's *Pasolini: il corpo della città* (Milan: Edizioni Unicopli, 2001).

19. Lino Micciché, *Pasolini nella città del cinema* (Venice: Marsilio, 1999).

20. Angelo Restivo, *The Cinema of Economic Miracles: Visuality and Modernization in the Italian Art Film* (Durham, N.C.: Duke University Press, 2002).

21. *Casabella continuità* 251 (May 1961). The special issue included a long essay by Francesco Tentori, "Quindici anni di architettura" (Fifteen years of Italian architecture), 34–55. The issue and Tentori's essay were attempts to understand, account for, and criticize the development of Italian architecture and urban planning since the end of World War II.

22. Marvin Trachtenberg, *Dominion of the Eye: Urbanism, Art, and Power in Early Modern Florence* (Cambridge: Cambridge University Press, 1997).

23. Clark, *Painting of Modern Life,* 17.

1. A Short History of the Roman Periphery

1. Italy's capital had first been Turin. The capital moved to Florence in 1865, then on to Rome after the city was finally conjoined to the rest of the nation. For a brief description of the planning of Florence as capital, see Paolo Scattoni, *L'urbanistica dell'Italia contemporanea: dall'unità ai giorni nostri* (Rome: Newton and Compton Editori, 2004), 16–18.

2. Robert C. Fried, *Planning the Eternal City: Roman Politics and Planning Since World War II* (New Haven: Yale University Press, 1973), 19. Much of the general information in the historical outline that I narrate below I owe to Fried's account and to numerous other sources, prominent among them: Italo Insolera, *Roma moderna: Un secolo di storia Urbanistica, 1870–1970,* new ed. (Turin: Einaudi, 1993), and Franco Ferrarotti, *Roma: da capitale a periferia* (Bari: Editori Laterza, 1974).

3. Fried, *Planning the Eternal City,* 21. For an excellent and economical introduction to the deep-seated problems of Roman urbanism, focusing on the Rome of the Popes and ending at unification, see Wolfgang Braunfels, *Urban*

Design in Western Europe: Regime and Architecture, 900–1900, trans. Kenneth J. Northcott (Chicago: University of Chicago Press, 1988), 340–65.

4. In some sense, then, the construction industry was not a "real" industry in the same sense as, for instance, the steel industry. Italian construction workers, many former peasants from the surrounding countryside, were often trained on the job to perform a variety of functions; there was no strict division of labor.

5. This eastern expansion plan was the first of many attempts to push the city's development in that geographical direction. Developing eastward would have meant freeing the city's core from the congestion that plagues it to this day. Eastern expansion was understood as vaguely anticlerical, since it was oriented away from the Vatican which lay across the Tiber to the west. (The Vatican, of course, had staunchly opposed the movement for national unity.) In this sense, eastern expansion was symbolically progressive. But eastern expansion also made good sense because it would have begun a healthy trend of asymmetrical urban development, as opposed to the concentric rings of "oil stain" development that has ensued naturally and has caused the city center always to be that place through which all traffic must eventually flow.

6. For a detailed discussion of the complex considerations involved in building the Via Nazionale, see Manfredo Tafuri, "La prima strada di *Roma moderna:* Via Nazionale," *Urbanistica* 26, no. 27 (June 1959): 95–109. Viewed on a map it is clear that Corso Vittorio Emmanuele II and Via Nazionale do not actually meet. The Via del Plebiscito "completes" Corso Vittorio Emmanuele II's connection to Piazza Venezia, while Via Nazionale is connected to the piazza by Via Magnanapoli and Via Sant'Eufemia. Nevertheless, together (with the help of the aforementioned streets that connect them) the two large streets form a slightly curved east-west axis that runs from the Tiber all the way to the Piazza della Reppublica and Termini station just beyond that. This is today the route (running from Termini to the Tiber) of the number 64 bus, infamous for its pickpockets.

7. Insolera, *Roma moderna,* 135–36.

8. Also called "spontaneous borgate." See Franco Martinelli, *Roma nuova: borgate spontanee e insediamenti pubblici* (Milan: Franco Angeli, 1988).

9. Fried, *Planning the Eternal City,* 22–24.

10. Insolera, *Roma moderna,* 35.

11. Ibid., 65–67; Diane Ghirardo, "City and Suburb in Fascist Rome 1922–43," in *Urban Forms, Suburban Dreams,* ed. Malcolm Quantrill and Bruce Webb (Chicago: Center for the Advancement of Studies in Architecture, 1993), 51–52.

12. Mount Testaccio, sometimes referred to as one of Rome's hills, is literally composed of potsherds, fragments of broken amphora discarded near to where they were unloaded by the Tiber, which accumulated during ancient Roman times.

13. Insolera, *Roma moderna,* 67.

14. In time Testaccio developed as a very cohesive working-class community and a center for left-wing political sentiment.

15. Quoted in Ferruccio Trabalzi, "Low Cost Housing in Twentieth-Century Rome," in *Out of Site: A Social Criticism of Architecture*, ed. Diane Ghirardo (Seattle: Bay Press, 1991), 134–35. Usually, "the centuries of decadence" in fascist rhetoric refers to the Renaissance and the baroque, oddly enough. Late medieval Italy was often privileged as the heroic period of the communes. Here, however, Mussolini effectively is decrying everything that was built in the intervening years between the ancient Roman empire and the moment at which he is speaking.

16. Insolera, *Roma moderna*, 128.

17. That is, the Italian dominion over the Mediterranean and the lands touching it.

18. Ghirardo, "City and Suburb," 56. For recent and valuable work on the fascist redeployment of symbols, particularly signifiers of ancient Rome, see Simonetta Falasca-Zamponi, *Fascist Spectacle: The Aesthetics of Power in Mussolini's Italy* (Berkeley: University of California Press, 2000), esp. 89–99.

19. Insolera, *Roma moderna*, 133.

20. Ghirardo, "City and Suburb," 56.

21. Ibid., 54.

22. Insolera, *Roma moderna*, 136–37. Later, private speculators would intentionally build large apartment houses past gas and electric lines because land was cheaper further out, but the city would then be forced to bring the services to the development, immediately raising the value of the buildings. Another useful source on the subject of the fascist borgate is Paolo Angeletti and Lucia Ciancarelli et al., eds., *Case Romane: La periferia e le case popolari* (Rome: Clear Editions, 1994).

23. Insolera, *Roma moderna*, 135.

24. Pierre Sorlin, *European Cinemas, European Societies, 1939–1990* (London: Routledge, 1991), 119, 124. Sorlin's account of the film's geography is lively and important but does not seem particularly researched, especially in regards to his several remarks on the history of the fascist borgate.

25. In the scene in which Ricci and his wife, Maria, go to reclaim their bicycle from the pawn shop (by hocking their matrimonial linen), Maria gives their address at Val Melaina, which might have served to anchor the geography of the film for spectators in 1948 who would have been unfamiliar with this particular location.

26. Insolera, *Roma moderna*, 139–40. (Unless otherwise noted, all translations, both here and elsewhere, from material written in Italian are my own.) Of course the film's black and white does not permit us to recognize the yellow of the plaster or the green of the shutters.

27. Such an attitude toward the film is, to some degree, warranted by the fact that all of the people playing members of the Ricci family were in fact non-professionals, "found" living in the various working-class districts of Rome. I have not discovered in my research whether any of these people were literally found in Val Melaina. Sorlin goes to some lengths in explaining his belief that the film represents Ricci as an immigrant to Rome from central Italy and Maria as someone displaced from the center to the borgate by the fascist sventramenti. The

evidence for this interpretation lies in the fact that Ricci does not speak Roman dialect, but as Sorlin goes on to explain, this fact might be simply a product of the Italian production method of dubbing dialogue in postproduction. He hedges his bets by saying that the Riccis and their neighbors "could be an entire resettled population or perhaps a combination of Romans and peasants." He argues that Maria seems Roman because she "appears to be more at ease" in the center of Rome, whereas Ricci seems "extremely nervous," a condition that finally leads Sorlin to conclude that he "is probably an immigrant" (121). I think Sorlin runs the risk of overpsychologizing the acting styles in his interpretation. Given that the borgate were originally built to house Romans displaced by fascist sventramenti, I prefer to entertain this imaginary scenario. That said, reading Ricci as a displaced Roman or as an immigrant from the countryside is a minor hermeneutic problem. The real point is that, regardless of where he comes from, this is where he lives.

28. Because the borgate were located so far outside the city, they might also be seen as attempts at urbanizing (what had been) the countryside. The very population that made up *il popolo romano* was drained from the city and installed in apartment blocks towering over fields and pasture land. One might almost say that Rome itself was moved to the borgate. The new neighborhoods eventually acted as forces of urbanization, drawing the city toward their dense population centers as the city was (already) moving out toward them (Insolera, *Roma moderna,* 141).

29. Ibid., 136–37.

30. Ibid., 140.

31. On internal immigration and the fascists' efforts to stop it, see Anna Treves, *Le migrazioni interne nell'Italia fascista: Politica e realtà demografica* (Turin: Einaudi, 1976).

32. Also mention should be made of the formation of the magazine *Casabella* during this period, which under the editorial direction of Giuseppe Pagano often espoused rather enlightened attitudes toward lower-class housing and urban planning. See Giuseppe Pagano, *Architettura e città durante il fascismo,* ed. Cesare De Seta (Rome: Editori Laterza, 1990).

33. Of course, situating EUR to the south reinforced Mussolini's aforementioned dream of Rome's advance, from Piazza Venezia and the Forum to the Tyrrhenian Sea and the mare nostrum.

34. For a comprehensive history of EUR, see Italo Insolera and Luigi di Majo, *L'EUR e Roma dagli anni trenta al duemila* (Rome: Editori Laterza, 1986).

35. Insolera, *Roma moderna,* 187; Paul Ginsborg cites slightly different figures: 1,961,754 in 1951 and 2,188,160 in 1961. Cf. *A History of Contemporary Italy: Society and Politics, 1945–1988* (London: Penguin Books, 1990), 220. For a concise and yet analytically useful discussion of the growth of urban centers in the twentieth century, refer to the chapter entitled "Myth of the Megalopolis," in Lewis Mumford's classic *The City in History* (Middlesex: Penguin, 1966), 598–646, esp. 607–22. Mumford links much of the city's growth to the rise of bureaucracy as much as industry, an interesting analysis when applied to the case of Rome.

36. Ginsborg, *History of Contemporary Italy,* 212, 213.

37. Ibid., 210–53. Another useful history of the economic miracle which investigates not just economic changes but also their concomitant cultural changes is Guido Crainz's *Storia del miracolo italiano: culture, identità, trasformazioni fra anni cinquanta e sessanta* (Rome: Donzelli Editore, 1996).

38. A skyscraper in Rome is a building several stories in height, not dozens as is the case with the American skyscraper.

39. Ginsborg, *History of Contemporary Italy,* 246.

40. Crainz offers a concise account of the changes wrought on Italian cities in the postwar period (*Storia del miracolo italiano,* 124–32).

41. *The Roof* will be discussed in subsequent chapters.

42. Ivone Margulies's recent essay in her edited collection is a much-needed addition to scholarship on the film. See "Exemplary Bodies: Reenactment in *Love in the City, Sons,* and *Close Up,*" in *Rites of Realism* (Durham, N.C.: Duke University Press, 2003), 217–44.

43. This area is the setting of *Mamma Roma,* though in that film we do not see these shanties.

44. Eleanor Clark, *Rome and a Villa* (New York: Pantheon, 1974), 5.

2. "Rome, Ringed by Its Hell of Suburbs"

1. Barth David Schwartz, *Pasolini Requiem* (New York: Vintage, 1995), 126.

2. Quoted in ibid., 127.

3. Not really his own because Pasolini, a child of the middle class (his mother's background was petit bourgeois, his father a military officer supposedly descended from minor Ferrarese nobility), was brought up to speak the standard Italian of the educated classes, the kind taught in school. As well, as I have mentioned, his Friulian is really an invention.

4. John Ahern, "Pasolini: His Poems, His Body," *Parnassus* 11, no. 2 (Fall/ Winter and Spring/Summer 1983–84): 108.

5. Schwartz, *Pasolini Requiem,* 126–29. Enzo Siciliano says the book was published in 1943. I do not know what accounts for this discrepancy; Siciliano, *Pasolini: A Biography,* trans. John Shepley (New York: Random House, 1982), 61. Contini was a major figure in Italian letters and his review was enormously important to Pasolini's own sense of personal accomplishment and to his ability to find work in Rome after his disgrace in Casarsa. For an account of the significance of the review, see Robert S. C. Gordon, *Pasolini: Forms of Subjectivity* (Oxford: Oxford University Press, 1996), 12–14.

6. This impact is the object of some controversy in Pasolini studies. Pasolini's first major biographer, Enzo Siciliano, a friend and literary critic and scholar, claimed that Rome's impact on Pasolini was immediate, ecstatic, and traumatic (see Siciliano, *Pasolini,* 151–54). Zygmunt Baranski develops a more nuanced approach to Pasolini's first years in Rome and in his very carefully argued essay, "Pasolini, Friuli, Rome (1950–1951): Philological and Historical Notes," which appears in a volume Baranski himself edited, *Pasolini Old and New: Surveys and Studies* (Dublin: Four Courts Press, 1999), 253–80. Baranski argues that close

attention to the chronology of Pasolini's output reveals a writer suspended (both in terms of style and content) between the world he has left behind and the city he now finds himself in. Baranski singles out Siciliano in particular, among other Pasolini scholars, for developing what Baranski sees as an overheated understanding of the effect Rome had on Pasolini's literary production in the very early 1950s. However, Baranski might have an overheated understanding of Siciliano, given that Siciliano himself says that in Pasolini's first Roman writings, "[t]he Friulian world and the Roman world shade into one another" (Siciliano, *Pasolini,* 155). Siciliano comments on several other transpositions that Pasolini performed between Friuli and Rome. Although I do not want to get too far ahead of my own argument here, I do want to flag this debate at the very outset of the analyses of Pasolini's poetry that follow. I think Baranski's very subtle genetic criticism and its historic precision give us a more careful picture of the shifts (small and large) in Pasolini's work as he moves from Friuli to Rome. However, in the evidence that I want to emphasize here, especially in Pasolini's first Roman poems, I think we witness a rather important stylistic shift taking place.

7. Ahern, "Pasolini," 105. The original Friulian reads:

> Sère imbarlumìda, tal fossâl
> 'a crès l'àghe, 'na fèmine plène
> a ciamina pal ciamp
>
> Jo ti recuàrdi, Narcìs, ti vèvis il colôr
> de la sère, quànt lis ciampànis
> 'a sùnin di muàrt.

Original Italian quoted from Pasolini, *Bestemmia: tutte le poesie,* vol. 3, ed. Graziella Chiarcossi and Walter Siti (Milan: Garzanti, 1993), 10.

8. The rural imagery could be used as evidence to claim that the poem exhibits a type of realism. The same might be said of the poem's being written in dialect. However, Pasolini's use of dialect, as argued above, seems more aimed at an elevation than a lowering of tone, the lowered tone being a recognized trope of realist literature. As well, the rural imagery also links the poetry to Pascoli who, despite his fragmentary rural imagery, is not what we might normally call a realist. Furthermore, the invocation of Narcissus clearly suggests this poem belongs elsewhere than in the canon of realist literature. Still, it is valuable, especially considering the number of contradictions in Pasolini's work, to remain sensitive to these tensions.

9. Schwartz, *Pasolini Requiem,* 64.

10. Edmund Wilson, *Axel's Castle* (New York: Scribner's, 1931), 64.

11. Ahern, "Pasolini," 106.

> Xe Domenega! Mi son so'o
> in un barcheta sul Lèmene
> El Burìn el xe de ve'udo
>
> Tuti i fa festa e mi so'o
> meso nudo sul cuòr del Lèmene
> scaldo i me strassi al sol de ve'udo

> No gò un scheo, son paròn so'o
> dei me cavei de oro sul Lèmene
> pien di pissìogoe de ve'udo.
> El xe pien de vizi el me cuòr so'o. (*Bestemmia*, 3:140)

Ahern's fine translation loses, perhaps necessarily, the effect of repetition in the ultimate word in each line. This form links the poem to medieval Provençal lyrical forms like the sestina and later lyrical forms like the villanelle. (I don't think the poem's form has a particular name.) Ezra Pound was intrigued by the sensual sounds of Provençal poetry, of which Pound authored some magnificent translations. It is likely Pasolini would have been aware of this work and there is detectable in the Friulian experiments some kinship to Pound's archaicizing interests. See Hugh Kenner, *The Pound Era* (Berkeley: University of California Press, 1971), 76–93, 110–20.

12. In this sense they are not unlike the Japanese haiku, another poetic form highly prized by Pound and other modernists.

13. Schwartz, *Pasolini Requiem*, 220.

14. Both Schwartz and Enzo Siciliano, Pasolini's major biographers, name September 30 as Saint Sabina's feast day (Schwartz, *Pasolini Requiem*, 220; Siciliano, *Pasolini*, 131). However, liturgical calendars that I have consulted list her feast day as August 29. I do not know to what this inconsistency is to be credited. Perhaps Ramuscello had its own tradition of honoring the saint on a different day.

15. Schwartz, *Pasolini Requiem*, 223.

16. Cited in ibid., 223. Interestingly, the article identifies Pasolini as a poet and places him in the company of Gide and Sartre. We might imagine that both of these gestures might have been some small consolation to Pasolini during this time of enormous duress.

17. See n. 6 above.

18. Anthony Oldcorn, "Pasolini and the City: Rome 1950, A Diary," *Italian Quarterly* 21–22, nos. 82–83 (Fall 1980/Winter 1981): 109–10.

19. Ibid., 113.

> Adulto? Mai—mai come l'esistenza
> che non *matura*—resta sempre *acerba*,
> di splendido giorno in splendido giorno—
> io non posso che restare fedele
> alla stupenda monotonia del mistero.
> Ecco perché, nella felicità,
> non mi sono mai abbandonato—ecco
> perchè nell'ansia delle mie colpe
> non ho mai toccato un rimorso vero.
> Pari, sempre pari con l'inespresso,
> all'origine di quello che io sono.

Original Italian quoted from *Bestemmia*, 3:297. The poem's use of the words *matura* and *acerba*, "ripe" and "unripe," respectively, may also be understood as residual presence of the rural in Pasolini's (now urban) poetry.

20. Here and in the rest of the poetry that I will be analyzing later, I make no distinction between the speaker of the poem and Pasolini himself. I understand that this lack of distinction amounts to a New Critical heresy; however, Pasolini insists on the deeply autobiographical significance and rigorously personal resonance of his poetry. It would be counterintuitive, not to mention unnecessarily obfuscatory, to refer to the "I" of the poems as "the speaker" and not "Pasolini." As Robert S. C. Gordon has noted, "Pasolini does indeed . . . constantly offer himself up for display in his work, but to such a degree that conventional mediation is cast aside; he is personally, bodily present within language" (Gordon, *Pasolini*, 2).

21. Probably this neighborhood was spared because it lies safely between the Corso Vittorio Emmanuele and the Via del Teatro del Marcello, two thoroughfares already privileged by Rome's modern planners.

22. Oldcorn, "Pasolini and the City," 114.

> [. . .]—fresco e inerte un motore si allontana
> sul selciato umido—grida e rigrida
> il venditore, con il suo carretto—
> sotto i bucati inquieti, è un coro
> disarmonico, cieco. (*Bestemmia*, 3:300)

23. We know from biographical accounts that he has made initial forays into the borgate—sexual errands—but he has yet to describe these places in these, his earliest Roman writings.

24. Oldcorn, "Pasolini and the City," 113.

> Quando piú chiara la felicità
> della gente, nei vicoli, risuona
> contro pareti grondanti di sole,
> e passano carretti, tra fanciulli,
> gattini, giovani abbracciati—come
> echeggia più fondo nel pensiero,
> squallido alone delle cose,
> il destino. . . . E se più vivo un suono contro
> la morte—una canzone, un grido
> di bambino—si leva . . . se più dolce, stinto
> a una stupita nube si fa il sole,
> sulla strada . . . no! non lo puoi pensare . . . (*Bestemmia*, 3:299)

25. I admire Oldcorn's translations quite a lot, and only pick at and around them in order to further my own interpretive project. I don't suggest that they are at all inadequate.

26. Oldcorn, "Pasolini and the City," 118.

> [. . .]e sulle periferie, da Testaccio
> a Monteverde, stagna stanco e humido
> un vibrare di voci passanti
> e motori—sperduta incrostazione
> del nostro mondo sul muto universo. (*Bestemmia*, 3:312)

27. Many of Pasolini's later letters become all very business-like, concerning themselves with publishing deals, the constant annoyances of filmmaking, and so on.

28. Letter to Silvana Mauri, February 11, 1950, Rome, in *The Letters of Pier Paolo Pasolini,* vol. 1, *1940–1954,* ed. Nico Naldini, trans. Stuart Hood (London: Quartet Books, 1992), 331 (hereafter *Letters*).

29. Letter to Silvana Mauri, spring 1952, Rome, in *Letters,* 371.

30. Letter to Silvana Mauri, summer 1952, Rome, in *Letters,* 380 (emphasis mine).

31. I will discuss the subject of allegory in Pasolini's work in my conclusion.

32. Later Pasolini would begin to theorize "concrete facts" as being signs of themselves, a more complicated take on matters than what we see mentioned in this letter. For an example of this theoretical position, see Pasolini, "Res Sunt Nomina," in *Heretical Empiricism,* ed. Louise K. Barnett, trans. Ben Lawton and Louise K. Barnett (Bloomington: Indiana University Press, 1988), 255–60. The title of this essay means "things are names," that is, signs.

33. Rohdie, *Passion of Pier Paolo Pasolini,* 109.

34. Siciliano, *Pasolini,* 173. I would imagine that Baranski would find this a rather too convenient attitude to strike. Nonetheless, so much was happening in such a compressed period of time that, unless one's objective is to establish a precise chronology of events, then I think the "simultaneous whirlpools" approach is legitimate.

35. Albert Moravia, *The Woman of Rome,* trans. Lydia Holland (New York: Farrar, Straus and Cudahy, 1949), 9.

36. Ibid., 214. Piazza Esedra is now referred to as Piazza della Repubblica.

37. *The Ragazzi,* trans. Emile Capouya (Manchester, England: Carcanet Press, 1986), 8. This translation was first published by Grove Press in 1968.

38. Because (as mentioned above) the novel is set during the end of the German occupation and the first years of the *dopoguerra,* Pasolini's evocation of it is more down at the heel than it actually might have appeared in the mid 1950s when the novel was published.

39. *The Ragazzi,* 14.

40. Ibid., 57.

41. David Ward, *A Poetics of Resistance: Narrative and the Writings of Pier Paolo Pasolini* (Madison, N.J.: Fairleigh-Dickinson Press, 1995), 60.

42. Pasolini, "Dal vero," *Alì dagli occhi azzurri* (Milan: Garzanti, 1996), 103–10. *Alì dagli occhi azzurri* was orginally published in 1965.

43. Pier Paolo Pasolini, *Stories from the City of God: Sketches and Chronicles of Rome, 1950–1966,* ed. Walter Siti, trans. Marina Harss (New York: Handsel Books, 2003), 165 (hereafter *Stories*). Subsequent page numbers appear in the text.

44. The Christian Democrats were the center-right-wing party of the DC (Democrazia Cristiana) and dominated political life from 1948 up through the early 1960s.

3. "Scandalous Desecration"

1. Geoffrey Nowell-Smith, "Pasolini's Originality," in *Pier Paolo Pasolini,* ed. Paul Willemen (London: BFI, 1977), 11. To my mind, this short article, published only two years after Pasolini's death, remains one of the most interesting and acute discussions of Pasolini's filmmaking to be found anywhere.

2. A recent study which pays some long overdue attention to the role that the city of Rome plays in *Roma città aperta* is an eponymous monograph on the film by David Forgacs (London: BFI, 2000).

3. In Italian such a floating barge is called a *galleggiante.* One of Pasolini's early urban vignettes is set on one of these: "The Drink," in *Stories,* 8–13.

4. Nowell-Smith maintains that Pasolini's uniqueness is found precisely in his system of editing, a claim with which I feel sympathy. Here is Nowell-Smith on Pasolini's editing style: "The image track in *Accattone* really does consist literally of images, loosely linked to each other via the content of what is being narrated, but visually dislocated from each other and, singly, often bizarre" ("Pasolini's Originality," 10).

5. P. Adams Sitney, *Vital Crises in Italian Cinema: Iconography, Stylistics, Politics* (Austin: University of Texas Press, 1995), 180. Sitney's book is, ten years after it was published, still the best study of the general period of postwar Italian filmmaking to be published in English.

6. Marcia Landy, *Italian Film* (Cambridge: Cambridge University Press, 2000), 176. "Mistakenly" because there is no crosscutting; the Bernini statue and *Accattone* appear in the same shot.

7. Restivo, *Cinema of Economic Miracles,* 54–55. Restivo emphasizes the fact that the Castel Sant'Angelo was used as a prison in medieval Rome. Restivo also points out that the bridge and the castle both receive their name from the legend that the Emperor Constantine had visions of an angel appearing above the castle that led him to declare Christianity the official religion of the Roman Empire (interestingly another example, like the Via della Conciliazione, of a typically Roman accord between temporal and ecclesiastical power). Restivo interprets the shots in which the bridge and the castle are visible as signs of a "contamination" of the "center with the periphery." In this I think he is right; however, he does not take into account the irony that I find more compelling: borgatari like *Accattone* may very well have lived near this bridge prior to the aforementioned sventramenti, a fact that would complicate his reading somewhat. We both obviously share a dissatisfaction with the way that, in Restivo's words, "none of the recent criticism of the film bothers to identify the location ... [of the scene] beyond stating that *Accattone* jumps from a bridge 'with angels.'" I recommend that readers consult his reading of the spatiality of *Accattone* (52–56).

8. Maurizio Viano, *A Certain Realism: Making Use of Pasolini's Film Theory and Practice* (Berkeley: University of California Press, 1993), 73.

9. In the case of his film *Theorem* (*Teorema,* 1968), for instance, the film and its "novelization" (for lack of a better word) confound any attempt to settle questions of autonomy and primacy. Book and film are parallel artifacts; neither is properly the source of the other, or else each is the source for the other.

10. Pier Paolo Pasolini, *Accattone, Mamma Roma, Ostia* (Milan: Garzanti Editore, 1993). The description of the children as angels might provoke skepticism about my argument against the metaphorical reading of the bridge sequence. I think, though, that the screenplay is literary and metaphorical, and occasionally, as in this case, clichéd in a way that the film is not.

11. The screenplay does not indicate an exact location, nor is it possible to tell the location from the film itself, but clearly we are *fuori le mura*—outside the walls.

12. The use of the Bach here is an interesting and complex issue. Clearly the relation of the music to the narrative context and the camera movement, as well as the obvious violence of Pasolini's appropriation of the music, all contribute to the strangeness of this scene. Although I do not choose to pursue in any detail Pasolini's use of music in this book, we can at least be certain that he is suggesting this film's narrative as a type of "passion" story.

13. *Accattone, Mamma Roma, Ostia*, 96.

14. Pasolini, "Confessioni tecniche," *Uccellacci e uccellini* (Milan: Garzanti, 1966), 44.

15. Pasolini's screenplay only denotes the location as "strada miserabile," or miserable street (*Accattone, Mamma Roma, Ostia*, 111). But, as mentioned at the end of the last chapter, this is the neighborhood Pasolini discusses in his article "The Concentration Camps," therefore we know his knowledge of the place is specific, despite the generic designation in the screenplay. For further documentation of the location, see Michele Mancini and Giuseppe Perrella in *Pier Paolo Pasolini: corpi e luoghi* (Rome: Theorema Edizioni, 1981), 389. For photographs and a basic account of the borgata, see Italo Insolera, "La Capitale in espansione," *Urbanistica* 29, nos. 28–29 (October 1959): 46–47; Piero Ostilio Rossi, *Roma: Guida all'architettura moderna, 1909–2000* (Rome: Editori Laterea, 2000), 74–78. Although it has no illustrative photographs, another good source is Marcello Ricci, "L'architettura delle borgate negli anni trenta," in *Case Romane*, ed. Angeletti et al., 20–23.

16. This information is all rehearsed in the sources cited in the previous footnote. An aerial photograph reproduced in Rossi (*Roma*, 78) shows very clearly the Gordiani's isolation; empty fields surround it on all sides. By the time Pasolini was making *Accattone*, the city had since grown out toward it somewhat.

17. Insolera, "La Capitale in espansione," 46.

18. Balilla was the name of the fascist boy's brigade. Pasolini's use of the name is clearly directed at resuscitating the memory of fascism which he believed to be very much alive, only going under an assumed name—that of neocapitalism. Almost all of the essays in Pasolini's *Lutheran Letters*, trans. Stuart Hood (New York: Carcanet, 1987), for example, give evidence of his belief that postwar neocapitalism was a continuation—and a more potent version—of fascism.

19. Balilla makes the sign of the cross once more, at the film's very end, but this second time he does it in reverse, rendering the gesture, perhaps, heretical.

20. The shot most readily brings to mind a similar one from the work of Visconti. Toward the end of *La terra trema* (1948)—the only great Italian film to

feature the exclusive use of nonactors—when 'Ntoni and his brothers are forced to apply for fishing work after the loss of their craft, there is visible on the wall behind the mocking foreman an inscription quoted from Mussolini: "Decisamente verso il popolo"—"Decisively towards the people." The irony could not be more bitter or more acute. In *Accattone* the sense of the "found" inscription is not ironic. Rather it serves as a marker of the specific context of deprivation and urban crisis that is the subtext, or the horizon of the film.

21. For a discussion of optical point of view and camera work, see Edward Branigan, "Formal Permutations of the Point of View Shot," *Screen* 16, no. 3 (Autumn 1975): 54–64, and also by Branigan, *Point of View in the Cinema* (Berlin: Mouton, 1984), 103–21.

22. Stephen Heath, *Questions of Cinema* (Bloomington: Indiana University Press, 1981), 51.

23. "Tu te ne porti di costui l'etterno / per una lagrimetta che 'l mi toglie . . ." ("For just one tear / you carry off his deathless part"), *Purgatorio,* V, lines 106–7, trans. Allen Mandelbaum (New York: Bantam, 1984), 70.

24. Kevin Lynch, *The Image of the City* (Cambridge: MIT Press, 1960), 4–5. Interestingly, Lynch's study appeared in print in 1960, one year before *Accattone* was released. I do not suggest Pasolini's awareness of the book—in fact, I would wager he knew nothing of it. But clearly both Lynch and Pasolini must be seen to be participants in an investigation going on throughout Europe and America into the redefinition of urban space in the post–World War II period of economic prosperity in the west.

25. Fredric Jameson makes significant reference to Lynch's work in the conclusion to the first chapter of *Postmodernism, or the Cultural Logic of Late Capitalism* (Durham, N.C.: Duke University Press, 1993), 51–54. Jameson is interested in Lynch's notion of "cognitive mapping"—a complex activity described in the above quotation from Lynch. Jameson argues that the postmodern redefinition of space—which he interprets as a move into the sublime—prevents such cognitive mapping (of both actual physical space and of cultural-economic forces) from being performed. He suggests that the way out of postmodernity's paralyzing "spatial" and "social confusion" is to find a means of performing "global cognitive mapping" (54). Presumably—although Jameson does not make this clear—such mapping would be dependent on yet another, as-yet-unforeseen redefinition of space that would force space out of the sublime, which, by definition, cannot be represented—mapped, if you will.

26. Again, Nowell-Smith, on Pasolini's approach to editing, argues that *Accattone* displays an "almost total lack of any internal system of narration" ("Pasolini's Originality," 10).

27. Such an understanding of the binary opposition between realism and modernism animates much politicized film theory, particularly that theory produced in the 1970s, a theory that in many ways fed on and was stimulated by the creative work of leftist postwar filmmakers like Godard and Pasolini. An interesting and illustrative example of this understanding of the relationship between realism and modernism is Colin MacCabe's essay, "Realism and the

Cinema: Notes on Some Brechtian Theses," in *Tracking the Signifier, Theoretical Essays: Film, Linguistics, Literature* (Minneapolis: University of Minnesota Press, 1985), 33–57. This essay first appeared in *Screen* 15, no. 2 (Summer 1974). *Screen* was, in the 1970s, the major outlet for this sort of theoretical work that privileged Brechtian modernism over "transparent" realism.

28. I owe my use of the term *sticky* to my friend and colleague Victoria Coulson and her work on Henry James. I doubt I use it in exactly the same way she would, but the debt is there all the same. See "Sticky Realism: Armchair Hermeneutics in Late James," *The Henry James Review* 25 (2004): 115–26.

29. Clark, *Painting of Modern Life*, 29, 30.

30. Italy's national film school (now called the Scuola Nazionale di Cinema).

31. Pier Paolo Pasolini, "An Epical-Religious View of the World," *Film Quarterly* (Summer 1965): 42–43. Franco Citti is the nonprofessional actor and native of the borgate who played the title role in *Accattone*. Pigneto is an area of the periphery where several scenes of *Accattone* were shot.

32. Central Rome, of course, is also contaminated, a pastiche: Christian churches cobbled out of ancient Roman spoglie (fragments of ruins); baroque facades masking medieval structures, and so on. The periphery plays out this same drama of juxtaposition, only in a very shoddy register. As well, we might see contamination at work as all the way back in the Friulian poems in which a rural dialect is married to a sophisticated poetic undertaking. It is important to see how contamination is a consistent procedure in Pasolini's work, but also how this procedure is radicalized in the context of the Roman periphery.

33. Schwartz, *Pasolini Requiem*, 357.

34. Ibid. Pasolini tells his own version of the story quite colorfully in *Accattone, Mamma Roma, Ostia*, 27–40.

35. Luigi Chiarini, "Neo-Realism Betrayed," in *Springtime in Italy: A Reader in Neorealism*, ed. David Overbey (London: Talisman, 1978), 208.

36. We could make a similar argument for some of the work of Visconti.

37. Pasolini, quoted in Sitney, *Vital Crises in Italian Cinema*, 174. This passage appears originally in an essay called "Nota su *Le notti*" that Pasolini published in "*Le notti di Cabiria*" di *Federico Fellini*, ed. Lino Del Fra (Modena: Cappelli, 1965), 228–34.

38. Pasolini, quoted in Oswald Stack, *Pasolini on Pasolini* (Bloomington: Indiana University Press, 1969), 42. Pasolini's criticism was echoed in the 1970s by a devastating article by Mario Cannella, "Ideology and Aesthetic Hypotheses in the Criticism of Neo-Realism," *Screen* 14, no. 4 (Winter 1973–74): 5–60. The general thrust of Cannella's argument is to fault neorealism and the anti- (or perhaps simply post-) fascist culture to which it belonged for contenting itself with merely differentiating itself from fascism without going further to rethink the basic social and economic formations of Italian culture. Thus the antifascist Resistance was installed uncritically as a foundational myth, observed by Italians on the right and the left, of the new Italian republic, which began in 1948. This apotheosis of antifascism as the master discourse of postwar Italy rings false, though, when one considers that many of the functionaries, officials,

bureaucrats, and civil and criminal laws of the fascist period very quietly weathered the transition to republican government. Cannella sees the hagiography of neorealism performed by its critics as participating in a similar whitewash. He blames neorealism and especially the movement's exegetes for repeating in the realm of aesthetics the same error committed in the domain of the political in postwar Italy, namely failing to recognize that "in order to create the conditions under which fascism will never again arise meant then and means now to construct socialism" (26). I encountered Cannella's very strident, unforgiving article as a graduate student when I was reading through hundreds of articles on a bibliography for a doctoral examination in Italian film history. The article, which when I read it seemed to explain so much and so definitively, has had a limited afterlife in film studies. Its reading of neorealism (like Pasolini's, as I will explain below) is very narrow. However, there is something appealing about its take-no-prisoners Marxist critique, however shortsighted and limiting that might be, and I can't help referring to it here, if only as a way of making visible the trace it left on my earlier (callow) understanding of Italian film history and neorealism. For an insightful revisionist account of neorealism, cf. Alfonso Canziani, *Gli anni del neorealismo* (Florence: La Nuova Italia Editrice, 1977), 15–32.

39. Roberto Rossellini, *My Method: Writings and Interviews,* ed. Adriano Aprà (New York: Marsilio, 1995), 35. These quotations do not give justice to all that Rossellini had to say on the subject, but they do clearly mark his difference from Pasolini.

40. For a brief introduction to leftist responses to neorealism, see Ugo Finetti, "Cenni sulla critica marxista e il neorealismo," in *Il neorealismo cinematografico italiano,* ed. Lino Miccichè (Venice: Marsilio, 1999), 262–73. Many on the Italian left in the 1950s felt that filmmakers had abandoned the cause of neorealism prematurely. Often Visconti's *Senso* has been used as a marker for this falling away. For an instance of such criticism, see Chiarini, quoted above.

41. On the difficulty of ever deciding what neorealism even was, see Lino Miccichè, "Per una verifica del neorealismo," in *Il neorealismo cinematografico italiano,* ed. Miccichè, 7–28.

42. Nowell-Smith, "Pasolini's Originality," 10.

43. Cesare Zavattini, "Some Ideas on the Cinema," in *Film: A Montage of Theories,* ed. Richard Dyer MacCann (New York: E. P. Dutton, 1966), 218.

44. Ibid., 218.

45. Ibid., 218–19.

46. André Bazin, *"Umberto D.:* A Great Work," in *What Is Cinema,* vol. 2, ed. and trans. Hugh Gray (Berkeley: University of California Press, 1971), 82.

47. He uses this term often, for instance, in the interview quoted above: Pier Paolo Pasolini, "An Epical-Religious View of the World."

48. Bazin articulates a theory of realist cinema in which the cinema must, in a sense, submit itself to the profilmic (i.e., the world, or the real) rather than seek to remake the world or to make judgments about it. He prizes the Italian neorealists in this respect because "[t]hey never forget that the world *is,* quite simply, before it is something to be condemned" (Bazin, "An Aesthetic of Reality:

Neorealism [Cinematic Realism and the Italian School of the Liberation]," in *What Is Cinema?*, ed. and trans. Gray, 2:21). Orson Welles and Jean Renoir also figure importantly in Bazin's attempt to articulate this aesthetic. His most important essays in this regard are the essay just quoted, as well as "The Evolution of the Language of Cinema" and "The Virtues and Limitations of Montage," both in *What Is Cinema?*, vol. 1, ed. and trans. Hugh Gray (Berkeley: University of California Press, 1967), 23–52.

49. See Pasolini, "The Written Language of Reality," and "Quips on the Cinema," both in *Heretical Empiricism*, ed. Louise K. Barnett, trans. Ben Lawton and Louise K. Barnett (Bloomington: Indiana University Press, 1988), 197–222, and 223–43 respectively.

50. All of the Pasolini literature, almost without exception, preoccupies itself with this theoretical contention of Pasolini's. Readers may refer to several essays published in Patrick Rumble and Bart Testa, eds., *Pier Paolo Pasolini: Contemporary Perspectives* (Toronto: University of Toronto Press, 1994), and Baranski, ed., *Pasolini Old and New*, cited above, as well as to the useful discussion of Pasolini's film theory in Robert S. C. Gordon's *Pasolini: Forms of Subjectivity*, also cited above.

51. "Quips on the Cinema," 225.

52. One could interpret, however, this last, small gesture of compassion as insufficient (to cancel the social critique that takes up most of the rest of the film). One could also reasonably argue that De Sica intends the spectator to absorb such an awareness of insufficiency. To do so would mean to interpret De Sica as an ironist, something I don't think he is. He is, however, at his most ironic in *Miracle in Milan* in which, after showing no solution to the problems of the underhoused shantytown dwellers in the film, he has these characters fly off into the heavens on broomsticks. This film is, therefore, a very bitter fable, one whose caustic critique is perhaps slightly camouflaged by its elements of fantasy. Here and in all of my discussions of De Sica and neorealism I must thank Laura Rascaroli who has encouraged me to think in a much more complicated way about these issues.

53. Interestingly, that structure is encountered early on in the discussion of Pasolini's story, "Studies on the Life of Testaccio." This ending also echoes a piece that Pasolini published in 1959, "Roman Deaths," a kind of series of vignettes intended as the subject for a film. Each vignette takes place on or around a bridge in Rome; each also ends in death. The story moves from center to periphery: each successive story is set at a bridge further from the center than the last. See *Stories*, 85–98.

54. Naomi Greene, *Pier Paolo Pasolini: Cinema as Heresy* (Princeton, N.J.: Princeton University Press, 1990), 25.

55. Ibid. She argues that its bleakness is similar to but exceeds that of *Bicycle Thieves* and Visconti's *La terra trema*.

56. I realize I may be charged with serious overreading here—and perhaps not only here. However, the way in which Pasolini so rigorously (even doggedly) observes spatial continuity in the long traveling shot sequences makes

his decisions to flout spatial-geographical continuity, as he does here and in the sequence of the funeral procession in the Borgata Gordiani, all the more interesting as objects of interpretive speculation.

57. Pasolini quoted in Stack, *Pasolini on Pasolini,* 132.

58. I do not know of a neorealist film in which a scene is filmed in one long, stationary take.

59. The reader should refer to the Bazin essays cited above. Bazin rarely singles out the long take as such, or by name, but its significance to his theory of cinematic realism (in Italian neorealism, as well as in Welles and Renoir) is implicit; witness, for instance, the praise he bestows on Renoir for making cinema that "would permit everything to be said without chopping the world up into little fragments" ("Evolution of the Language of Cinema," 38) or his contentment that Italian neorealists left themselves "free to use the camera unfettered by the microphone," which allowed them to "enlarge the camera's field of action and its mobility with, consequently, an immediate raising of the reality coefficient" ("Aesthetic of Reality," 30). In Anglo-American film studies there is often detectable a slippage between Bazin's understanding of neorealism and of the films themselves, which is problematic. Furthermore, Bazin, in his understandable excitement over what were to him at the time the most exciting and revolutionary of films, often tends to overvalue the formal radicality of neorealist films.

60. It should be borne in mind that these long moving takes, despite their prominence in *Accattone* and *Mamma Roma,* do not appear again to any great effect in Pasolini's later work. They are an enormous, significant exception to his aesthetic, which tends to favor abrupt cutting between still (though often shakily handheld) shots of varying duration (though his shots are never very short, either). It is telling that the long sequence shots appear only in his two films that expressly take as their subject and setting the Roman periphery

61. Stack, *Pasolini on Pasolini,* 39. Also see "The Fear of Naturalism," in *Heretical Empiricism,* ed. Barnett, 244–46.

62. Pasolini, "Is Being Natural?," in *Heretical Empiricism,* ed. Barnett, 241.

63. Ibid.

64. I find this a very difficult place in Pasolini's work and I can't explain satisfactorily where this fulmination comes from, or why he seems intent on forgetting what were some of the most interesting formal features of his first two films. When Pasolini wrote "Is Being Natural?" in 1967 he was moving in the direction of a politically charged cinema predicated on allegory. This movement will be the subject of my conclusion. It is difficult, as well, to take a theoretical text written by Pasolini some six years after *Accattone*'s release and use it anachronistically as a heuristic for that earlier piece of work, but I hope my reasons for doing so will become clear later in this chapter.

65. Jean-Luc Godard, in Jean Domarchi, Jacques Donio-Valcroze, Jean-Luc Godard, Pierre Kast, Jacques Rivette, and Eric Rohmer, "Hiroshima, notre amour," in *Cahiers du Cinéma: The 1950s: Neorealism, Hollywood, New Wave,* ed. Jim Hillier (Cambridge: Harvard University Press, 1985), 62.

66. Trabalzi, "Low Cost Housing in Twentieth-Century Rome," 137.

67. Later in the film *Accattone* does try his hand at hard labor, but he gives up before even finishing a single day's work.

68. Siegfried Kracauer, *Theory of Film: The Redemption of Physical Reality* (New York: Oxford University Press, 1965), 63–64.

69. Bazin, "*Umberto D.*," 81.

4. Pasolini, the Peripheral Sublime, and Public Housing

1. Pasolini, *Bestemmia,* 4:475.

> Correvo nel crepuscolo fangoso
> dietro a scali sconvolti, a mute
> impalcature, tra rioni bagnati
> nell'odore del ferro, degli stracci
> riscaldati, che dentro una fetida
> polvere, tra casupole di latta
> e scoli, inalzavano pareti
> recenti e ormai scrostate, contro un fondo
> di stinta metropoli.
>   Sull'asfalto
> scalzato, tra i peli di un'erba acre
> di escrementi e spianate
> nere di fango—che la pioggia scavava
> in infetto tepore—le dirotte
> file dei ciclisti, dei rantolanti
> camion di legname, si sperdevano
> di tanto in tanto, in centri di sobborghi
> dove già qualche bar aveva cerchi
> di bianchi lumi . . .

2. Dante invented this form, which is composed of interlocking rhyming iambic tercets: aba bcb cdc, and so on. (In Italian each three line unit is called a *terzina*.) The form obviously refers to the Holy Trinity and fits in neatly with Dante's tripartite schema for his *Divine Comedy* with its Inferno, Purgatory, and Paradise. Pasolini's loose terza rima only occasionally interlocks; even so the composition in tercets express an implicit Dantean premise, especially to an Italian audience. Although not central to my concerns here, I should point out that Dante's *Divine Comedy* was a work of not only spiritual autobiography, but also civic and political critique, aimed squarely at making an intervention in contemporary Florentine political life. Thus Pasolini's nod to Dante also underlines his own ambitions of becoming a "poeta civile," a voice of authority on contemporary political and cultural life in twentieth-century Italy.

3. Jewell, *The Poeisis of History,* 33. I would argue that the "escape" from "a classic fixedness of literary forms" is itself consonant with any number of modernist aesthetic practices.

4. Ibid., 33.

5. Pasolini, *Pier Paolo Pasolini: Poems,* ed. and trans. Norman MacAfee (New York: Noonday Press, 1996), 25 (hereafter *Poems*).

6. Bertolucci's first job in cinema was as assistant director on the set of *Accattone.*

7. *Poems,* 25–27.

8. Ibid., 27.

9. Though to read *The Waste Land* as only or merely dystopic is limiting.

10. The callous skin that the inhabitant of the metropolis must grow in order to survive is discussed by Georg Simmel: "[T]he metropolitan type— which naturally takes on a thousand different modifications—creates a protective organ for itself against the profound disruption with which the fluctuations and discontinuities of the external milieu threaten it"; "The Metropolis and Mental Life," in *On Individuality and Social Forms,* ed. Donald N. Levine (Chicago: University of Chicago Press, 1971), 326.

11. Georg Simmel on this condition: "Social life in the large city as compared with the towns shows a great preponderance of occasions to see rather than to hear people. . . . Before the appearance of omnibuses, railroads, and streetcars in the nineteenth century, men were not in a situation where for periods of minutes or hours they could or must look at each other without talking to one another" (quoted in Vidler, *Warped Space,* 69).

12. *Poems,* 29.

13. "PERMESIVANELACITTÀDOLENTE,/PERMESIVANEL'ETTERNODOLORE,/ PER ME SI VA TRA LA PERDUTA GENTE."Inferno,Canto III, 1–3. *TheDivineComedy*of Dante Alighieri, trans. Allen Mandelbaum (New York: Bantam, 1982), 21.

14. Schwartz, *Pasolini Requiem,* 252.

15. *Poems,* 29–33.

16. What linguistically would be referred to as a velar aspirate.

17. "dove si perdeva/ la città fra i tuguri . . ."

18. *Poems,* 33–35. MacAfee uses the word "slum" as a translation for both "periferia" (31) and "borgo" (33). This conflation is consonant with the slippage that occurs in common usage between "periphery" and "borgate."

19. Ibid., 51.

20. Ibid., 51–53.

21. Immanuel Kant, *The Critique of Judgment,* trans. J. H. Bernard (Amherst, N.Y.: Prometheus Books, 2000), 102. Interestingly, Lewis Mumford says of the megalopolis something very apropos of what I am describing here in regards to the Roman periphery and the sublime of boundlessness: "The form of the metropolis is formlessness, even as its aim is its own aimless expansion" (Mumford, *The City in History* [New York: Harcourt, Brace and World, 1961], 619). Formlessness, in and of itself, does not produce an experience of the sublime; formless boundlessness, however, would seem to meet the conditions necessary to induce an experience of the sublime, as this is theorized by Kant.

22. Kant, *Critique of Judgment,* 101–2.

23. Ibid., 102–3.

24. In Kantian aesthetics, of course, beauty is always purposive, but without a purpose.

25. Kant, *Critique of Judgment*, 103.

26. Ibid.

27. Ibid., 119. To follow Kant properly, there is no sublime object per se. However, occasionally, in a kind of shorthand, I may use the term to refer to that object which gives rise to an awareness of the sublime. I hope the analytic philosophers among my readers will excuse this transgression.

28. Kant, *Critique of Judgment*, 119.

29. Ibid., 119–20.

30. Jean-François Lyotard, *The Inhuman* (Stanford, Calif.: Stanford University Press, 1991), 98.

31. Kant, *Critique of Judgment*, 120.

32. Pasolini, *Lutheran Letters*, 10–11.

33. We can be sure of Pasolini's familiarity with the Romantic tradition of describing Rome as something sublime. The title poem of *The Ashes of Gramsci* is set in the Protestant cemetery where Keats and Shelley (and, of course, Gramsci) are buried. The poem makes explicit reference to the tradition of English Romantic graveyard poetry. Jewell is quite good on this subject (*Poeisis of History*, 23–52).

34. Percy Bysshe Shelley, "Prometheus Unbound" (preface), *Shelley's Poetry and Prose*, 2nd ed., ed. Donald H. Reiman and Neil Fraistat (New York: W. W. Norton, 2002), 206. In his poem "Adonais," written in memory of Keats, who died in Rome, Shelley calls Rome "at once the Paradise, / The grave, the city, and the wilderness" (*Shelley's Poetry and Prose*, 425).

35. *The Letters of Percy Bysshe Shelley*, vol. 2, ed. Frederick Jones (Oxford: Clarendon Press, 1964), 84–85.

36. Lord Byron, "Childe Harolde's Pilgrimage," in *With Byron in Italy*, ed. Anna Benneson McMahan (London: T. Fisher Unwin, 1907), 80–81.

37. George Eliot in *Middlemarch* gives a powerful account of her heroine Dorothea Brooke's bewildering, sublime experience of Rome on her honeymoon:

"[Dorothea] was beholding Rome, the city of visible history, where the past of a whole hemisphere seems moving in funeral procession with strange ancestral images and trophies gathered from afar.

"But this stupendous fragmentariness heightened the dream-like strangeness of her bridal life . . .

"To those who have looked at Rome with the quickening power of a knowledge which breathes a growing soul into all historic shapes, and traces out the suppressed transitions which unite all contrasts, Rome may still be the spiritual centre and interpreter of the world. But let them conceive one more historical contrast: the gigantic broken revelation of that Imperial and Papal city thrust abruptly on the notions of a girl who had been brought up in English and Swiss Puritanism, fed on meagre Protestant histories and on art chiefly of the hand-screen sort; a girl whose ardent nature turned all her small allowance of knowledge into principles, fusing her actions into their mould, and whose quick emotions gave the most abstract things the quality of a pleasure or a pain; a girl who had lately become a wife, and from the enthusiastic acceptance of untried duty found herself plunged in tumultuous preoccupation with her personal lot. The weight of unintelligible Rome might lie easily on bright nymphs to whom it formed a background for the brilliant picnic of Anglo-foreign society; but Dorothea had no such defence against deep impressions. Ruins and basilicas, palaces and colossi, set in the midst of a sordid present, where all that was living and warm-blooded seemed sunk in the deep degeneracy of a superstition divorced from reverence; the dimmer but yet eager Titanic life gazing and struggling on walls and ceilings; the long vistas of white forms whose marble eyes seemed to hold the monotonous light of an alien world: all this vast wreck of ambitious ideals, sensuous and spiritual, mixed confusedly with the signs of breathing forgetfulness and degradation, at first jarred her as with an electric shock, and then urged themselves on her with that ache belonging to a glut of confused ideas which check the flow of emotion. Forms both pale and glowing took possession of her young sense, and fixed themselves in her memory even when she was not thinking of them, preparing strange associations which remained through her after years. Our moods are apt to bring with them images which succeed each other like the magic-lantern pictures of a doze; and in certain states of dull forlornness Dorothea all her life continued to see the vastness of St. Peter's, the huge bronze canopy, the excited intention in the attitudes and garments of the prophets and evangelists in the mosaics above, and the red drapery which was being hung for Christmas spreading itself everywhere like a disease of the retina;" *Middlemarch* (London: Penguin, 1994), 187–89. Eliot, of course, is not a Romantic; *Middlemarch* was published first in 1872. However, clearly her description of Dorothea's experience is based not only on her (Eliot's) direct observation, but also on her reading of the Romantics. Also, Kant himself attributes to St. Peter's the ability to evoke an impression of the sublime (Kant, *Critique of Judgment*, 112). Eliot knew something of German philosophy, so it is possible that she is giving us, as it were, textbook Kant.

38. Ottavio Mark Casale, ed. and trans., *A Leopardi Reader* (Urbana: University of Illinois Press, 1981), 80–81.

39. Sergio Poretti, 'Monumenti sommessi,' in *Guida ai quartieri romani INA Casa,* ed. Margherita Guccione et al. (Rome: Gangemi Editore, 2002), 11. This book was produced in connection with a show; together they mounted a major occasion for the reconsideration of the successes and failures of this ambitious housing scheme.

40. Peter G. Rowe, *Civic Realism* (Cambridge: MIT Press, 1997), 106. Also see Ginsborg, *History of Contemporary Italy,* 246–47, and the aforementioned Guccione et al., *Guida ai quartieri romani INA Casa.* The excellent photographs that illustrate this last book give a sense of the way these buildings have weathered the years since their construction. Perhaps the most comprehensive overview

of INA Casa, although written from an official point of view that is only slightly critical, is Luigi B. Anguissola, ed., *I 14 anni del Piano INA Casa* (Rome: Staderini Editore, 1963). The book is rich in photographs and architectural drawings, with a brief synopsis of each INA Casa project. INA stands for Istituto Nazionale Abitazioni (National Housing Institute). *Casa,* of course, means "house."

41. Insolera, *Roma Moderna,* 187.

42. Cited in Mafredo Tafuri, *History of Italian Architecture, 1944–1985* (Cambridge: MIT Press, 1989), 16.

43. Ibid., 16.

44. Anguissola, ed., *I 14 anni del Piano INA Casa,* 6.

45. Ibid., xxi.

46. Ibid., xxi.

47. Ibid., xxii–xxiii. This was the second aspect. The other two aspects were: 1) the plan's intention of alleviating unemployment and homelessness, and 3) the plan's involvement of a number of agencies (public and private), architects, designers, and so on—that is, that it was an "opera di tutti," or, everyone's work.

48. Anguissola, ed., *I 14 anni del Piano INA Casa,* xxiii.

49. Insolera, *Roma Moderna,* 189.

50. Interestingly, the only other INA Casa project that gives the Tiburtino a run for its money in terms of amount of critical attention bestowed on it is the La Martella project in Matera in the southern Italian region of Calabria, begun in 1951 and completed in 1954. I will turn briefly to this project in the conclusion.

51. Zevi first put forth his argument for organic architecture in his *Verso un'architettura organica* (Rome: Einaudi, 1945). *Architecture as Space* (New York: Horizon Press, 1974), published in Italy in 1948 under the title *Saper vedere l'architettura* (How to look at architecture), more widely known to Anglo-American readers, may also serve as introduction to Zevi's championing of the "organic."

52. Maristella Casciato, "Neorealism in Italian Architecture," in *Anxious Modernisms,* ed. Sarah Williams Goldhagen and Réjean Legault (Cambridge: MIT Press, 2000), 33. The designers working on Tiburtino included Carlo Aymonino, Mario Fiorentino, Federico Gorio, Giulio Menichetti, and Michele Valori, among several others. Tafuri separates Italian organic architecture proper from the Roman school, but we might think of organic architecture as providing a kind of theoretical backdrop to architectural developments during the period. See Tafuri and Francesco Dal Co, *Modern Architecture,* vol. 2 (New York: Electa/ Rizzoli, 1976), 334–35.

53. Tafuri and Dal Co, *Modern Architecture,* 2:333

54. Casciato, "Neorealism in Italian Architecture," 32. Casciato does not take into account fascism's frequent privileging of rural culture as well as the regime's rather complicated relationship to architectural modernism, especially in the latter years of its hegemony. D. Medina Lasansky's recent book, *The Renaissance*

Perfected: Architecture, Spectacle, and Tourism in Fascist Italy (University Park, Pa.: Penn State University Press, 2004), is an interesting addition to the scholarship on fascist architecture and demonstrates that fascism was not only about privileging either modernism on the one hand or classical Rome on the other.

55. Saverio Muratori and Mario De Renzi were the designers of this project. I will be discussing them a bit later on in this chapter, particularly Muratori.

56. This information is available in several places, but especially good sources for facts, dates, names, and building information are Rossi, *Roma*, and Guccione et al., eds., *Guida ai quartieri romani INA Casa*

57. Rowe, *Civic Realism*, 108.

58. But as I have mentioned before, there is no real consensus about the larger body of neorealist cinema or about when it ended, though most scholars agree that *Rome, Open City* is the first full-fledged neorealist film.

59. Fascist architecture was actually characterized by the interaction of three architectural schools: Futurism, Novecentism, and Rationalism. Earlier fascist projects were more clearly modernist, in line with the main currents of avant-garde architecture of Europe, such as the Bauhaus. Later projects, like the E '42 (EUR) section of Rome, combined modernist building techniques with heavy allusions to the classical past. Nevertheless, in general, fascist architecture was never sympathetic to variety or disorder of the sort that was programmed into Tiburtino. For a helpful overview of architecture during the years of fascism, see Dennis P. Doordan, *Building Modern Italy: Italian Architecture, 1914–1936* (Princeton,. N.J.: Princeton Architectural Press, 1988).

60. Luchino Visconti, "Anthropomorphic Cinema," in *Springtime in Italy*, ed. Overbey, 84.

61. Giuseppe De Santis, "Towards an Italian Landscape," in ibid., 126.

62. We will leave to the side here some questions that come to mind: Did not the immigrants leave their rural villages? Why give them back what they had chosen to leave? Did the Tiburtino enact a sadistic theater of simulation? Furthermore, many of the inhabitants of Tiburtino we might suppose to have come from Rome—people who were pushed into the periphery by the sventramenti and who wished to move out of the borgate. What the village-like morphology of the Tiburtino would have meant to these inhabitants we do not know. This might be an interesting subject of empirical research, something that should be done soon while some of the project's first inhabitants are still alive. We have evidence of one imagined response in Pasolini's *A Violent Life*, which I will turn to shortly.

63. For an English translation of this work, see *The House by the Medlar Tree*, trans. Raymond Rosenthal (Berkeley: University of California Press, 1984).

64. Mario Alicata and Giuseppe De Santis, "Truth and Poetry: Verga and the Italian Cinema," in *Springtime in Italy*, ed. Overbey, 135.

65. Most commentators on this article make notice of its title's similarity to Vasco Pratolini's novel *Cronaca dei poveri amanti* (A story of poor lovers, 1947) and Antonioni's film *Story of a Love Affair* (*Cronoca di un amore*, 1950). All of these

titles reflect Zavattini's interest in cronaca, or the chronicle of everyday life of the sort found in newspapers, as the source for neorealist screenplays. See Zavattini, "Some Ideas on the Cinema."

66. Carlo Aymonino, "Storia e cronaca del Quartiere Tiburtino," *Casabella* 215 (April–May 1957): 20.

67. Ludovico Quaroni, "Il paese dei barocchi," *Casabella* 215 (April–May 1957): 24; Tafuri, *History of Italian Architecture*, 17; Tafuri and Dal Co, *Modern Architecture*, 333; Giovanni Astengo, "Dormitori o comunità?," *Urbanistica* 10–11 (1952): 4.

68. Rossi, *Roma*, 173; Casciato, "Neorealism in Italian Architecture," 34–36; Reichlin, "Figures of Neorealism in Italian Architecture" (Part I), *Grey Room* 5 (Fall 2001): 92; Tafuri, *History of Italian Architecture*, 17.

69. Pier Paolo Pasolini, *A Violent Life*, trans. William Weaver (New York: Pantheon, 1968), 168–69.

70. Ibid., 174–76.

71. The narration here displays properties of "*free* indirect discourse," a favorite theoretical concept and practical technique of Pasolini's, in which the third-person narrator's voice meshes with or is mimetic of the consciousness of a character's psychology. See Pasolini, "Comments on Free Indirect Discourse," in *Heretical Empiricism*, ed. Barnett, 79–101.

72. Interestingly, Pasolini's *Una vita violenta* was adapted as an eponymous film by Paolo Heusch and Brunello Rondi and released in 1962, the same year as *Mamma Roma*. The Heusch/Rondi film was released first. This film was also set in the Tuscolano II and not in the Tiburtino Quarter, as might have been expected. The film is a faithful adaptation of the novel. Its use of the INA Casa setting is straightforward, unlike Pasolini's use of it in *Mamma Roma*, the subject of the next chapter. Unfortunately, I know very little about the production history of *Una vita violenta*, apart from having seen it and read some of the contemporary reviews. It would be interesting, for instance, to know who got to the Tuscolano II first—Heusch and Rondi or Pasolini—and why. But it is clear from the variety of Pasolini's writings that I have analyzed from the 1950s that he knew very well the INA Casa projects built in the Roman periphery. As I mentioned in chapter 2, the design of the Villa Gordiani project that he discusses in "The Concentration Camps" was presided over (with Mario De Renzi) by Saverio Muratori who, as I will explain shortly, was also one of the main architects at the Tuscolano II.

73. Tafuri, *History of Italian Architecture*, 61.

74. Rowe, *Civic Realism*, 111–12.

75. In fact, the infill is not tufo, but bricks that have a coloring similar to tufo, but I'm actually rather unsure whether any resemblance to tufo should be interpreted as an intentional effect. Since its use as a signifying element is so central to Rowe's analysis, it is strange that he should misidentify this basic property of the buildings' materials and materiality.

76. Rowe, *Civic Realism*, 112.

77. Paolo Angeletti, "La periferia e le case popolari," in *Case Romane,* ed. Angeletti et al., 15.

78. Rowe, *Civic Realism,* 112.

79. Insolera, *Roma Moderna,* 194–201.

5. *Mamma Roma* and Pasolini's Oedipal (Housing) Complex

1. This is the term Italians use for late nineteenth- and early twentieth-century building style that is in other countries would be called art nouveau, although the term is also used to describe buildings of a more neoclassical character.

2. The two films seem related to and differentiated from each other in a way similar to Pasolini's first two novels' similarities and differences. As I have explained above, while both novels were written in Roman dialect, *The Ragazzi* is a more radical experiment in dialect and narrative form. Everything is told in dialect and the narrative energy is more diffuse, focused (or focalized, we might say) as it is through a chorus of characters. *A Violent Life,* on the other hand, moves in and out of dialect and its narrative focuses on a central protagonist, Tommaso Puzzilli. The first novel is set in the borgate, while the second begins there and then moves into the milieu of the INA Casa housing projects. *Accattone* is set entirely in the world of the borgate and, while it does have a central character, Accattone, its narrative allows more room for seemingly pointless digression (e.g., a long scene in which Accattone and his friends attempt to swindle another of their acquaintances into preparing dinner for them). In *Mamma Roma* the narrative plots the "rise" and fall of its central characters, Mamma Roma and her son Ettore, with ruthless efficiency. These characters move into an INA Casa project, like Tommaso in *A Violent Life.* One difference between *A Violent Life* and *Mamma Roma* that sets them far apart is the fact that in the novel Tommaso undergoes a political awakening through his exposure to communist ideology and dies as the result of an act of self-sacrifice. Ettore in *Mamma Roma* undergoes no such political transformation and dies at the hands of the state after attempting a crime of petty thievery. On the ideological differences between the two novels, see Joseph Francese, "Pasolini's 'Roman Novels,' the Italian Communist Party, and the Events of 1956," in *Pier Paolo Pasolini,* ed. Rumble and Testa, 22–39. Francese argues that the more hopeful outlook in *A Violent Life,* embodied by Tommaso's development of class consciousness, represents an attempt on Pasolini's part to draw closer to PCI orthodoxy after the rough treatment *The Ragazzi* received at the hands of Italian Marxist critics who found the novel's supposed nihilism incompatible with an ideology of class solidarity. I would actually question this interpretation, which seems a bit facile. I think it more likely that Pasolini was consciously trying to force an experiment: the contamination of the proper socialist-realist plot with his own aesthetic of the periphery.

3. Schwartz, *Pasolini Requiem,* 361–64. At one of *Accattone*'s premieres, a group of young neofascists disrupted the screening, even hurling rotten fennel

at the screen. The word for fennel in Italian, *finocchio,* is also a derogatory slang word for male homosexual.

4. Stack, *Pasolini on Pasolini,* 55.

5. Schwartz, *Pasolini Requiem,* 397.

6. The two most famous ideal city views are the so-called Urbino and Baltimore panels of unknown authorship, produced in the sixteenth century. On this subject, see Hubert Damisch, *The Origin of Perspective* (Cambridge: MIT Press, 1995). Scamozzi's set design (completed 1585) for Palladio's Teatro Olimpico is another reference point for ideal city views.

7. This latter building is the most recognizable element of the EUR landscape and can be seen from some distance. It makes a brief but important appearance in *Rome, Open City.* The building and the neighborhood of EUR become, in the postwar period, tropes through which directors have sought to think through Italy's relationship both to the fascist past and to postwar modernity. So I argue in research that I am conducting at the moment.

8. The interior shots in the church are actually not San Giovanni Bosco, but some other church that I have not yet been able to identify. The exterior of the church also features significantly in an important scene in Fellini's *Nights of Cabiria,* on which (as I have explained above) Pasolini collaborated. The scene in which Cabiria's suitor (who it turns out is really her seducer and would-be murderer) proposes marriage to her is shot in the piazza in front of the church—then hardly more than a rather desolate construction site (*Nights of Cabiria* was released in 1957; *Mamma Roma* in 1962). The church appears prominently in the background throughout the scene in which her suitor convinces her (dishonestly) that his marriage proposal is sincere. Perhaps the melancholy, unfinished nature of the site is meant to comment ironically on Cabiria's chances for happiness with this man. Regardless of whatever Fellini meant by using this location, we can be sure that Pasolini would have remembered its use when choosing locations for *Mamma Roma.* In *Nights of Cabiria* the location seems chosen for its shabby picturesqueness. In *Mamma Roma* the landscape of which the church is a part operates in a different register. Comparing the scene from *Nights of Cabiria* to what we see in *Mamma Roma* is also useful for gauging how very densely this neighborhood was developed in only five years' time. The piazza on which the church sits was also used as the location for the character Steiner's house in Fellini's *La dolce vita.*

9. *Accattone, Mamma Roma, Ostia,* 268. Another clue to Pasolini's thinking: in the screenplay, the description goes on to say that mother and son enter the entranceway and "head toward one of its infinite number of entrances" (268). Clearly the idea that the building would have infinite doorways suggests that—for Pasolini—the Tuscolano II displays a kind of limitlessness that recalls the rows of windows of the Rebibbia prison as described in "The Tears of the Excavator." I can only explain why the screenplay would describe the building as "dark red" (in Italian: *vinaccia*) by suggesting that perhaps at the that time he was composing the screenplay he was thinking of setting the film at the Tiburtino

Quarter. This latter possibility seems, in fact, likely given the earlier discussion of *A Violent Life*'s setting in the Tiburtino, where there are buildings with dark red plaster.

10. Stack, *Pasolini on Pasolini*, 51–52.

11. *Accattone, Mamma Roma, Ostia*, 270. The film's being shot in black and white also conflicts with the emphasis on color in this screenplay indication. The original Italian reads: "Rosa, giallo, come di latta, come di zucchero, si stendono, oblique, a raggera, a zig-zag, le infinite file delle case popolari nuove. Qualcuna perpendicolare, qualcuna orizzontale, affondano nell'orrizonte estivo, cieco di sole, brulicante di nubi."

12. In fact, the description sounds closer to those offered of the Quartiere Tiburtino in *A Violent Life*, discussed in the last chapter. Also see n. 10 above.

13. *Accattone, Mamma Roma, Ostia*, 293. "Sotto il sole, ardente, di un mezzo-giorno, o quello, quieto, di un meriggio, si sparge, immenso, il panorama della periferia di Roma, bruno, biancastro, immenso informe."

14. Millicent Marcus, *Italian Film in the Light of Neorealism* (Princeton, N.J.: Princeton University Press, 1986), 52. Obviously Magnani herself and the film's title function as allusions to Rossellini's film.

15. *Stories*, 128–31.

16. Although in this shot the dome is not visible as in the anaphoric cityscape.

17. *Accattone, Mamma Roma, Ostia*, 270 .

18. The film hints that Ettore is physically unwell long before he is imprisoned.

19. Pasolini, "10 giugno," "Le poesie di *Mamma Roma* [The Poems of *Mamma Roma*]," *Accattone, Mamma Roma, Ostia*, 400. The Italia: "vedo/le nubi stracciarsi sugli attici/degli altari a sei piani di Cecafumo . . ."

20. "23 April," in ibid., 397. "Sono altari/queste quinte dell'Ina Casa." The word "quinte" refers to theater wings, which I have translated rather loosely. The reference is, I believe, to the sort of perspectival stage design suggestive of an ideal city that I mention above.

21. Micciché, *Pasolini nella città del cinema*, 116. Maurizio Viano discusses the difficulty in reading this sequence of shots as expressive of point of view, but his argument maintains that the shots of the landscape differ from one another by virtue of being photographed with different lenses (cf. Viano, *A Certain Realism*, 92–93). Viano's discussion of this sequence is useful; he suggests that Pasolini "mixes" objective and subjective shots so that their status becomes undecidable, though I think he reads too much in to the possibility of the shots being taken with different lenses. I elaborate my own understanding of this problem below.

22. Here Micciché and I part ways somewhat, for, if I understand him correctly, he seems to attribute the view of the landscape not to the character's actual vision, but to her conscience: the view belongs not to the character's "eyes but to the conscience" (116). Belonging to the conscience would seem to render the shot subjective, but Micciché does not make this point clear.

23. Micciché, *Pasolini nella città del cinema*, 116 (emphases in original).

24. Lynch, *Image of the City*, 3. Lynch's positivist approach to city planning needs to be examined more closely. He invests great significance in the fact of being able to picture (image or imagine) the city. His belief in the self-evident value of the city-as-visible deserves some critique: being able to visualize coherently one's surroundings does guarantee a release from alienation embodied by those surroundings. *Mamma Roma* would seem to prove this—as would, say, Seaside, Florida.

25. Viano, *A Certain Realism*, 93.

26. Note the eponymous strategies of both titles, another way Pasolini cues an awareness of his intertextual strategies.

27. Most critics of the film also point out the obvious intertextual relationship to *Rome, Open City*, particularly in regards to the fact that both films end on a panorama of Rome. In the case of the Rossellini film, what we see is central Rome with the dome of St. Peter's presiding over all as a synecdoche and symbol of grace, harmony, and positive (i.e., not fascist) Italian national identity. The rewriting of this shot posed by *Mamma Roma*'s final domed cityscape should by now be apparent to the reader.

28. Tafuri, *History of Italian Architecture*, 16.

29. This incredible preproduction research is documented and discussed in Michele Gandin, ed., *Il tetto di Vittorio De Sica* (Bologna: Cappelli Editore, 1956). The book includes texts by De Sica, a preproduction diary, photographs of possible actors (taken from the streets), and other fascinating material.

30. On this project, see Rossi, *Roma*, 183; Reichlin, "Figures of Neorealism in Italian Architecture (Part 2)," *Grey Room* 6 (Winter 2002): 110–33.

31. Reichlin, "Figures of Neorealism in Italian Architecture (Part 2)," 120.

32. Late in the production of this book I saw for the first time Luigi Zampa's 1947 film *L'onorevole Angelina* (The honorable Angelina), starring Anna Magnani as the eponymous heroine, a woman of the borgate who leads the women of her neighborhood in a series of protests against the miserable conditions in which they are forced to live. Produced relatively early in the period of neorealism (coming before *Bicycle Thieves*, for instance), the film capitalizes on the persona Magnani developed in her portrayal of Pina in *Rome, Open City*. Much of *L'onorevole Angelina* is shot on location in the Borgata Pietralata, a fascist borgata similar to the Borgata Gordiani, built in the mid-1930s. (Pietralata serves as one of the principal settings in *A Violent Life*.) The action of the film comes to a crisis when Angelina leads her neighbors in illegally occupying a new middle-class apartment block that is being built near the borgata. Magnani's portrayal of a woman of the borgate insisting on a better home for her family and her fellow citizens must also have been on Pasolini's mind when he chose the actress to play Mamma Roma. *L'onorevole Angelina* is in many ways a remarkable film, especially given its documentation of conditions at Pietralata. (The fascist constructions have since been demolished.) However, despite the film's exposure of poverty and under-housing, it resolves itself comically and more or less happily, not unlike *The Roof*.

33. Debord, *Society of the Spectacle*, 23.

Conclusion

1. The actor who plays Stracci is the same actor, Mario Cipriani, who plays Balilla in *Accattone*.

2. According to legend, when Fellini set out to make his ninth film he hit a creative block and so began making a movie that thematized this very problem, thus the name, *8½*.

3. The poem is "10 giugno" (*Accattone, Mamma Roma, Ostia*, 400–401).

4. Pasolini's "Palestine" in fact consisted of parts of the state of Israel and the kingdom of Jordan.

5. Noa Steimatsky's elegant and informative essay on *The Gospel* is among some of the best pieces of writing on Pasolini that I know: Steimatsky, "Pasolini on *Terra Sancta:* Towards a Theology of Film," *The Yale Journal of Criticism* 11, no. 1 (1998): 239–58. I owe much to Steimatsky's understanding of the interaction between Pasolini and the landscape, articulated here and in our many conversations.

6. Casciato, "Neorealism in Italian Architecture," 36. For discussions of La Martella, see Casciato, "Neorealism in Italian Architecture," 36–40; Tafuri, *History of Italian Architecture*, 24–25; Tafuri and Dal Co, *Modern Architecture*, 333–34; and the volume *Esperienze urbanistiche in Italia* (Urbanist experiences in Italy) (Rome: Istituto Nazionale di Urbanistica, 1952). This book has an introduction by the industrialist Adriano Olivetti, who played a central role in drawing attention to the situation in Matera and bringing the people and resources together to create La Martella.

7. Casciato obviously thinks it was a huge success. She is nearly hagiographic in her estimation of La Martella's "eloquent witness to the twin souls, rational and sentimental, that animated Italian Neorealist architecture" (40).

8. "The Other Face of Rome," in Pasolini, *Stories*, 217–18.

9. Pasolini's political attitudes and his growing despair over what he saw as the triumph of consumer capitalism are very much on display in two books of collected essays: *Scritti corsari (Pirate writings)* and *Lettere luterane (Lutheran letters),* both collected in his complete works, edited by Walter Siti, *Saggi sulla politica e sulla società* (Milan: Mondadori, 1999). The latter book has also been translated: *Lutheran Letters,* trans. Stuart Hood (New York: Carcanet, 1987).

10. This is not a view I share at all, but it is stultifyingly ubiquitous in the Antonioni literature.

11. *The Eclipse* is better known in the Anglo-American context by its translated title, whereas *L'avventura* and *La notte* are usually not translated.

12. Often the buildings are rather bleak, impersonal—generically modern if not always rigorously modernist.

13. This by now is a familiar cinematic technique—or even a trope—in the Pasolinian oeuvre.

14. For a useful and brief history of the Autostrada, see Enrico Menduni, *L'autostrada del sole* (Bologna: il Mulino, 1999).

15. Henri Lefebvre, *The Production of Space*, trans. Donald Nicholson-Smith (Oxford: Blackwells, 1995), 52.

16. "An Interview: How Beautiful You Were, Rome," *Stories,* 226.

17. And of course the countrysides of almost every country in the world, or at least the West.

18. "New Linguistic Questions," in *Heretical Empiricism,* ed. Barnett, 3–22.

19. Ibid., 14.

20. Ibid. Interestingly, there is a chapter in Menduni's history of the autostrada entitled "Tra Fanfani e Pasolini" (Between Fanfani and Pasolini) which gives us a sense of the way in which Pasolini's name clings to the history of the autostrada and is also central to a general critique of postwar Italian modernization.

21. Angelo Restivo privileges the Autostrada as a mode through which notions of space were redefined in the 1960s and he goes on to connect this to analyses of films by Pasolini and Antonioni. See Restivo, *The Cinema of Economic Miracles,* 61–76.

22. The framing here recalls the shot of *Accattone* on the Ponte Sant'Angelo.

23. Theodor Adorno, "Commitment," in *Aesthetics and Politics* (London: Verso, 1977), 194. The flavor of Adornian critique permeates much of Pasolini's late essays, particularly *Pirate Writings* and *Lutheran Letters.* His last film, *Salò,* is made, I think, under the sign of Adorno.

24. Tafuri, "La prima strada di Roma moderna: Via Nazionale," *Urbanistica* 29, no. 27 (June 1959): 95–109.

25. Pasolini, *Lutheran Letters,* 49. The most complete consideration of these films in English is Patrick Rumble's *Allegories of Contamination: Pier Paolo Pasolini's Trilogy of Life* (Toronto: University of Toronto Press, 1996), a careful and interesting study of a period in Pasolini's work that has been written off by other critics (cf. Viano, *A Certain Realism,* 263–93).

26. Pasolini, *Lutheran Letters,* 49.

27. Schwartz, *Pasolini Requiem,* 607.

28. The footage at Orte became part of a television documentary that Pasolini collaborated on called *Pasolini e la forma della città* (Pasolini and the form of the city, 1974). Also referred to as *La forma dell'Orte* (The form of Orte).

29. Translation cited from Viano, *A Certain Realism,* 260.

30. Ibid.

31. Fredric Jameson, *The Geopolitical Aesthetic: Cinema and Space in the World System* (Bloomington: Indiana University Press, 1992), 5. Jameson's theorization of third world narratives as inescapably allegorical of the development of the postcolonial nation state was first articulated in his essay, "Third-World Literature in the Era of Multinational Capitalism" (1986), published in *The Jameson Reader,* ed. Michael Hardt and Kathi Weeks (Oxford: Blackwell, 2001), 315–39. This article was immediately attacked for, basically, its Eurocentrism, most notably in Aijaz Ahmad's essay, "Jameson's Rhetoric of Otherness and the 'National Allegory,'" in *In Theory: Classes, Nations, Literatures,* ed. Aijaz Ahmad (London: Verso, 1992), 95–122. This latter position was then criticized from a Marxist perspective by Neil Lazarus in his essay "Fredric Jameson on 'Third-World Literature':

A Defence," in *Fredric Jameson: A Critical Reader,* ed. Sean Homer and Douglas Kellner (Basingstoke: Palgrave MacMillan, 2004), 42–61. Clearly this genealogy indicates how very fraught is the subject of allegory and the third world.

32. Michael Murrin, *The Veil of Allegory: Some Notes Toward a Theory of Allegorical Rhetoric in the English Renaissance* (Chicago: University of Chicago Press, 1969) 15, 55.

Index

John David Rhodes is lecturer in literature and visual culture in the Department of English at the University of Sussex.